REITs

Building Profits
with Real Estate
Investment Trusts

JOHN A. MULLANEY

John Wiley & Sons, Inc.
New York • Chichester • Weinheim • Brisbane • Singapore • Toronto

Copyright © 1998 by John A. Mullaney

Published by John Wiley & Sons, Inc.

Library of Congress Cataloging-in-Publication Data:

Mullaney, John A.
    REITs : buildings profits with real estate investment trusts /
John A. Mullaney.
        p.   cm.
    Includes index.
    ISBN 0-471-19324-0 (cloth : alk. paper)
    1. Real estate investment trusts—United States.   I. Title.
    II. Series.
    HG5095.M85   1997
    332.63'247—dc21   97-14586

To my brother Tom, who,
through a kidney transplant
on July 23, 1997, enabled me
to resume a healthier and more normal life
and
to my uncle, George Quinn,
for the courage and strength he
has demonstrated in his battle against cancer

CONTENTS

Contents

Contents

ACKNOWLEDGMENTS

I STARTED WORKING on this book in early 1996 with several goals in mind. One was to write a book that would present a comprehensive overview of the real estate investment trust industry; a second goal was to provide readers with an understanding of the dynamics of the real estate business; a third was to leave potential REIT investors with realistic expectations of the returns they could expect from their investments in the industry; and a final goal was to get the book published by a major and well-respected publishing company. I feel confident I have accomplished all of these goals. This would not have been achieved, however, without the support and cooperation of a number of people.

First, I must thank the investor relations personnel employed by the 200 public real estate investment trusts who provided me with a vast amount of information on their companies. This information, which included annual and quarterly reports, article reprints, press releases, filings with the Securities and Exchange Commission, and analysts' reports, enabled me to prepare summaries for each of the major REITs in the industry.

I am also indebted to Lori VanLonkhuyzen and Chris Lucas of the National Association of Real Estate Investment Trusts (NAREIT), who provided me with data on such topics as the industry's performance and size, and to the many business writers across the country employed by the publications mentioned in Chapter 19 (as well as other news organizations and publications) whose informative and well-researched articles on REITs and real estate provided me with many ideas for this book.

My gratitude is extended to the individuals who reviewed the book prior to its publication and provided me with both endorsements as well as excellent feedback: Charles Barbo, Chairman and CEO of Shurgard Storage Centers; Ina Fritsch, President of Fritsch Financial Services; Tim Peterson, Senior Vice President of Post Properties; Anne Ravetti, Investor Relations Manager of Meridian Industrial Trust; and Peter Wheeler, President and COO of Commonwealth Equity Services. My thanks also to a former boss, Nell Browning, who was able to break away from the beautiful sunsets at her retirement home in Pegosa Springs, Colorado, to critique the book.

This project turned out to be longer than I expected. During much of the time, I also suffered from a kidney disease that placed me on dialysis. To get through it, I had the support and encouragement of a number of people: first, my family; my father Joe and stepmother Jane, my brothers Joe Jr., Paul, and Tom, and my sister Mary; second, my cousin Kerry DePalo, whose many thoughtful letters provided me with encouragement, and my uncle, George Quinn, who has taught me true courage and faith through his battle with cancer; and third, special friends such as Meg Beller, Bill and Donna Cupleo, Pete Lyons, Betty McKenna, Michael and Martha Murray, Marty and Catherine Parkes, Jim and Betty Seward, Stan Sobczyk, F.S.C., Mike Weber, and Denise Vasconcelos and Lars Beggren (all the way from Brazil).

Finally, a special word of thanks to Jacque Uriniyi of John Wiley & Sons, who championed my book through her company and enabled me to accomplish my goal of having it published by a major publishing firm, and to Donna King at Progressive Publishing Alternatives for her patience in working with this first time book author. They and their respective staffs have been great.

INTRODUCTION

MOST BOOKS ON real estate propose to tell you how to make a fortune buying and managing your own rental properties. Not this book. Instead, I will introduce you to a far more convenient way to make money in the real estate marketplace: real estate investment trusts.

Real estate investment trusts, or REITs as they are more commonly called, are not new. They have been around since 1960; however, in the 1990s, their numbers have more than doubled, and they have taken on a new look. Today, there are REITs that invest in all types of properties, from apartment communities to upscale shopping malls to golf courses. They offer individual investors the opportunity to diversify their portfolios into an asset class that provides a wide range of benefits and they offer something that has traditionally not been associated with real estate investments: liquidity.

Real estate investment trusts are public companies whose stock trade on one of the major exchanges: the New York, American, or NASDAQ. They invest primarily in existing properties, which generate immediate profits. Because REITs are required by law to distribute 95 percent of their taxable income, most of these profits are paid out to shareholders on a quarterly basis in the form of dividends. This makes REITs especially appealing to income-oriented investors. Real estate investment trusts generate a dividend yield that is competitive with fixed income alternatives, such as Treasury securities, bonds, and certificates of deposit. They also offer an added benefit: capital appreciation potential. Unlike fixed income investments, REITs have the potential to increase their cash flow. They do this by raising rents at the properties they own. This leads to an increase in their dividends, and to higher share prices.

This combination of benefits, high dividend yields and increasing share prices, enabled REITs to outperform the Standard & Poor's 500 in five of the first seven years of the 1990s. This is quite a feat considering the fact that this has been one of the better decades in the stock market's history. It is even more impressive after you account for the fact that in the early 1990s, the real estate industry was mired in a deep recession.

Because of their high yields, REITs are also considered good defensive stocks. This means that in a bear market, they should hold their value better than most stocks.

All REITs are not the same, however. They vary in risk and growth potential. In 1995, for instance, the average return for REITs investing directly in real property was 15.3 percent. Returns for individual trusts, meanwhile, ranged from a negative 33 percent to a positive 78 percent; 1996 was no different. The average equity REIT returned 35.3 percent, while individual equity REIT returns ranged from a negative 44 percent to a positive 92 percent.

The message is clear; in order to successfully invest in this marketplace, you must understand the industry, the players, and the factors that dictate success. This book is designed to provide you with such an understanding.

The task, however, can be formidable. As a result of the industry's dramatic growth in the 1990s, there are approximately 200 REITs from which to choose. I will try to make your effort a more manageable one by providing tips on what to look for in REITs and what to avoid; by explaining terminology that is particular to the REIT industry, terminology that will help you better understand how to gauge a REIT's operating results; by outlining how the REITs of the 1990s differ from those of past decades; and by providing you with a framework for developing a REIT portfolio that meets your individual investment needs.

For those of you who invested in real estate limited partnerships in the 1980s and have experienced nothing but regret since, I will explain some of the key differences between REITs and partnerships that I believe make REITs more appealing.

I will cover the various segments of the REIT industry, who the major players are in each segment, and what their competitive strategies are. I will also provide some insight into how they determine which real estate markets to buy in and what properties to buy.

While the focus of this book is to provide you with the information necessary to make sound investment decisions in the REIT marketplace, I realize that some of you will want to leave these decisions to the pros; therefore, included is a listing of mutual funds that specialize in real estate investments.

Regardless of the direction you take, the fact that you are making the effort to learn more about real estate investment trusts should serve you well. That's because REITs have clearly emerged as the real estate investment of choice for individual investors. The statistics bear that out. Since the start of the decade, the industry's stock market value has grown more than tenfold, from $9 billion to approximately $100 billion. By the end of the 1990s, it is expected to easily surpass the $140 billion mark.

Most analysts, meanwhile, expect that real estate markets in the foreseeable future will be more stable than they were in the 1980s, when massive overbuilding led to one of the worst downturns in the industry's history. There is more discipline in the marketplace now, which should preclude the supply of properties from getting out of line with demand.

All of this makes the prospect of investing in REITs look very attractive at this time, and by making an investment in the industry, you will be able to realize all of the benefits associated with real estate without having to endure the hassles of being a landlord.

CHAPTER ONE

What Are
REITs?

YOU COME IN CONTACT with it every day—possibly an apartment property in which you live, an office building where you work, or a neighborhood grocery center where you shop. It is called commercial real estate. Nationwide, it is a $3.2 trillion industry.[1] However, have you ever wondered who owns these properties? Maybe an insurance company, a major pension plan, or a group of wealthy individuals?

Why not you? That's right. You could own a share of the apartment property you live in, the office building where you work, or the shopping center where you purchase your groceries every week; and, you can do it with a relatively modest amount of money.

How? Through real estate investment trusts. Real estate investment trusts, or REITs, are publicly-traded companies which invest in and manage portfolios of commercial properties or mortgage loans. For the individual investor, they represent one of the few ways, and arguably the most practical way, to invest in real estate that was once the exclusive domain of the very wealthy and institutions.

Today, there are REITs that invest in just about every type of commercial property in existence: apartment buildings, regional malls, neighborhood shopping centers, office complexes, industrial parks, health care facilities, hotels, motels, self-storage properties, factory outlet centers, and, even golf courses. These REITs invest on an all cash basis, with modest borrowings, or through an exchange of stock. They buy properties directly or through joint ventures with

1

other investors. Some develop properties, some just buy existing real estate.

Since 1992, the REIT industry has experienced historical growth. From 100 companies, it has expanded to over 200 firms. From $44 billion in assets, it has grown in total size to more than $140 billion. And, from a stock market value of around $9 billion, it has skyrocketed to almost $100 billion.[2]

In 1991, REIT investments comprised less than 4 percent of all the funds invested directly in U.S. real estate by institutional investors.[3] By mid-1996, that percentage had increased to 22 percent.[4] What caused this growth spurt was the real estate recession, some say depression, of the late 1980s and early 1990s. At the time, private real estate companies which had managed to make it through the downturn in tact still had a major problem: they lacked capital. Capital to not only refinance debt on their existing properties, but also to grow their organizations. There were a lot of very attractive properties on the market at the time, and they were available for bargain prices; however, the traditional suppliers of capital to the industry—banks, insurance companies, pension plans, and foreign investors—were too busy trying to salvage their own portfolios to consider any new investments in real estate.

For private real estate firms, the future looked bleak. Then, in late 1991, Kimco Realty, a New York-based private real estate company, took a bold step to solve its financing dilemma: it went public. That was not an easy decision for a private real estate firm. Real estate people tend to be rather entrepreneurial and independent by nature. When you run a privately-held company, you are in control. When you go public, you give up a lot of that control. Your decisions are second guessed by stock analysts, business writers, and shareholders. The value of your company is not necessarily dictated by the value of your assets or even your profits, but rather by how favorably your firm's operations are viewed in the capital markets.[5]

Despite all of these obstacles, Kimco elected to take the plunge into the public marketplace. It raised $135 million in its initial public offering. That was not an insignificant sum of money in 1991 since, at the time, real estate was one of the most difficult investments to sell. Kimco used this newfound capital to snap up some prized real estate that was going untouched in the market. Other private real estate companies took note. A number of them soon followed Kimco's lead; slowly at first, then in droves.[6]

In the two year period of 1993 through 1994, close to 100 private real estate companies went public. They raised more than $16 billion in their initial offerings. Total capital raised by the industry exceeded $33 billion. It was an all time record. Never before had so many REITs been formed in a two year period, and never had so much money been raised.[7]

This wave of new REITs changed the complexion of the industry. A number of the most prominent real estate companies in the nation are now publicly-owned real estate investment trusts. They include companies such as Taubman, a developer and manager of some of the most upscale shopping malls in the nation; Post Properties, whose name is synonymous with high quality apartments in Atlanta; and Public Storage, a major player in the self storage business.[8]

The industry has also attracted some of the heavyweights of the business world; including people like Sam Zell, who has made billions in the real estate industry and who has used his wealth and reputation to become a takeover artist in the broadcasting, sporting goods, and airline industries; Bill Sanders, a founder and former partner in the well-known institutional real estate firm of LaSalle Partners, who now controls three separate REITs and has significant interests in at least three others;[9] and Richard Rainwater, who formerly ran the investment operations of the Bass Brothers and who now heads one of the largest REITs in the country.[10]

REIT REQUIREMENTS

Before we get too far with our discussion of today's REIT industry, let us take a step back and cover some of the basics of the industry, such as how REITs are structured.

REITs can be either public or private enterprises. Public REITs are open to the general public and are listed on one of the major securities exchanges. Private REITs are generally restricted to parties that REIT management wants as co-owners (such as friends, family, and business associates) or perhaps just to institutional investors. In this book, we will devote our attention exclusively to public REITs.

REITs are set up as corporations or business trusts. In recent years, most have been established as corporations because the laws governing corporations are generally more uniform and established than those governing trusts. The corporate REIT issues stock, while the business trust issues shares of beneficial interest.

The key difference between REITs and other public companies is in how they are taxed. In three simple words: they are not. They are not taxed at the federal level and, in most cases, not at the state level. Most of the profits made by REITs are distributed to shareholders, who then pay the tax bill. Other public companies are taxed on their profits. If they pay out any dividends to shareholders, then the shareholders are responsible for paying taxes on these dividends. That results in double taxation.

Why were REITs given this preferential tax treatment? Well, it was to put real estate investment trusts on the same footing, at least tax wise, with mutual funds.[11] Like REITs, mutual fund profits flow through directly to their shareholders; however, just as there are certain rules mutual funds must follow to qualify for this favored tax treatment, REITs must also meet certain guidelines:

- At least 75 percent of their assets must be invested in real estate, shares of other REITs, government securities, or cash;
- A minimum of 75 percent of their income must come from real estate investments,
- At least 90 percent of their income must be from real estate investments or from dividend, interest, or capital gains.
- They must pay out to shareholders at least 95 percent of their taxable income annually, and
- No more than 30 percent of their annual income can come from the sale of properties held less than four years. (This precludes a REIT from engaging in the sale of real estate as part of its business or trade; such as a homebuilder developing and selling single family homes.)

When REITs were created, the federal government also wanted to make sure they were open to small investors; therefore, other provisions of a REIT include the fact that 100 or more persons must own its shares and no more than 50 percent of the trust can be owned by five or fewer individuals during the last half of each taxable year.

Other than their special tax treatment, REITs look very much like other public companies. They issue stock; common, and sometimes preferred and convertible. They are listed on one of the secu-

4

rities exchanges: the New York, American, or NASDAQ. They have a board of directors (or trustees), a majority of whom must not work for the REIT, who are responsible for ensuring that the interests of the shareholders are protected.

TYPES OF REITs

There are three types of real estate investment trusts: those which invest in mortgages, those which invest directly in real property, and those which do both.

In the past, mortgage REITs invested in loans on existing properties, as well as construction and development loans. Most of today's mortgage REITs, however, loan money only to the owners of existing properties. Their portfolios usually consist of first mortgage loans and/or investments in mortgage pools, which are groups of mortgage loans (usually on residential properties) packaged by agencies such as the Government National Mortgage Association (GNMA), Federal National Mortgage Association (FNMA), or by investment banks.

Mortgage REITs usually generate a higher dividend yield than equity REITs. This is because mortgage REITs have limited potential to increase in value. Some of their loans may contain what are known as equity participations, which entitle the REIT to an added return if the mortgaged property's cash flow increases or its value appreciates during the term of the loan. If you invest in a mortgage REIT, however, you invest primarily to receive a high current dividend and not for any appreciation potential. Normally, the only way the stock price of a mortgage REIT increases in value is if interest rates decline. Alternatively, if interest rates increase, the share price declines. This points out the primary risk of investing in mortgage REITs, namely interest rate risk.

By way of example, if a REIT acquires a portfolio of mortgage loans when the market rate of interest is 8% and rates subsequently increase to 10 percent, then the portfolio's value, and the stock price of the REIT, would decline by approximately 20 percent. (The actual level of change would be influenced by other factors, such as the maturity of the mortgages and their quality.) Likewise, if interest rates decline, the portfolio of loans would increase in value.

To offset the risk of rising interest rates, most mortgage REITs today invest a substantial percentage of their funds in variable rate mortgages. The interest rate on variable rate mortgages can be reset periodically to adjust to changing market interest rates, thereby reducing interest rate risk.

The second type of REIT, called an equity REIT, purchases ownership interests in real estate. Most focus their investments on one type of property (such as office buildings), and some limit their investments further to a particular region of the country (such as the Southeast).

The benefits of investing in equity REITs vary. Some equity trusts provide a high current dividend return, but have limited growth potential. Real estate investment trusts that enter into certain types of leases called triple net leases fall into this category. Other equity REITs provide a lower current return, but have greater appreciation potential. Trusts which engage in a significant amount of new property development are an example of this group. Like mortgage REITs, the share prices of equity REITs will fluctuate with changing interest rates; however, because equity REITs have the ability to increase their cash flow (by increasing property rents), they are less susceptible to interest rate risk.

The third type of REIT, called a hybrid, invests in both mortgage loans as well as real property. Most of the hybrid REITs are in the

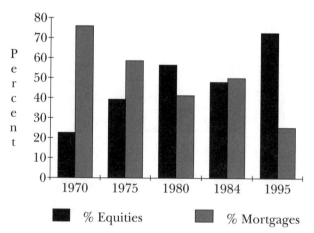

Exhibit 1-1   REIT Industry Investment Allocation SOURCE: National Association of Real Estate Investment Trusts

health care sector where they issue mortgage loans to health care operators as well as acquire ownership interests in properties leased to health care companies. This dual investment strategy results in hybrid REITs generating yields which are generally higher than equity REITs, but lower than mortgage REITs. Hybrid REITs have less growth potential than equity REITs, but greater appreciation potential than mortgage REITs.

Mortgage REITs dominated the industry in the 1970s (Exhibit 1-1). In the early 1980s, equity REITs took the lead, only to be replaced by mortgage REITs in the mid-1980s. In the 1990s, the focus has shifted back to equity REITs, and that is where we will focus much of our attention.

CHAPTER TWO

Past to
Present

THE REIT INDUSTRY TRACES its beginnings to the early 1900s when some New England businessmen, interested in profiting from the growing real estate industry, established what was known as The Massachusetts Trust. At first, these trusts were restricted to the very wealthy and focused on a specific marketplace: Boston.[1]

As the years went on, the general public joined in and the trusts expanded their investment activities west to cities such as Chicago, Omaha, and Denver. The Great Depression of the 1930s, however, put a damper on real estate investing, slowing the expansion of the Massachusetts Trust.[2] Then, in 1935, the Trust was dealt a fatal blow when the U.S. Supreme Court ruled that these trusts were not exempt from corporate taxation.[3]

The REIT concept lay dormant for more than two decades before it gained significant support in the real estate industry in the late 1950s. After several failed attempts to get legislation approved, the industry finally succeeded near the end of 1960.

Just a few months before his administration came to an end, President Eisenhower signed into law the Real Estate Investment Trust Act. The act recreated the tax advantages of investing in real estate through the trust format, and it reopened the door for individual investors of relatively modest means to invest in real estate.

The rush was on. The REIT industry raised close to $300 million in its first year and a half of existence. Then, without any notice, the bottom fell out. In May 1962, the stock market plummeted.

Real estate investment trust stocks were caught in the slide, declining in value by an average of 20 percent. The industry's high hopes were dashed. Capital raising sputtered, with less than $70 million being collected over the following four years combined.[4]

FIRST REIT BOOM

In the late 1960s, the REIT industry's drought came to an end in a big way. As part of its effort to reduce the level of inflation, the Federal Reserve Board increased interest rates in 1968. While that helped put the nation's economy back on more stable ground, it caused a host of problems for banks and savings and loans (S&Ls). At the time, the banks and S&Ls were restricted by law in what they could pay to attract deposits. As a result, many of their customers fled to higher paying money markets, bond funds, or GNMA funds. With fewer deposits, banks and S&Ls, which had traditionally taken care of the needs of the construction industry, curtailed their lending activity. This opened the door for REITs.[5]

Mortgage REITs soon hit the market. In 1968, three mortgage trusts; Associated Mortgage Investors, General Mortgage Investors, and Republic Mortgage Investors, sold $73 million in new shares and helped the REIT industry raise a then record of $110 million. Other mortgage trusts soon followed, first sponsored by mortgage bankers, and then by major insurance companies, commercial banks, and financial services firms. One billion dollars was raised in 1969, and more than $1.3 billion the following year. Connecticut General raised $120 million for its REIT, while Mutual of New York brought in $100 million for MONY Mortgage Investors. Major banks such as Chase Manhattan, Bank of America, Wells Fargo, and Philadelphia National also introduced trusts.[6]

Even after credit conditions eased in the early 1970s, mortgage REITs continued to expand. They were able to raise money not only through stock and debt underwritings, but through commercial banks as well. The banks, instead of getting back into the real estate lending business as direct competitors of REITs, elected to provide financing to the industry. Bank loans, which had represented just 11 percent of total REIT assets in 1969, rose to more than 56 percent of total assets by 1974.[7]

Meanwhile, the country's building boom continued, supplying

mortgage REITs with plenty of business. This encouraged a number of REITs to overextend themselves. The REITs engaged in the practice of borrowing short and lending long (in other words, the money they borrowed was due before the money they had loaned out). This strategy provided them with much of their profits, because they were able to lend money long-term at a rate that was higher than the rate they were paying on their short-term borrowings. The only problem was that the REITs either had to renew their financing or arrange new loans after the initial borrowings came due. This presented a rather significant risk: if interest rates rose, the cost of new debt could exceed earnings from the outstanding mortgages. In the end, that's exactly what happened.[8]

In 1973, the Federal Reserve once again tightened monetary policy, leading to higher interest rates. This action, combined with the oil embargo that same year, led to the worst national recession since the 1930s. Not only were trusts caught in the predicament of having to borrow money at higher rates, but many of their short-term loans were not being repaid. Builders who had received REIT financing to start construction projects were unable to complete them and defaulted on their loans.[9]

As their sources of profits soured, a number of mortgage trusts were unable to repay their lenders, the banks. Ironically, the REITs, which just a few years earlier had overtaken banks as the source of capital for builders, were now at the mercy of these same institutions for their own survival. Thirty REITs reportedly went out of business during this period.[10] Others dropped their trust status. The industry's asset base declined from almost $20 billion to less than $10 billion, and the number of REITs paying dividends dropped from a high of 154 in 1973 to a low of 68 at the end of 1975. Mortgage real estate investment trusts had overextended themselves, and they had paid for it.[11]

SECOND REIT BOOM

It was not until the real estate markets improved in the early 1980s that REITs recovered. Limited partnerships, however, proved to be the hot investment of the decade. Unlike REITs, partnerships were able to take full advantage of the generous tax benefits bestowed on the industry by The Economic Recovery Tax Act of 1981. These included shorter depreciation schedules for real property and the ability to pass through tax losses to investors, who then were able to utilize these losses to reduce their personal income tax liabilities. More than $81 billion in capital was raised by real estate limited partnerships during the decade, almost four times the amount raised by REITs.[12]

Real estate investment trusts and partnerships, however, were not the only players in the real estate business in the 1980s. Banks, S&Ls, insurance companies, pension plans, and foreign investors also took part in a big way. The influx of capital led to the biggest construction boom in the history of the United States. The results were devastating. Office vacancy levels reached all time highs, and the number of empty apartment units also set records in most major real estate markets.

This surge in building was compounded by another change in tax laws. The Tax Reform Act of 1986 once again altered the economics of investing in real estate. This time, though, it was the real estate partnerships which became less favorable and REITs which became more attractive. This was because the tax incentives introduced in the Economic Recovery Tax Act of 1981 were largely eliminated. Real estate investing would no longer be a tax motivated decision, but rather a profit motivated one. This played into the hands of REITs, but it also devastated the real estate industry as it eliminated from the marketplace one of the key players in the 1980s buildup: the tax-motivated investor. The supply of real estate was at an all time high, and the 1986 tax act provisions had reduced the level of demand.[13]

The real estate industry was headed for the worst recession in its history. Its toll would be felt throughout the country. The famous savings and loans crisis soon followed; then came the downfall of a number of prominent banks. Insurance companies and foreign investors retreated from the real estate business, and many real estate limited partnerships, especially the tax-oriented ones, declared bankruptcy. REITs were also impacted by the real estate recession. Few new ones were created, and capital raising declined.

Once again, though, prospects were about to change, brought on largely by a relatively minor provision in the 1986 tax act. The government had decided to allow most REITs to develop and manage their own properties. Previously, REITs were required to contract out these services to third parties. This would make a big difference to a lot of private real estate companies that had previously discarded the notion of becoming a REIT because they had no interest in being passive investors in their industry.

THIRD REIT BOOM

By 1992, many private real estate companies had started to seriously consider the option of going public. Real estate markets throughout the country were beginning to recover and there were a lot of properties available for prices well below those seen just a few years earlier. The only problem for these privately-owned companies was not having access to capital to take advantage of these unique market conditions. The solution eventually became apparent: go public.

In 1993 fifty companies became REITs, raising more than $9.3 billion. Total capital raising for the industry, both initial and secondary offerings, surpassed $18.3 billion. It was the biggest capital raising year in the industry's history, and it was followed by the second largest in 1994, with more than $7.1 billion in initial equity capital and $14.7 billion in total funds raised (Exhibit 2-1).[14]

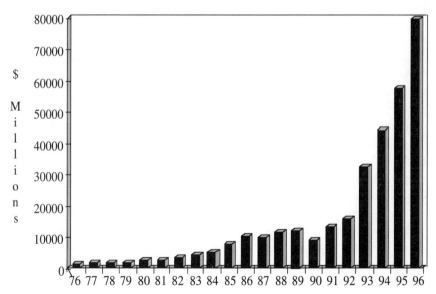

Exhibit 2-1 REIT Industry Equity Capitalization 1975–1996 SOURCE: National Association of Real Estate Investment Trusts

13

The REIT industry's stock market value grew from $15.6 billion in 1992 to more than $45 billion by the end of 1994. There were more than 220 REITs in existence, 95 of which had gone public in either 1993 or 1994.[15] They not only propelled the REIT industry into the spotlight on Wall Street, but they also changed its makeup. Before 1993, mortgage REITs generally dominated the industry. Today, the industry is dominated by equity REITs.

In the past, REITs were passive investors; they would buy the properties, but other firms would manage them. REITs were compared to mutual funds, and rightly so. Both invested in certain assets, but left the management of those assets to others. Most of today's REITs are fully integrated firms, which means they not only acquire their own properties, but they actively manage them as well. They may even build them.

The industry today is also high specialized. In the past, diversification was believed to be the key to building a successful REIT. Again, REITs were compared to mutual funds. You invested in a mutual fund because you wanted to own an interest in a diversified portfolio of stocks. REITs offered the same thing. Invest in a REIT and you could own an interest in a diversified portfolio of real estate. This was all well and good when REITs were passive investors, but today's actively managed REITs prefer to be more focused both in terms of the types of properties in which they invest, as well as where they invest. This enables them to better understand the dynamics of the real estate they buy and the markets they buy in.

Real estate has traditionally been a local business. Local real estate companies understood the markets in which they operated, and their lenders, the local banks, did as well. One of the reasons why the industry got out of line in the 1980s is because so many real estate developers and their lenders went national. The developers and lenders went from one market to another and, without fully understanding the supply/demand parameters in those markets, built one new property after another. The outcome of those efforts is now a painful part of real estate history in the United States.

Another aspect of many of today's REITs that is different from those of yesteryear is their structure. A significant number of today's REITs have been formed as UPREITs. The term UPREIT stands for umbrella partnership REIT. It is simply a legal structure under which the REIT does not own properties directly, but rather through a partnership. The principal reason for this structure is that it enables private real estate owners to form REITs with properties they already own without incurring a tax liability. If they sold these properties to the REIT for cash or even exchanged these holdings for REIT shares, they would have to pay taxes on their profits.

Under the UPREIT structure, the REIT sponsor transfers the real estate to a partnership in exchange for what are called operating partnership (OP) units. At the same time, the REIT takes the capital it has raised from investors in the public marketplace and acquires units in the same partnership. Both parties share in the profits of the partnership in proportion to their ownership interests.[16]

While the UPREIT structure is more complicated than that of a traditional REIT, Wall Street has generally endorsed the structure because it has encouraged a number of experienced and high quality real estate companies to go public. In fact, since this structure was introduced in 1992, more than 75 percent of new REITs have taken this form.[17] If these sponsors did not have the UPREIT option available to them, many would have remained private.

There is a disadvantage to the UPREIT structure, however. That is the potential for conflict of interest. While this structure enables the original owners to retain their lower tax basis in the transferred properties, public investors buy in at a higher tax basis. When the time comes for the REIT to consider a sale, the differing tax liabilities of the two parties could result in a conflict of interest between the public investors and the principals. Ideally, the presence of independent members on the board of directors should avoid this conflict of interest. Of course, this all depends upon how truly independent the board members are.[18]

REITs VERSUS LIMITED PARTNERSHIPS

Besides the many differences with REITs of the past, today's real estate investment trusts also differ in many respects from the real estate limited partnerships which were so prominent in the 1980s.[19] For those of you who may have invested in one or more of these partnerships and, as a result, have vowed never to invest in another real estate venture, let's take a look of some of the advantages today's REITs have over last decade's partnerships:

Management Experience

Today's REITs are managed by experienced real estate professionals, most of whom helped found the organizations, acquire the trusts' properties, and define strategy. Many limited partnerships, on the other hand, were started by individuals whose expertise was more in the structuring and marketing of the partnerships than in the acquisition of properties.

Shareholder Power

REIT shareholders exercise greater control over management through their election of a Board of Directors as well as their ability to introduce certain matters for a vote of all shareholders at the company's annual meeting. Limited partners had minimal power over the general partners (GPs) because they did not elect anyone to act on their behalf in the management of partnership affairs, and if the GPs failed to meet their responsibilities, the investors' only viable option was to remove them.

Management Ownership

Most REIT managers have substantial ownership interests in their companies. In many instances, these interests were simply transferred over when their privately-owned companies went public. The general partners of limited partnerships normally invested only a nominal sum (usually around $100) in the partnership in order to collect a stated percentage (normally 10 to 15 percent) of the partnerships' annual cash distributions and a share of the profits when the partnership's properties were sold.

Specialization

The vast majority of REITs are focused by geography, asset type, or both. This enables them to gain a better understanding of the markets in which they operate and/or the segment of the real estate industry in which they focus. This specialization enables REITs to develop more clearly defined investment strategies. Limited partnerships, while often focused by asset type, rarely focused their operations geographically. In the end, this generally resulted in sub-par performance since the sponsors were not able to fully appreciate the dynamics of each of the market areas they had entered.

Debt

REITs usually limit the amount of debt they undertake to 50 percent or less of their total market value. This is in contrast to many limited partnerships that leveraged their acquisitions with up to 80 percent debt. When real estate went through its downturn in the late 1980s and early 1990s, many of these partnerships lost their properties to lenders.

Capital Raising

REITs raise capital when they need funds to purchase properties they have already identified for acquisition or to pay off short-term debt that has been used to buy properties. If a REIT's management believes the marketplace is overpriced or overbuilt, they are under no pressure to make any new investments. Limited partnerships, meanwhile, were generally always out raising money from investors. Under their bylaws, they were required to invest this capital within a certain time frame. Additionally, if they failed to make any new acquisitions for a significant period, it generally hurt their capital raising efforts; therefore, there was considerable pressure on partnership sponsors to invest funds even if market conditions were less than favorable.

Cost of Capital

The cost of raising equity capital is less for REITs than for limited partnerships. REITs sell stock in offerings which typically are sold out in a day to a few days, and normally receive $.92 to $.94 of every dollar raised. Limited partnership offerings were available for sale in the marketplace for up to a year and involved extensive marketing efforts. Marketing costs and sales commissions regularly totaled 12 to 14 percent of capital raised; therefore, limited partnerships had only $.86 to $.88 of every dollar raised available for investment.

17

Valuation

Real estate investors are more likely to know the true value of their REIT investment. Since analysts, pension fund managers, and mutual fund companies are constantly evaluating public REITs, the share price of these trusts should approximate their true value. Limited partnerships, meanwhile, were not subject to such analysis and typically did not provide investors with any valuations.

Tax Reporting

A REIT investor receives an IRS Form 1099 which indicates the amount and type of income received during the year. This is the same form that is sent out by mutual funds companies and banks to their customers. Partnership investors receive a more complicated IRS Schedule K-1.

Liquidity

Perhaps the biggest difference between REITs and limited partnerships is liquidity. REIT shares are traded as stock on one of the major exchanges. There is generally a ready market for such shares, especially for the larger REITs. By law, only a certain percentage of limited partnership interests could change hands each year for a partnership to retain its status. While certain secondary markets for limited partnership interests have developed over the years, investors have generally incurred a significant loss when they have sold their interests in these markets.

While the real estate limited partnerships being sold here in the 1990s may not have some of the drawbacks of their predecessors, they still lack one key element which gives REITs the edge: liquidity.

One thing I have learned over the years is that most investors are reluctant to give up access to their money. They might say they are willing to, but the reality is that they are not. This makes the option of investing in REITs the most practical way for individual investors to participate in the real estate marketplace.

CHAPTER THREE

Running
a REIT the
Right Way

IN SEPTEMBER 1995, THE board of directors of Property Capital Trust sent a letter to its shareholders recommending that they vote to approve a plan of liquidation for the trust. Why would a REIT vote to sell its assets and close up shop at a time when the industry is experiencing an unprecedented revival? Because Property Capital Trust did not fit the profile of today's REIT.

Property Capital Trust was formed in 1969. Like most other REITs started at the time, and those formed throughout the 1970s and 1980s, Property Capital Trust was a passive entity that acquired interests in a diversified portfolio of real estate. This approach does not meet the standard for today's REITs. The model REIT today is one that is actively managed, specializes in one property type and, in many instances, focuses its efforts in a specific region of the country. Property Capital Trust not only failed to meet this profile, it did not believe it could successfully revamp its operations to do so. As a result, it elected to go out of business.

The fate of Property Capital Trust illustrates the importance of meeting the standards of today's REIT industry. The Tax Reform Act of 1986 permitted REITs to be actively managed operations and that is what the market looks for in current REITs. For most REITs formed since 1992, that is not a problem. They were previously fully-integrated private real estate companies that not only acquired real estate, but also managed it, and sometimes developed or redeveloped it.

These fully-integrated REITs offer shareholders more than just an interest in a portfolio of real estate. They offer the opportunity to benefit financially from all phases of the real estate business. That's because REITs cannot only save money by developing and managing their own assets but, in many cases, they can do it better than third parties. Many REITs provide these same services to other property owners as well. This works to their benefit on several fronts.

First, it not only brings in additional revenue, but it also increases the REIT's profit margins. The more properties a company has under management, the greater its economies of scale. In other words, while it might take 100 people to manage 15 properties, a REIT might be able to take on the management of 15 additional properties by hiring only 75 more people. In this scenario, the REIT would double its revenues, but its expenses would increase by only 75 percent.

Second, it provides REIT management with a larger knowledge base. The more properties a firm manages, the more experience it gains resolving the various issues that come with the job. Issues such as deciding what capital improvements will benefit the bottom line the most, what lease packages will maximize revenue, and how occupancy rates will be impacted by different levels of rent increases.

Third, it provides the REIT with a potential supply of acquisitions. The best property to buy is often the one that presents no surprises. While REITs conduct extensive analysis on all acquisitions, it is sometimes difficult to truly understand the inner workings of a property until you actually manage it.

This additional experience also enables the management of a REIT to determine the most effective means of gaining a competitive advantage in the marketplace. The real estate industry is no different from other industries; it is very competitive. To gain an edge, you must operate your business differently or better than your competition. Real estate companies can gain a competitive advantage a number of different ways. Sometimes the methods that are pursued will depend on the industry segment in which a company is focused (i.e., the office market versus the apartment market); however, they will usually include one or more of the following:

Targeting High Growth Markets—A number of REITs target cities where future population and job growth are expected to be above the national average. In these "high growth" markets, real estate should also increase at an above average rate. In recent years, cities such as Atlanta, Denver, Dallas, Las Vegas, and Phoenix have fit this profile.

Utilizing A Barrier To Entry—One of the biggest threats in the real estate business is the prospect of a developer buying a plot of land near your property and building a new and improved version of what you have to offer. By owning real estate in a market area where there are no sites available for development, you can alleviate this threat. Such a situation is called a barrier to entry; the developer cannot enter your market because there is no land on which the developer can build the new and improved property.

Buying for Less Than Replacement Cost—One of the ways a REIT can protect itself from new development is by purchasing property for less than its replacement value. Even if a developer is able to acquire nearby land and develop a newer version of what you offer, it will cost that developer more to build that property; therefore, the builder will have to charge higher rents to realize the same return on investment.

Becoming a Key Player in a Given Market—By focusing on one or a few specific markets, REITs are able to acquire more properties within each market, which can work to their advantage in leasing space. For instance, if a REIT owns a number of office properties in a city, there is a greater likelihood it will be able to take care of the space needs of a potential lessee than if it owned only one property in that city.

Owning a Prestigious Property—Owning the most prestigious property in town will always work to your advantage. It may be an office building that includes in its tenant base a city's most prominent law firms, a hotel that has a long and distinguished history, or a shopping mall that is a must see for visiting tourists. These "trophy properties" are the type of assets that command a premium above and beyond the value of their cash flow.

While most of today's REITs focus their investment activities in a particular geographical region of the country, there are still a number of markets within each region from which a REIT has to select. To determine which market or markets offer the best investment potential, REITs conduct a rather detailed analysis of each one. This analysis involves two steps: One is an evaluation of each market's economy to gauge its underlying strength and growth potential; the other is an appraisal of real estate conditions in each area.

A local economy can be very healthy, but the economics of investing in real estate might still be poor. This would be the case if there were an excess of vacant apartments in a marketplace where home ownership was still very affordable. This is known as a demand/supply imbalance. There is an excess supply of apartments and demand is not likely to be strong because home ownership is affordable.

In the short term, REITs focus on such factors as how much vacant space exists in a market, how fast that space is being leased, how much it is being leased for, and how much new space is being constructed. Longer term, however, REITs are more concerned with employment growth, cost of living, migration trends (whether people are moving in or out of the area), and household formations. These factors will influence the demand for all types of commercial properties within a community.

A REIT evaluates a local economy by focusing on the well-being and future growth potential of what are known as export companies. These are firms that sell their goods and/or services outside of the local market area (not necessarily outside the country) and, as such, bring wealth into the community. (Nonexport firms, or service sector firms, sell their goods and/or services locally and are largely dependent on the export companies for their business.)[1]

In a given marketplace, it is the export firms that generally influence the future demand for office space, retail facilities, and housing. Because there are a host of variables that can impact the future growth of these companies (such as the overall economy, international competition, and competition from other firms within the same industry), the REIT manager must be a well-informed businessperson in addition to being a real estate expert.

An evaluation of the local real estate market includes both a review of overall market conditions as well as a more detailed look at the segment in which the REIT invests, such as apartments, office buildings, or shopping centers. This analysis will focus on vacancy levels and absorption rates. The vacancy level will indicate how much space is available, while the absorption rate will reveal how much of this space is being leased. Both rates influence the amount of new construction that will be planned for a given market, at least under normal real estate market conditions.

In analyzing these factors, a REIT manager must look beyond just the raw data because the numbers don't always tell the whole story. For instance, while the overall office vacancy level in a particular market area might be high, certain sub-markets might be experiencing a shortage of supply. Likewise, while the overall market vacancy level for apartment properties might be above average, units oriented toward middle-income residents might be insufficient to meet demand. Both situations present opportunities for a REIT to develop new properties, even though overall market vacancy levels would not support such a decision.

Once a REIT completes its evaluation of the various markets within its targeted region, it will generally narrow its choices down to just a few. The real work then begins: finding the right properties to buy. What is "right" will vary from one REIT to another. Some REITs look for the premier properties in a market area—the cream of the crop. This is because they want to own only upscale properties. Other REITs, which have the requisite ability and experience, look for properties that need a facelift. This is because if they do their job well, these REITs can add significant value to the acquired property.

Some of the factors that all REITs evaluate when looking at a potential acquisition include its location (i.e., access to employment centers, schools, shopping centers, and highways), age, size, physical condition, amenity package, and rent levels. Buildings that are well-located and well-maintained will usually always be competitive in a marketplace. Alternatively, properties located in areas that have seen better days, that do not offer amenity packages that are competitive with those offered at new facilities, and that have suffered physical deterioration, will be at a competitive disadvantage.

Even if an identified investment property passes the first stage of analysis, there are more questions to be answered: Can it be operated profitably? If so, how profitable will it be? What will be the primary benefits that will be realized from the property: current income, capital appreciation, or a combination of the two?

To answer these questions, the REIT will perform a variety of financial studies, examining the property's potential profitability under various economic scenarios. In these studies, the REIT must account for the difference between evaluating properties with multiyear leases (office properties, retail facilities, and industrial buildings) and those with shorter term leases (hotels and apartments). For hotels and, to a lesser extent, apartments, the existing lease rates will be comparable with market rates because of their short term nature. For properties with longer term leases, market rates may have changed considerably between the time a lease was signed and the time it comes up for renewal.

REIT managers also need to be familiar with trends in the marketplace that impact their investment decisions and the way they manage properties. Apartment property owners need to understand the demands of business people who work from home (i.e., multiple telephone lines, apartments with office space, etc.). Retail property managers have to take into account the consumer trend toward value in the 1990s. Office building landlords must be able to accommodate the increasing technological needs of tenants.

As you can see, the task of buying investment real estate is a fairly involved one, and one that is usually beyond the ability of most individual investors. This is why REITs are such a practical way for individuals to invest in real estate. Within the industry, however, there are not only hundreds of REITs from which to select, there are a host of sectors to wade through. In subsequent chapters, we will examine each of these sectors; their potential investment benefits and risks, their characteristics, and the strategies employed by firms within each segment to gain a competitive advantage.

CHAPTER FOUR

The
Real Estate
Marketplace

ONE OF THE KEY differences between the REIT industry of the past and today's is the trend toward specialization. The vast majority of current REITs focus their efforts in a specific segment of the real estate industry. This presents a number of benefits to REITs, especially since most of the REITs that dominate today's industry were previously privately held firms that specialized in the ownership and management of a specific property type. For individual investors, however, the industry's specialization presents a dilemma. Which sector or sectors should they invest in?

Unfortunately, there's no simple answer. As is the case with so many investments, the right course of action depends on a number of factors, including your investment objectives, risk tolerance, and time frame. I will cover these topics in greater depth in a later chapter. For now, though, let us focus on the specific real estate sectors and how they compare to each other based upon their level of risk.

TYPES OF REAL ESTATE

In analyzing REITs, it is important to consider the risk level of each based upon the type of asset the company invests in, the amount of debt it utilizes, the level of diversification the REIT provides, the amount of new property development in which it is engaged, and the expertise and experience of the REIT's management team. The combination of these variables will determine how venturesome a given REIT can be.

Before you address most of these questions, though, you can perform an initial screening of REITs based upon the type of properties in which they invest. Different types of real estate present varying levels of risk based upon factors such as the stability of their income stream, the quality of their tenant base, the duration of their leases, the intensity of management oversight required, and the potential competition in the marketplace. Using these variables as a guideline, you can determine where a particular type of property lands on the risk spectrum. Higher risk properties will tend to be more management intensive, face significant competition in the marketplace, and offer shorter term leases. Lower risk properties, on the other hand, will usually require less management oversight, have fairly predictable income streams, and will normally attract a lot of attention from institutional investors.

In the real estate industry, the perceived risk level of a property is usually denoted by its capitalization rate. The capitalization rate is defined as the percentage by which a future income stream is divided to arrive at a property's current value.[1] The higher the capitalization rate, the higher the perceived risk of a property. For instance, a property with an annual net operating income of $100,000 and a 10 percent capitalization rate would be worth $1 million. (Net operating income is a property's cash flow before debt service payments.)

$$\frac{\$100,000}{10\%} = \$1 \text{ million}$$

Likewise, a property with the same annual net operating income but a 9 percent capitalization rate (meaning a lower perceived risk) would be valued at more than $1.1 million.

$$\frac{\$100,000}{9\%} = \$1,111,111$$

Exhibit 4-1 is a 1996 year-end analysis of capitalization rates showing how much rates can vary from one property type to another.

Within these property segments, capitalization rates will vary

Property Type	Capitalization Rate
Hotels	10.1%
Downtown Office	9.5%
Power Centers	9.5%
Community Centers	9.5%
Suburban Office	9.1%
Industrial	9.0%
Apartments	8.8%
Regional Malls	8.3%

Exhibit 4-1 Property Capitalization Rates SOURCE: Real Estate Research Corporation

from one real estate market to another. For instance, a 1995 national survey of capitalization rates for office properties revealed a range of 7.1 percent for San Francisco to 9.9 percent for Oklahoma City.[2] This reflects the perceived safety and appreciation potential of purchasing an office building in these respective cities.

Based upon real estate market conditions in the mid-1990s, Exhibit 4-2 shows the risk spectrum I propose for the various REIT sectors that we will examine in subsequent chapters.

Let's briefly review each asset type noted in the risk spectrum:

Land

Raw land is considered to have the greatest risk of all real estate investments because it provides no income stream and generates few

High Risk	Low Risk
Suburban Office	
CBD Office	Multifamily Residential
Shopping Centers	Manufactured Housing
Self-storage Centers	Industrial Properties
Hotels/Motels	Regional Malls
Raw Land	Commercial Net Lease

Exhibit 4-2 Property Risk Spectrum

27

tax benefits (because land is not depreciable). The primary, and in some cases the sole, benefit realized from this asset is capital appreciation.

Due to the substantial risk associated with raw land, successful land investments are expected to provide a high rate of return to investors. Alternatively, there is considerable downside risk with this investment. Because raw land generally does not generate any income prior to its development, the holding costs (i.e., property taxes, maintenance, and mortgage payments) must be paid out-of-pocket by the investor. Additionally, there is the risk that the land will not appreciate in value, resulting in both lost opportunity costs as well as actual cash losses.

There are no REITs that currently engage in pure land development. This is due to the fact that such investments do not generate any current income and the value of vacant land is difficult for the capital markets to evaluate. Many REITs do own undeveloped land in their portfolios, which they will either develop or sell. The balancing act in which these REITs engage is how much undeveloped land to retain. Because these holdings do not generate any current income, they reduce the current return REITs realize from their portfolios. Alternatively, land that is primed for development is a source of near term revenue growth for REITs, and can enhance the value of their shares.

Hotels and Motels

The operating nature of these properties, the short term nature of their leases, the relative ease of entry into the business (at least for smaller hotels/motels), and their susceptibility to economic downturns, make this asset type a higher risk investment.

Hotels and motels fall into two categories: transient facilities and destination locations. Transient hotels/motels are usually located on major highways or at airports and depend primarily on individuals in transit from one location to another. Destination facilities seek guests who will remain for at least several days, perhaps for a vacation, to attend a convention, or to conduct business in a particular city.

To gain a niche in the increasingly competitive hospitality marketplace, many hotel chains are targeting specific customers. The industry is now segmented along the following lines: luxury hotels, corporate-style hotels, mid-market hotels, limited service hotels, and economy budget hotels. The range extends from those seeking the finest, in terms of amenities, to those seeking the lowest cost.

While these properties are higher risk, they have an advantage in that they are able to more readily adjust their rates to market conditions due to their day-to-day leases.

Self-storage Centers

This asset type is categorized as a higher risk property for several reasons: Leases are generally short term; competition in the marketplace can be substantial due to the relatively low cost of buying and building such properties; and, because these facilities are operating businesses, they are somewhat management intensive.

Self-storage centers meet the needs of individuals to store large bulky objects for which space is lacking in today's smaller apartments and the need for businesses to find inexpensive storage space. Access to a significant customer base is important; this is why these facilities are generally located either within or on the fringes of heavily populated areas.

The typical complex is a series of "bare bones" buildings divided into individual rental units of all shapes and sizes; therefore, construction costs are usually minimal.

Shopping Centers

The shopping centers in this category include neighborhood, community, and power centers. The neighborhood shopping complex serves a three to five mile area, while the community center and power centers can serve up to a fifteen mile area.

The neighborhood shopping center provides for the sale of convenience goods (i.e., food, drugs) and personal services (i.e., dry cleaning, hair salons). It is usually built around a supermarket as a main tenant. A community shopping center usually includes a supermarket as well, but will also be built around a junior department store or major discount store. The power center, meanwhile, will include one or more "big box" or superstore retailers that specialize in a particular line of products, such as toys, office supplies, electronics, home accessories, or building supplies.

Shopping centers are considered higher risk investments today because there are too many of them in the United States. Additionally, they are always subject to changing consumer preferences.

Office Buildings

Throughout much of the 1980s, office buildings were the favored investment of institutional investors due to their competitive return and the projected future demand for this asset type. The overbuilding that occurred in this sector in the 1980s, combined with corporate cutbacks that have continued into the 1990s, however, have put a dent into the popularity of office buildings.

Prospects have improved in the mid-1990s as demand for office space has started to catch up with supply. That has revived investor interest in office properties. Initially, this interest was based largely on economics—the ability to acquire such properties at a price substantially below their replacement value. This is still largely true for office buildings located in central business districts (CBD).

For suburban office properties, the investment rationale has changed. It is based upon the demand/supply outlook. The demand for suburban office space in the 1990s has outpaced that of CBD office properties. Some companies have decided that they do not need to pay the higher rents of downtown office buildings, while others have determined that a suburban location is more convenient for their workforce.

Office buildings offer some measure of security because they generally have longer term leases (usually three to five years) and new properties often take years to plan, get approved, and build.

Multifamily Residential

Apartment properties bounced back quicker from the 1980s' overbuilding than office properties for several reasons. One reason is that overbuilding in the apartment sector was not as severe as it was for office properties. Secondly, demand remained stronger throughout the late 1980s and early 1990s, allowing it to catch up more rapidly with the available supply.

There are generally two types of apartment properties: high-rise complexes and garden-level communities. The high-rise properties tend to be located in more densely populated areas and have higher rents. The garden-level apartments are located in suburban locations.

Apartment properties can also be segmented by price. Upscale communities charge higher prices, but also provide the best in terms of amenities. Multifamily properties geared toward moderate income renters tend to have few, if any, amenities but offer more affordable rents.

Residential properties can be quite management intensive and, depending upon such variables as the composition of tenants, the age of the complex, and local weather conditions, may require substantial capital expenditures. Turnover at apartment properties also tends to be high.

The demand for apartment units is generally more predictable than it is for other types of commercial real estate, and the relatively short term nature of the leases provides apartment owners with greater flexibility in increasing rents.

Manufactured Housing

The manufactured housing sector has traditionally not attracted a significant amount of attention from the investment community, because these properties, which have customarily been known as mobile home parks, did not have the best of reputations.

REITs that focus in this market segment, however, invest in well-established and higher-end manufactured home communities. Most of these communities have all of the amenities associated with quality apartment properties and have become quite popular with retirees. The fact that manufactured home communities have minimal resident turnover and capital expenditure requirements gives this asset type an edge over apartment properties on the risk scale.

31

Industrial Properties

Industrial properties have gained increasing recognition in the 1990s as a viable real estate investment by institutional investors. This is due to the stable returns they have generated over the years, as well as the fact that they have not been prone to overbuilding.

The key to success for most of these properties is their proximity to transportation routes. This is why industrial parks are found close to airports and train lines. These properties are used for warehousing, distribution, assembly, or manufacturing.

Industrial facilities require little management oversight because they are usually leased to single tenants and are subject to net leases, which require the tenant to pay all of the operating costs of the property.

Regional Malls

Shopping malls come in two varieties: the regional center and super regional center. The regional center is based around one or two major department stores and provides for the sale of general merchandise, apparel, furniture, and home furnishings. The super regional center, meanwhile, is built around three or more major department stores and can range in size up to more than one million square feet.

The regional mall will generally serve residents living within 20 minutes of the site, while the super regional mall serves residents from several area communities and in some cases, those in an entire marketplace.

While malls have been impacted by the consumer trend toward value in the 1990s, they are still considered an attractive investment. This is because overbuilding is normally not a problem in this segment of the industry. Major anchor tenants are usually locked into long term mall leases and are not able to jump from one center to another. This restricts the ability of mall developers to build competing facilities.

Despite this safeguard, existing mall owners are still under pressure to retain market share. This means they must closely monitor ever-changing consumer preferences and keep both the appearance and tenant base of their facilities up-to-date.

Commercial Net Lease

This classification is not actually a different property type, but rather a different type of real estate investment. The risk level of net lease investments is less due to the fact that the operating risk of the property is transferred from the owner to the lessee, who is responsible for paying all of the costs associated with the asset. The primary risk of this investment is the creditworthiness of the tenant and the viability of the tenant's business.

Direct real estate investments made by health care REITs are generally always net leases to health care operators. Additionally, many retail property investments, especially single tenant facilities, are subject to net leases.

These risk classifications can shift as a result of changing real estate market conditions. For instance, in the early 1980s, office buildings were considered to be safer investments than they are in today's market. At the time, vacancy levels were low and the growing white collar employment rate meant strong demand. Here in the late 1990s, vacancy levels are still high in some cities, corporate cutbacks have reduced demand, and the increased technological needs of many businesses have made some older office buildings obsolete.

In considering these risk classifications, you should note that they pertain only to specific asset classes and not to individual REITs. When you invest in a given REIT, you are investing not only in its assets, but also in the geographical region in which it is focused, the investment strategy it is employing, and its management team. All of these factors impact the quality and risk of an individual REIT.

Therefore, this risk spectrum is only one of the factors you should consider in analyzing the appropriateness of a REIT for your investment dollars. Other factors to consider in evaluating a REIT and its holdings include:

The Tenant Base—The quality of a REIT's tenants is an important consideration in evaluating the safety of the income stream and the appreciation potential of its properties. This factor is especially key in analyzing retail REITs because the quality of tenants will determine the "traffic count" at their properties and the potential business volume realized by their centers. Because the REITs often participate in the increasing revenues of the retail operations, it is important that they attract popular tenants.

Terms of Existing Leases—The terms of existing tenant leases will, to a large extent, dictate whether a property has the potential to increase in value or to lose value. Key factors here include the duration of existing property leases, how the existing tenants' rental rates compare to current market rates, how much of the property's operating expenses are assumed by tenants, and whether current leases include any rent escalation clauses or participation in the tenants' increasing business profits or revenues. Many office building REITs have acquired properties in recent years that had rent levels well below current market rates, thus providing for potential increased cash flow when such leases are renewed.

Risks of Property Operations—The potential risks associated with operating a real property are numerous and can be impacted by such factors as the intensity of management required, the type of operations carried on at the facility (i.e., restaurant versus industrial property), the location of the property, and the capital improvements required. All of these factors can impact the potential revenues and/or expenses of a property.

Market Vacancy Levels/Absorption Rates—Vacancy levels/absorption rates can impact the future cash flow of a property. If a marketplace in which a REIT invests is overbuilt and there is little absorption of excess space, the REIT will have a difficult time maintaining its profit levels. Alternatively, a REIT that is focused on marketplaces where vacancy levels are low and absorption is strong, should be the beneficiary of increasing profit margins.

Construction Activity—Construction activity will determine the level of future competition in a given marketplace. Even if the current vacancy level is low, a host of new construction activity can change this situation in a relatively short period of time.

Demand/Supply

The last three factors discussed, a market's vacancy rate, absorption rate, and its new construction activity, have perhaps the most significant impact on the direction of real estate values. They determine the demand/supply balance within a real estate market. Traditionally, demand/supply has been one of two principal factors that has impacted property rents. The other is inflation.

Inflation increases the cost of building new properties. Higher prices for building materials, as well as higher labor costs, will require that new properties charge higher rents to cover the increased costs of construction. Owners of existing properties will also increase their rents because, in a high inflationary economy, their expenses will grow at a faster rate.

While inflation was one of the main reasons for investing in real estate during much of the 1980s, it has not been as prevalent a factor in the 1990s. Despite this fact, real estate values have still been on the rise nationally, primarily because demand for space has been increasing at a faster rate than the supply of new space. The demand/supply equation in real estate is comparable to that for other industries. If demand for a good exceeds its supply, either a price increase will reduce the level of demand or the supply will be increased to meet the higher demand. Alternatively, if the supply exceeds demand, either the price will be reduced to increase demand or the supply will be reduced.

In the real estate business, markets have traditionally gone through cycles. At a given point in time, there is an excess of supply, then demand increases and exceeds the supply of new space. Occupancy levels and rents increase to a point at which new construction becomes feasible. New properties are then built until market conditions result in an oversupply of space. At this stage, the process starts all over again.

The cyclical nature of property development is illustrated in Exhibit 4-3 which shows a comparison of newly constructed apartment units for two separate six year periods in Denver, San Antonio, Phoenix, Tulsa, and Oklahoma City.

The real estate cycle of the 1980s was more extreme than most other cycles. Tax incentives introduced in 1981 by the Economic Recovery Tax Act, low cost capital from S&L deregulation and tax exempt bond financing, and high inflationary expectations fueled the overdevelopment which occurred in the early to mid-1980s. At the time, the market generally ignored such basic questions as what the current yield on new property development would be and whether new rental projects would be profitable. Today, these artifi-

The Real Estate Marketplace

City	1981–1987	1988–1994
Denver	38,221	8,675
San Antonio	43,278	2,626
Phoenix	111,896	18,120
Tulsa	17,021	848
Oklahoma City	25,466	180

Exhibit 4-3   Construction of New Apartment Units SOURCE: REIS Reports, Inc.

cial stimuli are gone and the main focus of investors is the current yield on capital.

These yields, however, will vary from one property type to another. The reason for the variances has to do with the factors I've already mentioned: the differing risk levels of the various types of real estate, their potential for appreciation, and their ability to adjust rental rates to current market rates. The following chapters examine these factors for each of the main property sectors within the REIT industry.

CHAPTER FIVE

Multifamily Residential

THE MULTIFAMILY RESIDENTIAL SECTOR is one of the largest in the REIT industry today, representing about 20 percent of the total market value of the industry.[1] At the end of 1996, multifamily REITs owned 650,000 apartment units nationwide, up from just 50,000 in 1991.[2]

Unlike REITs in some other sectors, multifamily REITs usually focus their operations in specific geographical areas of the country. Their objective is to become a dominant player in one or a select number of markets, as opposed to developing a geographically diversified portfolio of investments. This is due to the fact that the demands of tenants tend to be local in nature. Apartment units that appeal to residents in the Northeast, for instance, may not appeal to renters in the Southwest. Therefore, an apartment property owner must be familiar with the preferences of each marketplace in order to successfully compete.

The multifamily marketplace itself can be segmented along the lines of property type, tenant composition, amenity package, and price.[3]

Multifamily REITs generally invest in two types of properties: high rise and garden style. High-rise apartment buildings are most often found in densely populated, older urban centers, such as New York City, Boston, Philadelphia, Chicago, and Washington, D.C. They are usually built in locations that are convenient to public transportation, work places, and retail facilities. Garden-style properties, meanwhile, tend to be found in newer cities, such as Atlanta,

Los Angeles, Houston, and Dallas. This is because the garden-style apartment property is a creation of the suburbs, which exist in abundance in these cities. They are usually two to three stories in height; are located on open, well-landscaped sites; generally contain amenities such as a pool, tennis courts, and/or fitness centers; and have ample parking.

Although apartment properties are open to both families and adults, most cater to the adult market. They do this primarily by offering just one and two bedroom units, which are usually too small for most families. Adult-oriented properties are generally easier to manage, and there is usually less wear and tear on the property. Also, because most families ideally want to own their own home, during periods when market conditions for buying a home are favorable, family-oriented units can be difficult to rent. Single persons and young married couples, meanwhile, tend to live in an apartment because of their lifestyle needs, economics, or because they are simply not ready to settle into a home.

Apartment complexes generally target different economic classes of residents based upon the quality of the property and the level of amenities offered. Some properties offer the basics: a quiet, pleasant surrounding or a convenient location. Others offer resort-style pools, tennis courts, indoor basketball and racquetball courts, and state-of-the art fitness centers.

The "bare bones" properties would appeal to middle-income residents because their rents are usually lower. Alternatively, upper-income renters would tend to reside in a community that contains a full amenity package. Multifamily REITs cater to both economic classes. There are advantages and disadvantages in each case.

The middle-income market is the larger of the two, but it is more sensitive to rent increases. The upper-income group is less sensitive to rent increases, but individuals in this group are more apt to enter the home ownership market when the appropriate time comes (i.e., marriage, decision to settle down, etc.). Specific market conditions will also influence the investment appeal of owning properties that cater to one economic class or the other. This is because the income level of renters, as well as the quality of job opportunities in a market area, will impact the type of apartments that will be supported. Higher income levels and a significant number of professional job opportunities, for instance, will create a need for "luxury" apartments in a given marketplace.

The most difficult aspect of managing an apartment property is tenant turnover. Unlike office buildings and retail properties where tenants normally sign multiyear leases, apartment renters sign leases of one year duration or less. As a result, tenant turnover can be high—often as much as 60 to 70 percent of the tenant base each year. This makes multifamily residential properties highly management intensive and costly to maintain.

Owning apartment properties does have its advantages:[4]

- The broad tenant base of apartment complexes tends to make cash flow fairly predictable because the relocation decision of one or a few tenants has a minimal impact on the overall profitability of the property.

- Tenant improvement costs are both more predictable and smaller than they are for other properties, such as office buildings.

- For investors, the value of apartment properties can be more accurately analyzed. That's because apartment leases are short term; therefore, they reflect current market rates and the true earning power of the property. This compares to longer term leases for office buildings and retail facilities, where existing tenants may be paying rates that are well above or below current market rates.

- It is generally easier to predict demand for apartment units than for other property types because information on the factors that dictate demand (demographics and economic conditions) are readily available.

Demand for multifamily apartment units is dictated by two factors: household formation and the likelihood that newly formed households will rent. Household formations, which can include a newly married couple or an individual moving out on his or her own, can be very cyclical and are normally related to job formations and consumer confidence. A strong economy where there are plenty of employment opportunities will result in more household formations.[5]

The likelihood that newly formed households will rent instead of purchasing depends on their ability to afford a home and their desire to own. Whether or not a household can afford to buy will be dictated largely by the level of home prices in a given market area and by mortgage rates. The desire to own a home, meanwhile, is subject to a variety of concerns; including the responsibilities of owning a home, interest in settling down, and the proximity of affordable homes to the workplace.

In the early 1980s, demand for apartment units was strong. From 1980 to 1985, rental household formations generally increased from year to year, reaching a peak in 1985 of more than 800,000. Since then, however, they have declined.[6] The drop-off in household formations in the late 1980s led to a decline in demand for apartment units at an inopportune time: just as an excess supply of units had come onto the market. The result was apartment vacancy levels of historic proportions toward the end of the decade, as shown in Exhibit 5-1.[7]

By 1991, however, the demand/supply cycle for apartments turned favorable again. As economic growth accelerated, rental demand rose, while new construction was virtually nonexistent.

To meet renewed demand, new apartment construction has resumed in a number of markets throughout the country (Exhibit 5-2). This time around, however, the new development activity is not expected to come close to the frenzied levels of the mid-1980s. Granted, various markets may still become overbuilt and underbuilt from time to time because even with the best planning, it is difficult

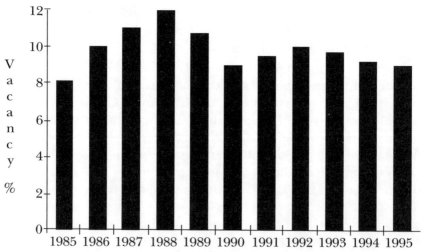

Exhibit 5-1   National Apartment Vacancy Rates SOURCE: U.S. Census Bureau

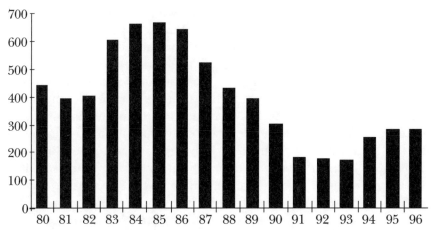

Exhibit 5-2 U.S. Multifamily New Construction (in thousands of units) SOURCE: U.S. Census Bureau

to precisely match demand and supply in any given year. However, it is still a safe bet that the market corrections will be less severe.

A key reason why new property development should not be a problem this time around is because there will be less of a need to build new properties. That is due to the fact that the number of new household formations this decade is not expected to match the average 540,000 rental household formations of the 1980s. The reason: the aging population of the United States. These demographic trends point to a more difficult environment for apartment owners for the remainder of the 1990s. This makes it even more imperative that the REITs that focus in this sector of the industry devise and implement strategies that will enable them to gain a competitive advantage. Obtaining this advantage, though, can be difficult.

Most apartment REITs try to make the task a more manageable one by focusing their efforts in a particular region of the United States. This enables them to gain a solid understanding of the markets in which they operate and the competitive forces in those markets.

A number of multifamily REITs attempt to gain an edge by concentrating their operations in high growth markets. Cities such as Atlanta, Phoenix, Las Vegas, and Dallas have been targeted by REITs such as Post Properties (Atlanta), Evans Withycombe (Phoenix), Oasis Residential (Las Vegas), and AMLI Residential (Dallas) due to their future growth prospects.

Other REITs have selected markets where there are significant barriers to entry. One such barrier is buying a property in an "in-fill" location where large-scale new construction is virtually nonexistent due to a lack of land suitable for development or due to strong anti-growth sentiment among the local population. Avalon Properties has been successful with this strategy in the Northeastern United States (primarily New England) and in the mid-Atlantic states; Charles E. Smith Residential Realty has employed it in Washington D.C.; and Bay Apartment Communities and Essex Property Trust have both utilized it to their advantage in San Francisco. It is not a coincidence that all four companies have extensive experience developing properties in their respective markets, and have been successful in acquiring and re-zoning available land.

Columbus Realty specializes in developing new apartments in Uptown Dallas, an area which is immediately adjacent to the downtown business district. Its properties, which cater to a more upscale tenant base, are mid-rise buildings constructed in close proximity to shops and restaurants. Columbus Realty's development activities are part of an effort to transform Dallas from a 9-to-5 work city to a lively, 24-hour metropolis.

By developing in these "in-fill" locations, REITs are able to bring new apartment units to areas where the current supply of units consists primarily of older properties. These new communities are generally able to charge a premium over existing market rents and experience rapid lease-up, since there is pent-up demand in the marketplace for such product.

Another multifamily REIT uses a different version of the barrier to entry to its advantage. Irvine Apartment Communities owns the sole rights to develop apartment properties in the nation's largest master planned community, Irvine Ranch. Irvine Ranch spans more than 90 square miles and three major cities in southern California. Through its ownership of the existing supply of multifamily properties on the Ranch and its development rights, Irvine Apartment Communities has a monopoly in this sub-market.

A more seldom used method utilized by multifamily REITs to gain a competitive advantage is through financing. Multifamily property investors have access to tax-exempt debt. This below market-rate financing reduces the cost of operating a community; however, there is a price tag. In order to receive this debt, a multifamily REIT must set aside a certain percentage of its apartment units (usually 20 percent) at affordable rents. Affordable rents are based upon a percentage of an area's median income. So, there is a trade-off, but if the interest rate savings from the tax-exempt financing is greater than the reduced revenue from the set-aside units, the tax-exempt financing can be very attractive. One REIT which specializes in securing this type of financing for its properties is Ambassador Apartments. In fact, this Chicago-based company calls itself "The Tax-Exempt Bond REIT" to clearly identify its strategy.

A competitive strategy, which has been employed for more than 20 years by Post Properties in Atlanta, but which is being increasingly employed by a number of other multifamily REITs, is the creation of a brand image. The brand image strategy has, of course, been utilized effectively in a number of other industries, including restaurants, hotels, and retail. In the multifamily industry, the concept is the same: Use the REIT's name to market a standardized product to consumers. This strategy is used primarily by REITs that engage in new property development, because it enhances their ability to offer a standardized product in the marketplace.

Regardless of how attractive an apartment property is, though, there is another aspect of a multifamily REIT's operations that plays a key role in the success or failure of its communities: customer service. A multifamily REIT must take care of its customers, the residents of its apartment properties. This has led a number of REITs to develop mission statements to motivate their employees. Gables Residential says it is "taking care of the way people live." Mid-America Properties "strive(s) relentlessly to please our customers by presenting choice homes within outstanding apartment communities." Oasis Residential wants "to be uncompromising in our resolve to serve our residents." Post Properties plans "to provide the superior apartment living experience for our residents." AMLI Residential aims to "provide an outstanding living environment for our residents."

Some of these REITs convey their company's business philosophy through formalized instruction. Gables Residential has Gables University through which its employees participate in sessions on customer service, operations, performance, and delivering exceptional service.

Post Properties has formed Post University, a partnership between the company and the Michael J. Coles School of Business at Kennesaw College in Atlanta. In courses led by the faculty of the

School of Business, Post Properties managers take courses on team building, marketing communication, accounting, time management, conflict resolution, customer service, and creative problem-solving.

This formalized instruction is just not for show. Apartment REIT managers must understand their customers, their lifestyles and location preferences, if they are to successfully provide the living environments their tenants demand. Earning resident satisfaction, increasing rents as market conditions allow, maximizing rent collections, and maintaining high occupancy levels, enable a multifamily REIT to maximize its revenue and profits.

Ensuring that residents are satisfied is a key to sustaining high occupancy levels. It not only eliminates the cost of preparing an apartment for a new resident, it reduces marketing expenses and allows on-site personnel to spend more of their time taking care of the needs of existing residents. (One apartment REIT estimates that each move out costs it an average of two months rent as a result of the expense of preparing the unit for a new tenant and the loss of rental income.)[8]

Pleasing future apartment residents is not likely to get any easier. This is because many of tomorrow's tenants will rent not because of economics, but due to a lifestyle choice. They may be individuals not interested in assuming the responsibilities associated with home ownership, or they may be professionals seeking to rent closer to work rather than buying farther away. Regardless of the reason, the fact is that these type of residents will be more demanding in the amenity package they will expect. They will require larger apartment units with such features as a washer and dryer, hardwood floors, upgraded interior finishes, and attached garages. They will also expect improved security measures, such as access gates, in-unit alarm systems, keyless entry systems, and better locks.[9]

Rapidly changing technology will also increase resident needs. As more economic transactions originate in the home and more business people operate out of their residences, apartment properties will have to adapt. Some communities already have through the introduction of multiple phone lines in apartment units and on-site executive business centers containing copiers, fax machines, computers, laser printers, and conference rooms.

There is little doubt that the multifamily sector will be one worth watching in the future. The ever-changing needs of residents, combined with technological developments, will make this segment of the REIT industry more competitive than ever before.

This increased level of competition has resulted in a number of smaller multifamily REITs being acquired by their larger brethren. In 1984, Holly Properties was acquired by Wellsford Residential. The following year, America First merged into Mid-America Apartment Communities. In 1996, REIT of California merged with BRE Properties, and United Dominion bought out South West Property Trust. That was followed in early 1997 with the acquisition of Paragon Properties by Camden Properties Trust and Wellsford Residential Property Trust being taken over by Equity Residential.

Some industry watchers believe we will witness even more consolidation in the years to come.[10] This will be necessary for multifamily REITs to attract more attention from institutional investors where size is of paramount importance. That means that the larger, publicly-owned REITs, with their access to low cost capital, will be in the forefront. They will not only have the option of expanding through the traditional methods of raising capital via stock and debt underwritings, but also by merging with or acquiring other public REITs.[11]

Companies such as Equity Residential Properties, Security Capital Pacific Trust, United Dominion Trust, Avalon Properties, Security Capital Atlantic, Post Properties, Merry Land and Investment, and BRE Properties are the dominant trusts in the multifamily sector; at least in terms of size. Many of these REITs took advantage of the increased interest in this segment in the early 1990s to expand their operations, and they are now some of the largest REITs in the industry.[12]

Another factor that will determine which REITs will be the premier multifamily companies in the future is property management. This is because in a more stable real estate environment, success will be realized more from a firm's ability to generate consistent and improved operating results at its properties, than from its ability to acquire real estate advantageously. This is where this sector of the REIT industry will offer investors the opportunity for capital gains.

While the number of newly formed households in the near future will be lower than it was during the 1980s, there will still be significant demand potential from several new classes of renters: the two income earning couple not interested in maintaining a home, individuals seeking to locate closer to work rather than owning further away, and the increasing number of retirees who will want to be freed from the burdens of home ownership and have more time to enjoy their postwork years.

To be successful in the future it will be imperative that multifamily REITs have not only the ability to buy properties right, but also the necessary skills to manage them effectively.

SUMMARIES

The summaries that follow in this chapter as well as subsequent chapters include the major REITs in each property segment, but not necessarily all of the REITs in these segments. I have included some basic information on each REIT, such as when they went public, the exchange where their stock trades, their symbol, and their web address (if any). For REITs that went public this decade, I have included their initial offering price so you will be able to analyze their stock performance in their first calendar year of operations.

I have also included my assessment of each REIT's competitive strategies, as well as other pertinent information regarding the REIT's history and/or operations. The annual return for each REIT is calculated by adding the increase or decrease in stock value to the annual dividend yield, which is based on the price of the stock as of January first. These return figures may likely vary from other performance data you may encounter on these same REITs, because some analysts assume that quarterly dividends are reinvested.

Multifamily REITs

AMLI Residential Properties Trust
125 South Wacker Drive, Suite 3100
Chicago, IL 60606
(312) 984-5037
(http://www.amlires.com)

Exchange: New York (AML)
Initial Public Offering: February 8, 1994
Initial Offering Price: $20.50
Geographical Focus: Southeast, Southwest, and Midwest

Competitive Strategies: Targeting high growth markets; marketing a brand name; new property development; and investing on a joint venture basis with institutional investors.

Target Market: Upper income

Special Notes: Was the successor to a company formed in 1980 to originate and manage limited partnerships that invested in apartment properties throughout the United States. Has joint venture investments with institutions such as Allstate Insurnace, Northwestern Mutual, The Rockefeller Foundation, The Ohio State Teachers Retirement System, and The New York State Common Retirement System.

Investment Performance:

	Close	Gain/Loss	Dividend	% Yield	Annual Return
1994	$18.75	—	$1.47	—	—
1995	$20.00	6.7%	$1.72	9.2%	15.9%
1996	$23.38	16.9%	$1.72	8.6%	25.5%

Ambassador Apartments, Inc.
77 West Wacker Drive, Suite 4040
Chicago, IL 60601
(312) 917-1600
(http://www.aah.com)

Exchange: New York (AAH)
Initial Public Offering: August 31, 1994
Initial Offering Price: $16.00
Geographical Focus: Southern United States
Competitive Strategies: Calls itself "The Tax-Exempt Bond REIT" as its special niche in the industry is its focus on securing tax-exempt housing bonds to finance property acquisitions and re-development.

Target Market: Middle income

Special Notes: Formed to continue the multifamily operations of The Prime Group, which was also responsible for Prime Retail (NASDAQ:PRME), a publicly-traded REIT focusing in the factory outlet business. Ambassador Apartments was initially called Prime Residential, but changed its name in early 1996.

Investment Performance:

	Close	Gain/Loss	Dividend	% Yield	Annual Return
1994	$15.88	—	$0.14	—	—
1995	$18.50	12.3%	$1.60	9.7%	22.0%
1996	$23.63	27.7%	$1.60	8.3%	36.0%

Apartment Investment and Management Company
1873 South Bellaire Street, Suite 1700
Denver, CO 80222-4348
(303) 757-8101

Exchange: New York (AIV)
Initial Public Offering: July 29, 1994
Initial Offering Price: $18.50
Geographical Focus: Southwest, South-central and Southeast
Competitive Strategies: Targeting high growth markets; identifying new acquisitions through third party property management operations; and purchasing properties for less than replacement value.
Target Market: Middle income
Special Notes: The company targets middle income renters because there is less new construction in the market segment and demand is more predictable since fewer tenants have the financial resources to buy a home.
Investment Performance:

	Close	Gain/Loss	Dividend	% Yield	Annual Return
1994	$17.25	—	$0.29	—	—
1995	$19.38	12.3%	$1.66	9.7%	22.0%
1996	$28.25	45.8%	$1.70	8.8%	54.6%

Associated Estates Realty Corporation
5025 Swetland Court
Richmond Heights, OH 44143-1467
(216) 261-5000
(http://www.aecrealty.com)

Exchange: New York (AEC)
Initial Public Offering: November 19, 1993
Initial Offering Price: $22.00
Geographical Focus: Great Lakes Region
Competitive Strategies: Highly focused geographically and new property development
Target Market: Middle and upper income
Special Notes: Successor to an organization founded in 1964 to build, manage, and own apartment properties in Cleveland, Ohio.
Investment Performance:

	Close	Gain/Loss	Dividend	% Yield	Annual Return
1993	$20.75	—	$0.19	—	—
1994	$21.00	1.0%	$1.60	7.7%	8.7%
1995	$21.50	2.4%	$1.72	8.2%	10.6%
1996	$23.75	10.5%	$1.80	8.4%	18.9%

Avalon Properties
15 River Road
Wilton, CT 06897
(203) 761-6500
(http://www.avalonprop.com)

Exchange: New York (AVN)
Initial Public Offering: August 24, 1993
Initial Offering Price: $20.50
Geographical Focus: Mid-Atlantic and Northeast
Competitive Strategies: New property development in "in-fill" locations; brand name marketing strategy; third party management operations; regional offices in Virginia, Massachusetts, and New Jersey, enable it to monitor local market conditions and interact more effectively with local officials on new property developments.
Target Market: Upper income
Special Notes: Formed to continue the business operations of Trammel Crow Residential Mid-Atlantic Group and Northeast Group. These groups were part of the operations of national real estate developer Trammel Crow, which was one of the largest owners and managers of real estate in the country during the 1980s.

Investment Performance:

	Close	Gain/Loss	Dividend	% Yield	Annual Return
1993	$20.50	—	$0.17	—	—
1994	$23.00	12.2%	$1.08	5.3%	17.5%
1995	$21.50	(6.5)%	$1.46	6.4%	(0.1)%
1996	$28.75	33.7%	$1.49	6.9%	40.6%

BRE Properties, Inc.
One Montgomery Street, Suite 2500
San Francisco, CA 94104-5525
(415) 445-6530
(http://www.breproperties.com)

Exchange: New York (BRE)
Initial Public Offering: 1970
Geographical Focus: Western United States
Competitive Strategies: To become the preeminent multifamily REIT in the western United States; to be recognized as a market leader in efficient operations, cash flow growth, and expansion of shareholder wealth; new property development capabilities; acquire existing properties and upgrade them.
Special Notes: Merged with REIT of California in March, 1996. As a result of this merger and property acquisitions, BRE doubled the size of its portfolio during the year from 5,475 units to 12,212 units. Plans to spend $500 to $600 million through the end of this century to acquire another 10,000 apartment units.
Target Market: Middle and upper income
Investment Performance:

	Close	Gain/Loss	Dividend	% Yield	Annual Return
1991	$14.19	22.7%	$1.20	10.4%	33.1%
1992	$16.19	14.1%	$1.20	8.5%	22.6%
1993	$16.82	3.9%	$1.20	7.4%	11.3%
1994	$15.44	(8.2)%	$1.20	7.1%	(1.1)%
1995	$17.82	15.4%	$1.26	8.2%	23.6%
1996	$24.75	38.9%	$1.33	7.4%	46.3%

2 for 1 stock split in 1996

Bay Apartment Communities
4340 Stevens Creek Blvd., Suite 275
San Jose, CA 95129
(408) 983-1500
(hhtp://www.bayapartmt.com)

Exchange: New York (BYA)
Initial Public Offering: March 17, 1994
Initial Offering Price: $20.00
Geographical Focus: San Francisco Bay area and Northern California
Competitive Strategies: New property development in "in-fill" locations; acquiring assets with reconstruction needs or properties that are undermanaged; and special investment opportunities.
Target Market: Upper income
Special notes: Built more than 5,000 residential units in the San Francisco Bay area during the 15 years preceding the formation of the REIT.
Investment Performance:

	Close	Gain/Loss	Dividend	% Yield	Annual Return
1994	$20.13	—	$1.20	—	—
1995	$24.25	20.5%	$1.55	7.7%	28.2%
1996	$36.00	48.5%	$1.61	6.6%	55.1%

Berkshire Realty Company, Inc.
Harbor Plaza, 470 Atlantic Avenue
Boston, MA 02210
(800) 343-0989
(hhtp://www.brireit.com)

Exchange: New York (BRI)
Conversion Date: June 27, 1991
Conversion Price: $8.00
Geographical Focus: Southeast
Competitive Strategies: Acquiring properties with repositioning, redevelopment, or rehabilitation potential; purchase of troubled mortgages with the potential for subsequent ownership of the underlying property.

Target Market: Upper and middle income
Special notes: Formed through the consolidation of two limited partnerships: Krupp Cash Plus III and Krupp Cash Plus IV.
Investment Performance:

	Close	Gain/Loss	Dividend	% Yield	Annual Return
1991	$ 8.63	—	$0.75	—	—
1992	$ 8.63	0.0%	$1.15	13.3%	13.3%
1993	$11.00	27.5%	$0.80	9.3%	36.8%
1994	$ 9.38	(14.7)%	$0.86	7.8%	(6.9)%
1995	$ 9.63	2.7%	$0.89	9.5%	12.2%
1996	$ 9.88	2.6%	$0.90	9.4%	12.0%

Camden Property Trust
3200 Southwest Freeway, Suite 1500
Houston, TX 77027
(713) 964-3555
(800)9-CAMDEN
(http://www.camdenprop.com)

Exchange: New York (CPT)
Initial Public Offering: August 1993
Initial Offering Price: $22.00
Geographical Focus: South
Competitive Strategies: Concentrated geographical focus in the state of Texas; targets high growth markets such as Houston, Dallas, Phoenix, and Denver; new property development capabilities.
Target Market: Middle and upper income
Special Notes: Successor to the Centeq Companies, which had been engaged in the ownership and development of properties based in Texas since 1980. Between its initial stock offering in mid-1993 and year-end 1996, the company's portfolio grew by more than three times its original $187 million size. In early 1997, it merged with The Paragon Group (NYSE:PAO), another publicly-owned REIT focused in the multifamily sector, bringing its asset base to more than $1.25 billion.

Investment Performance:

	Close	Gain/Loss	Dividend	% Yield	Annual Return
1993	$25.25	—	$0.28	—	—
1994	$24.88	(1.5)%	$1.76	7.0%	5.5%
1995	$23.75	(4.5)%	$1.84	7.4%	2.9%
1996	$28.63	20.5%	$1.90	8.0%	28.5%

Columbus Realty Trust
15851 Dallas Parkway, Suite 855
Dallas, TX 75248
(972) 387-1492
(http://www.columbusrt.com)

Exchange: New York (CLB)
Initial Public Offering: December 29, 1993
Initial Offering Price: $17.25
Geographical Focus: Dallas, Texas
Competitive Strategies: Concentrated geographical focus in Dallas, Texas; new property development in an established area in Uptown Dallas and in Los Colinas, a Dallas suburb.
Target Market: Upper income
Special notes: Columbus Realty's multifamily communities are of recent vintage. The company has specialized in developing properties in Uptown Dallas, an area immediately adjacent to the downtown central business district.
Investment Performance:

	Close	Gain/Loss	Dividend	% Yield	Annual Return
1993	$17.38	—	$ —	—	—
1994	$18.50	6.4%	$1.49	8.6%	15.0%
1995	$19.38	4.7%	$1.50	8.1%	12.8%
1996	$22.75	17.4%	$1.56	8.1%	25.5%

Cornerstone Realty Income Trust
306 East Main Street
Richmond, VA 23219
(804) 643-1761

Exchange: New York (TCR)
Initial Public Offering: April 18, 1997
Initial Offering Price: $10.50
Geographical Focus: Southeast
Competitive Strategies: Acquire under-performing assets at less than replacement cost and increase their value through improved management and selected renovations; maintain high occupancy levels by minimizing tenant turnover at its properties.
Target Market: Middle income
Special notes: Cornerstone Realty has regional offices in Virginia, North Carolina, and South Carolina. The company was founded as a private real estate firm in 1993.

Equity Residential Properties Trust
Two North Riverside Plaza
Chicago, IL 60606-2639
(312) 474-1300

Exchange: New York (EQR)
Initial Public Offering: August 18, 1993
Initial Offering Price: $26.00
Geographical Focus: National
Competitive Strategies: It is one of the largest REITs in the industry, which better enables it to tap the capital markets for lower cost capital and attract greater attention from institutional investors; its national portfolio of apartment properties insulates it from regional economic downturns; third party management operations; acquisition of sizable portfolios from other institutional investors reduces property acquisition costs.
Target Market: Middle income
Special notes: The successor to the multifamily property business of Equity Properties Management Corporation, an entity founded in 1969 and controlled by real estate investor Sam Zell. To manage its portfolio, Equity Residential operates six regional centers located strategically in Washington, D.C., Tampa, Dallas, Chicago, Denver, and Seattle. In early 1997, it acquired Wellsford Residential Prop-

erty Trust (NYSE: WRP), giving it a total stock market value of more than $3 billion.

Investment Performance:

	Close	Gain/Loss	Dividend	% Yield	Annual Return
1993	$31.88	—	$0.68	—	—
1994	$30.00	(5.9)%	$2.01	6.3%	0.4%
1995	$30.63	2.1%	$2.18	7.3%	9.4%
1996	$41.25	34.7%	$2.50	8.2%	42.9%

Essex Property Trust Inc.
777 California Street
Palo Alto, CA 94304
(415) 494-3700
(http://www.essexproperties.com)

Exchange: New York (ESS)
Initial Public Offering: June 13, 1994
Initial Offering Price: $19.50
Geographical Focus: Pacific Coast states
Competitive Strategies: New property development in "in-fill" locations; geographically focused in sub-markets where there are numerous constraints to development, have a high quality of life, a diverse and growing employment base, and a high cost of home ownership.
Target Market: Middle and upper income
Special Notes: The successor to Essex Property Corporation, which had been engaged in the acquisition, development, and management of properties in the Western United States since 1971. Recorded the highest overall return of all major multifamily REITs in both 1995 and 1996.
Investment Performance:

	Close	Gain/Loss	Dividend	% Yield	Annual Return
1994	$15.13	—	$0.91	—	—
1995	$19.25	27.3%	$1.70	11.2%	38.5%
1996	$29.38	52.6%	$1.72	8.9%	61.5%

Evans Withycombe Residential, Inc.
6991 East Camelback Road, Suite A200
Scottsdale, AZ 85251
(602) 840-1040

Exchange: New York (EWR)
Initial Public Offering: August 10, 1994
Initial Offering Price: $20.00
Geographical Focus: Arizona
Competitive Strategies: Focused geographically in high growth markets; new property development; third party management operations.
Target Market: Middle and Upper Income
Special notes: Successor to a company that was founded in 1977 and has grown to become the largest developer and manager of apartment properties in the state of Arizona.
Investment Performance:

	Close	Gain/Loss	Dividend	% Yield	Annual Return
1994	$21.00	—	$0.55	—	—
1995	$21.50	2.4%	$1.50	7.1%	9.5%
1996	$21.00	(2.3)%	$1.20	7.4%	5.1%

Gables Residential Trust
2859 Paces Ferry Road, Suite 1450
Atlanta, GA 30339
(770) 436-4600
(http://www.gables.com)

Exchange: New York (GBP)
Initial Public Offering: January 26, 1994
Initial Offering Price: $22.50
Geographical Focus: South and Southeast
Competitive Strategies: New property development; geographically focused in eight markets: Atlanta, Memphis, Nashville, Houston, Dallas, San Antonio, Austin, and Orlando; brand awareness strategy; third party management operations.
Special Notes: The company attempts to create communities which complement the neighborhoods where they are built. Gables prop-

erties contain added features such as access-controlled gates, additional closet space, nine foot high ceilings, and attached garages. Selected by Walt Disney Company in early 1997 to develop an apartment property in a town Disney is creating 20 miles south of Orlando, Florida.

Investment Performance:

	Close	Gain/Loss	Dividend	% Yield	Annual Return
1994	$21.50	—	$1.67	—	—
1995	$22.88	6.4%	$1.86	8.7%	15.1%
1996	$29.00	26.8%	$1.94	8.5%	35.3%

Home Properties of New York, Inc.
850 Clinton Square
Rochester, NY 14604
(716) 546-4900
(http://www.home properties.com)

Exchange: New York (HME)
Initial Public Offering: August 4, 1994
Initial Offering Price: $19.00
Geographical Focus: Upper New York state
Competitive Strategies: Acquisition of existing properties that the company can add value to through renovations and more intensive management; geographically focused in New York; third party management operations; focus in markets where there is little new construction.
Target Market: Senior citizens and middle income
Special Notes: Successor to Home Leasing Corporation, which was founded over three decades ago.
Investment Performance:

	Close	Gain/Loss	Dividend	% Yield	Annual Return
1994	$19.63	—	$0.26	—	—
1995	$17.13	(12.7)%	$1.66	8.4%	(4.3)%
1996	$22.50	31.4%	$1.69	9.9%	41.3%

Irvine Apartment Communities, Inc.
550 Newport Center Drive, Suite 300
Newport Beach, CA 92660
(714) 720-5500
(http://www.iac-apts.com)

Exchange: New York (IAC)
Initial Public Offering: December 1993
Initial Offering Price: $17.50
Geographical Focus: Southern California
Competitive Strategies: Owns exclusive rights to develop multifamily properties in the Irvine Ranch, the nation's largest master planned community located in Orange County, California; develops a variety of properties to meet the needs of young professionals, growing families, empty-nesters, students, and senior citizens; reduces operating expenses through centralized marketing and leasing efforts.
Target Market: Generally upper income
Special Notes: Its UPREIT partner is the Irvine Company, which has owned and developed the Irvine Ranch since 1864. The Irvine Ranch is home to more than 17,000 businesses, 175,000 residents, and 200,000 employees. With more than 52,000 acres still available for development, it is one of the most valuable development opportunities in the country.
Investment Performance:

	Close	Gain/Loss	Dividend	% Yield	Annual Return
1993	$17.88	—	—	—	—
1994	$16.38	(8.4)%	$1.11	6.2%	(1.8)%
1995	$19.25	17.6%	$1.39	8.7%	26.3%
1996	$25.00	29.9%	$1.44	7.5%	37.4%

Merry Land & Investment, Inc.
624 Ellis Street
Augusta, GA 30903
(706) 722-6756

Exchange: New York (MRY)
Initial Public Offering: 1981

Initial Offering Price: $7.50
Geographical Focus: Southeast
Competitive Strategies: It is one of the largest REITs in the industry; goal is to be the largest owner of high end apartments in the South; new property development capabilities; market concentration.
Target Market: Upper Income
Special Notes: Originally incorporated in 1966 as a subsidiary of the Merry Companies, a brick manufacturer, it became a separate publicly-owned corporation in 1981 and a REIT in 1987. From its inception as a separate public company in 1981 through the end of 1996, Merry Land & Investment provided its shareholders with an average annual compound return of 21.5 percent.
Investment Performance:

	Close	Gain/Loss	Dividend	% Yield	Annual Return
1991	$ 8.00	106.5%	$0.44	11.4%	117.9%
1992	$15.00	87.5%	$0.66	8.3%	95.8%
1993	$20.00	33.3%	$0.90	6.0%	39.3%
1994	$21.88	9.4%	$1.25	6.3%	15.7%
1995	$23.63	8.0%	$1.40	6.4%	14.4%
1996	$21.50	(9.0)%	$1.48	6.3%	(2.7)%

Mid-America Apartment Communities, Inc.
6584 Poplar Avenue, Suite 340
Memphis, TN 38138
(901) 682-6600
(hhtp://www.maapart.com)

Exchange: New York (MAA)
Initial Public Offering: February 4, 1994
Initial Offering Price: $19.75
Geographical Focus: Southeast and Central states
Competitive Strategies: Invests in second tier markets where the competition for properties is generally lower; acquires properties to which it can add value through refurbishment, more intensive management, and expansion; aggressive attitude toward expense control.
Target Market: Middle and upper income

Special Notes: Merged with another multifamily REIT, America First (AMEX:AFR), in mid-1995. Recorded the highest percentage increase in profits of all major apartment REITs in 1995.
Investment Performance:

	Close	Gain/Loss	Dividend	% Yield	Annual Return
1994	$26.75	—	$1.71	—	—
1995	$24.75	(7.5)%	$2.01	8.5%	0.0%
1996	$28.88	16.7%	$2.04	7.4%	24.9%

Oasis Residential, Inc.
4041 E. Sunset Road
Henderson, NV 89014
(702) 435-9800
(http://www.oasisres.com)

Exchange: New York (OAS)
Initial Public Offering: October 1993
Initial Offering Price: $21.75
Geographical Focus: Nevada
Competitive Strategies: Highly focused geographically in Las Vegas; strong new property development capabilities; brand awareness strategy.
Target Market: Middle income and Upper income
Special Notes: The successor to the real estate development and management business started by the company's chairman, Robert Jones, in 1976. The largest owner of apartment properties in Las Vegas.
Investment Performance:

	Close	Gain/Loss	Dividend	% Yield	Annual Return
1993	$24.88	—	$0.29	—	—
1994	$24.50	(1.5)%	$1.52	6.1%	4.6%
1995	$22.75	(7.1)%	$1.64	6.7%	(0.4)%
1996	$22.75	0.0%	$1.74	7.7%	7.7%

Post Properties, Inc.
3350 Cumberland Circle, Suite 2200
Atlanta, GA 30339-3363
(770) 850-4400

Exchange: New York (PPS)
Initial Public Offering: July 22, 1993
Initial Offering Price: $25.50
Geographical Focus: Southeast
Competitive Strategies: New property development capability with an in-house construction division; highly focused geographically with a concentration of properties in Atlanta; brand awareness strategy; third party asset and property management services.
Target Market: Middle and upper income
Special Notes: Successor to a company that was formed in 1971 and, since such time, has been continuously involved in developing and managing multifamily residential properties primarily in the Atlanta, Georgia, marketplace.
Investment Performance:

	Close	Gain/Loss	Dividend	% Yield	Annual Return
1993	$30.75	—	$0.77	—	—
1994	$31.50	2.4%	$1.80	5.9%	8.3%
1995	$31.88	1.2%	$1.96	6.2%	7.4%
1996	$40.25	26.3%	$2.16	6.8%	33.1%

Security Capital Atlantic, Inc.
6 Piedmont Center, Suite 600
Atlanta, GA 30305
(800) 201-0632

Exchange: New York (SCA)
Initial Public Offering: October 15, 1996
Initial Offering Price: $24.00
Geographical Focus: Southeast
Competitive Strategies: Size; new property development capability; focus on high growth markets; extensive research operations.
Target Market: Middle Income
Special Notes: Security Capital Atlantic was started as a private

REIT by investor William Sanders in 1993. Owns approximately a 15% interest in Homestead Village Properties (NYSE: HSD), a company which specializes in the development and management of extended stay hotels.
Investment Performance:

	Close	Gain/Loss	Dividend	% Yield	Annual Return
1996	$24.50	—	$2.30*	—	—

*Includes a special distribution

Security Capital Pacific Trust
7777 Market Center Avenue
El Paso, TX 79912
(800) 982-9293

Exchange: New York (PTR)
Initial Public Offering: 1963
Initial Offering Price: $10.00
Geographical Focus: Western half of the United States
Competitive Strategies: Size; new property development capability; focus on high growth markets; extensive research operations.
Target Market: Middle Income
Special Notes: Security Capital Pacific Trust was formed in March, 1995 as a result of the merger of two existing REITs: Property Trust of America and Security Capital Pacific. Property Trust of America was organized as a REIT in 1963, while Security Capital Pacific was previously a private REIT formed in 1993. Owns approximately a significant interest in Homestead Village Properties (NYSE: HSD), a company which specializes in the development and management of extended stay hotels.
Investment Performance:

	Close	Gain/Loss	Dividend	% Yield	Annual Return
1991	$10.00	42.9%	$0.64	9.1%	52.0%
1992	$14.00	40.0%	$0.70	7.0%	47.0%
1993	$20.00	42.9%	$0.82	5.9%	48.8%
1994	$18.00	(10.0)%	$1.00	5.0%	(5.0)%
1995	$19.75	9.7%	$1.15	6.4%	16.1%
1996	$22.88	34.5%	$3.40*	17.2%	51.7%

*Includes a special distribution

Charles E. Smith Residential Realty, Inc.
2345 Crystal Drive
Arlington, VA 22202
(703) 920-8500
(http://www.smithreit.com)

Exchange: New York (SRW)
Initial Public Offering: June 30, 1994
Initial Offering Price: $24.00
Geographical Focus: Washington D.C.
Competitive Strategies: Highly focused geographically; third party management operations; new property development capabilities.
Target Market: Middle and upper income
Special Notes: Successor to an entity that had been engaged in the development and management of real estate in the Washington D.C. area since 1946. The company's apartment properties come in a variety of styles: high rise mid-rise structures, and garden style. Some properties cater to middle income renters, while others are "luxury" complexes providing such amenities as exercise rooms, sauna and locker rooms, daily continental breakfast, and an activities director on site.
Investment Performance:

	Close	Gain/Loss	Dividend	% Yield	Annual Return
1994	$25.38	—	$0.48	—	—
1995	$23.63	(6.9)%	$1.92	7.6%	0.7%
1996	$29.25	23.8%	$1.98	8.4%	32.2%

Summit Properties Inc.
212 South Tryon Street, Suite 500
Charlotte, NC 28281
(704) 334-9905
(http://www.smtprop@ad.com)

Exchange: New York (SMT)
Initial Public Offering: February 15, 1994
Initial Share Price: $19.00
Geographical Focus: Southeast and Midwest
Competitive Strategies: Significant new property development capability; maintains a high quality of product; brand awareness strategy.

Target Market: Upper income
Special Notes: Successor to a company founded in 1981. Summit customizes its properties to fit a particular customer profile and geographic market. It designs and develops communities aimed at affluent professionals who have the ability to buy a home, but choose to rent because of flexibility and convenience.
Investment Performance:

	Close	Gain/Loss	Dividend	% Yield	Annual Return
1994	$19.25	—	$1.29	—	—
1995	$19.88	3.3%	$1.51	7.8%	11.1%
1996	$22.13	11.3%	$1.55	7.8%	19.1%

Town and Country Trust
100 South Charles Street, Suite 1700
Baltimore, MD 21201
(410) 539-7600
(http://www.tctrust.com)

Exchange: New York (TCT)
Initial Public Offering: August 23, 1993
Initial Offering Price: $22.00
Geographical Focus: Mid-Atlantic states
Competitive Strategies: Brand awareness strategy; focus on minimizing property level turnover, resulting in higher average occupancy levels.
Target Market: Middle income
Special Notes: Successor to a company which started its operations in 1979.
Investment Performance:

	Close	Gain/Loss	Dividend	% Yield	Annual Return
1993	$20.38	—	$0.17	—	—
1994	$14.25	(30.1)%	$1.60	7.9%	(22.2)%
1995	$13.00	(8.8)%	$1.60	11.2%	2.4%
1996	$14.63	12.5%	$1.60	12.3%	24.8%

United Dominion Realty Trust
10 South Sixth Street, Suite 203
Richmond, VA 23219-3802
(804) 780-2691
(http://www.udrt.com)

Exchange: New York (UDR)
Initial Public Offering: 1972
Geographical Focus: Southeast and Southern United States
Competitive Strategies: To be a dominant apartment owner in major markets in the Sunbelt; acquire newer communities at discounts from their replacement values and older or under-performing communities that can be upgraded and repositioned by capital improvements and more intensive management.
Target Market: Middle Income
Special Notes: Founded as a REIT in 1972. Through 1996, it had paid quarterly dividends to shareholders since inception and had increased the dividend payment every year for the prior 19 years. From 1980 through 1996, United Dominion provided shareholders with an average annual return of more than 20 percent. Merged with South West Property Trust (NYSE:SWP), another public multi-family REIT, at the end of 1996, making it the largest REIT owner of apartments in the Sunbelt.
Investment Performance:

	Close	Gain/Loss	Dividend	% Yield	Annual Return
1991	$10.32	38.7%	$0.63	8.5%	47.2%
1992	$12.63	22.4%	$0.66	6.4%	28.8%
1993	$14.25	12.8%	$0.70	5.5%	18.3%
1994	$14.38	0.9%	$0.78	5.5%	6.4%
1995	$15.00	4.3%	$0.90	6.3%	10.6%
1996	$15.50	3.3%	$0.96	6.4%	9.7%

Walden Residential Properties
One Lincon Center
5400 LBJ Freeway, Suite 400
Dallas, TX 75240
(972) 788-0510
(http://www.waldenresidential.com)

Exchange: New York (WDN)
Initial Public Offering: February 9, 1994
Initial Share Price: $19.25
Geographical Focus: Southeast and Southwest
Competitive Strategies: Purchase properties below their estimated reproduction cost; acquire apartments whose profitability can be enhanced through strategic capital improvements and more intensive property management.
Target Market: Middle Income
Special Notes: The Walden Group was formed in 1974 by company chairman Don Daeske. The company maintains regional offices in Atlanta, Austin, Dallas, Houston, Ft. Worth, and Tulsa. In May 1997, they announced an agreement to acquire Drever Partners, a private real estate company based in San Francisco and Houston, in a deal valued at almost $670 million. Drever's portfolio of 80 apartment communities would roughly double Walden's size and make it one of the largest multifamily REITs in the country.
Investment Performance:

	Close	Gain/Loss	Dividend	% Yield	Annual Return
1994	$17.88	—	$1.09	—	—
1995	$20.88	16.8%	$1.82	10.2%	27.0%
1996	$24.88	19.2%	$1.86	8.9%	28.1%

CHAPTER SIX

Manufactured Housing

A NOTHER SEGMENT OF THE residential marketplace is the manufactured housing industry. Traditionally known as mobile homes, the manufactured homes of today are much too permanent to be called "mobile." Improved construction standards, combined with significant cost advantages over site-built homes, has resulted in manufactured housing becoming a significant player in the residential marketplace.

From less than one percent of the total U.S. housing market in 1950, manufactured housing rose to seven percent of the total housing stock by the end of 1995. Most recently, the growth has been even more impressive. Since 1980, this industry segment has been the fastest expanding sector of the nation's housing market, representing almost 25 percent of all U.S. single family homes sales.[1] Exhibit 6-1 shows the remarkable growth in the manufactured housing industry.

While demand for manufactured housing has been strong, the supply side of the equation also makes manufactured home communities an appealing investment. Restrictive zoning laws, substantial start-up costs, and limited long-term financing make it difficult to develop communities.

In a number of markets, municipalities restrict the development of manufactured home communities. Even in the localities that are receptive to such development, the zoning process, with its permit filings, reviews, appeals, and final approvals, can often take years to

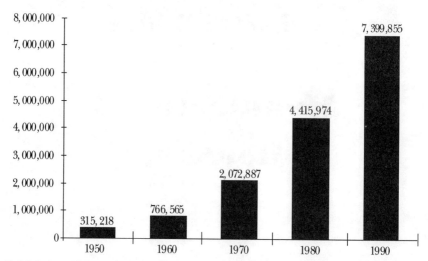

Exhibit 6-1 Manufactured Homes in the U.S. SOURCE: U.S. Department of Commerce

get through. Additionally, the cost of constructing a community's infrastructure is substantial and requires significant capital, which is often difficult to obtain.[2]

Leasing a new manufactured home community can also be challenging. One of the features of living in such a community is the benefit of interacting with neighbors. When a facility first opens, the number of residents will be limited, virtually eliminating one of the most important characteristics of such communities.

For all of these reasons, the REITs that focus in this sector purchase only existing properties. The type of properties they invest in normally contain many of the same amenities enjoyed by residents of luxury apartment complexes: pools, clubhouses, laundry facilities, children's playgrounds, fitness centers, athletic fields, and tennis courts. They are also constructed with basically the same infrastructure as regular home communities, with paved streets, curbs and gutters, underground utilities, cable television, and streetlights. Facilities located in retirement or resort areas often feature added amenities such as lakes and streams, shuffleboard courts, and RV storage areas.

Within a manufactured home community, the underlying land, utility connections, streets, and common areas are owned by the community. The residents lease their individual spaces and are responsible for acquiring and placing their own manufactured home on their leased site within the community.

The manufactured homes the residents buy today are a far cry from those of yesteryear. They can be custom built with the same amenities found in site-built homes; including modern kitchens, skylights, central air and heating systems, fireplaces, wall-to-wall carpeting, and bay windows. Some homeowners go one step further, adding fixtures such as garages, patios, and decks to their homes once they are placed in service within a manufactured housing community. Floor plans usually range from 950 square feet to as much as 2,200 square feet, providing as much living space as many site-built homes. Additionally, only manufactured homes are built to federal government standards.

These manufactured homes have numerous advantages over site-built homes. They can cost as little as 50 percent of a site-built home, they usually require a lower down payment, and the cost of land is less (because tenants rent instead of purchasing).[3]

Manufactured housing communities appeal to two different market segments: retirees and moderate income families. While most communities include both retirees and working families among their resident base, they generally cater to one group or the other. This is accomplished primarily through the amenities offered. An on-site clubhouse, shuffleboards, and tennis courts would appeal more to retirees; while pools, children's playgrounds, and athletic fields would tend to attract more families.

Manufactured home communities have proven to be a lure for retirees because it affords them the opportunity to own a residence in a community where they can maintain an active lifestyle. Moderate income families, meanwhile, are attracted to this housing alternative due to economics, because the cost of site-built homes is often out of their reach. Both groups are expected to increase in the future, as the baby boom generation matures and the number of moderate income working families escalates as a result of the increasing income disparity in the American workforce.

Communities that cater to retirees generally have more stable cash flows because retirees generally do not suffer financially during a recession. An economic downturn, however, could result in job loss or a decline in wages for working families, who will then be forced to seek alternative and less expensive housing.

Communities that cater to families, however, usually have the potential to generate higher rental rates because during good economic times, families have the ability to grow their incomes to cover rent increases. Most retirees, meanwhile, are dependent on income sources that are either fixed or are linked to increases in the inflation rate. Therefore, as a group, retirees are more sensitive to rent increases. Also, because retirees usually have more free time than working families, they are more capable of banding together to fight rental increases.

Some states actually limit the rental rate increases a manufactured housing community can impose. Two such states are California and Florida, which not coincidentally have some of the largest concentrations of manufactured housing communities in the country. Any limits, however, usually allow community owners to raise rates at the same level as inflation.

For owners of manufactured home communities, the limits on rental increases are offset by the stability of cash flow offered by these properties. Because manufactured homes are very expensive to relocate (usually $1,500 to $5,000, depending on the size of the home and the distance of the move), most homeowners stay put once they settle into a community. If they do elect to move, they usually sell their homes instead of relocating them. This results in annual physical turnover rates of only 3 to 5 percent at manufactured home communities versus 55 to 60 percent at apartment communities.[4]

Other features that make this market segment appealing include the fact that:[5]

- New construction is limited. Permits to construct communities can be difficult to obtain and the lease-up period for newly built properties is usually long; therefore, the possibility of overdevelopment in this market segment is limited,

- The percentage of tenants who take their homes and leave a community is less than one-tenth the turnover rate of most apartment complexes, thus providing a more stable income stream to community owners,

- Due to the limited amount of new construction and the high cost of relocating a manufactured home, communities are generally able to increase rents annually,

- Manufactured housing communities are less likely to suffer from "real" depreciation over time than apartment properties, retail facilities, hotels, and office buildings, because the major asset of such communities is the land they rent to residents and not physical structures,

• As site-built housing costs continue to escalate in the United States, manufactured homes will likely become an increasingly more attractive option for moderate income working families who want to own their own home,

• The cost advantages and the attractive living style of manufactured housing communities also make this alternative more appealing to the increasing population of retirees,

• Of the estimated 24,000 manufactured housing communities in the United States, less than 4 percent are owned by the 20 largest owners/operators of such communities and less than 300 are owned by the 4 publicly traded companies in this market segment. This highly fragmented marketplace of property owners makes buying opportunities more favorable because many properties are owned by families who, at some future point, may elect not to continue in the business.

The real question in this segment of the industry is how many existing manufactured home communities meet the acquisition criteria of the REITs that concentrate in this area. This criteria generally establishes that a property must be an upscale facility that is substantially leased and generating a solid return from its operations, or it must possess appreciation potential through improved occupancy, higher rental rates, and/or expansion.

Properties that have appreciation potential may include facilities that are undermanaged, communities that have not been well-maintained, or newly developed properties that are still in their lease-up stage.

The strategy of the existing manufactured housing REITs has been to acquire a core group of properties with solid occupancy levels and cash flow, and combine them with properties that offer some potential for appreciation through expansion or increased occupancy. The net result is that shareholders of manufactured housing REITs enjoy fairly predictable cash dividends from operations, along with the potential for capital gains from the expansion of existing properties or increased occupancy of recently acquired communities.

Longer term, if this segment of the industry is to grow, it may be necessary for manufactured housing REITs to either engage in new property development or acquire existing properties that need to be upgraded with some of the enhanced amenities that exist at facilities currently owned by these REITs.

Manufactured Home REITs

Chateau Communities, Inc.
6430 S. Quebec Street
Englewood, CO 80111
(303) 741-3707

Exchange: New York (CPJ)
Initial Public Offering: November 1993
Initial Offering Price: $20.00
Geographical Focus: National
Competitive Strategies: It is the largest REIT in this segment of the industry and one of the larger REITs in the country; third party management operations; seeks to invest in existing properties that offer the potential for increased revenues through rental rate increases, improved occupancy, and expansion.
Special Notes: Chateau Communities is the result of a merger between Chateau Properties and ROC Communities in February 1997. This merger created the largest manufactured housing REIT in the nation. Chateau was the successor to an organization founded in 1966 to develop, own, and operate manufactured housing communities. ROC Communities was formed in 1993 to continue the business of its predecessor company, ROC Properties, which had been engaged in the ownership and management of manufactured home communities since 1979.
Investment Performance:

	Close	Gain/Loss	Dividend	% Yield	Annual Return
1993	$21.88	—	$0.15	—	—
1994	$21.88	0.0%	$1.42	6.5%	6.5%
1995	$22.50	2.9%	$1.53	7.0%	9.9%
1996	$26.63	18.3%	$1.62	7.2%	25.5%

Manufactured Home Communities, Inc.
Two North Riverside Plaza
Chicago, IL 60606
(312) 474-1122

Exchange: New York (MHC)
Initial Public Offering: March 3, 1993
Initial Offering Price: $12.875
Geographical Focus: National
Competitive Strategies: Focuses on upscale communities—rental rates at its facilities are the highest among the public REITs focusing in this sector; by catering to senior citizens and acquiring properties that are geographically diversified, the company's portfolio will likely be more insulated from economic downturns than those of its competitors.
Special Notes: A successor to the manufactured home business operations started by Sam Zell in 1983.
Investment Performance:

	Close	Gain/Loss	Dividend	% Yield	Annual Return
1993	$21.50	—	$0.86	—	—
1994	$19.88	(7.5)%	$1.14	5.3%	(2.2)%
1995	$17.50	(11.9)%	$1.18	5.9%	(6.0)%
1996	$23.25	32.9%	$1.22	7.0%	39.9%

2 for 1 stock split in March, 1994

Sun Communities, Inc.
31700 Middlebelt Road, Suite 145
Farmington Hills, MI 48334
(248) 932-3100

Exchange: New York (SUI)
Initial Public Offering: December 15, 1993
Initial Offering Price: $20.00
Geographical Focus: Midwest and the Sunbelt states
Competitive Strategies: The company's acquisition criteria focuses on three types of situations: stabilized but undermanaged communities where rents and occupancy levels can be increased through more aggressive management, communities with expansion potential, and opportunistic lease-up acquisitions consisting primarily of newly developed properties.

Special Notes: Prior to its formation as a REIT in 1993, Sun Communities had been engaged in the ownership and management of manufactured housing communities through limited partnerships since 1975.

Investment Performance:

	Close	Gain/Loss	Dividend	% Yield	Annual Return
1993	$20.13	—	$0.08	—	—
1994	$22.50	11.8%	$1.78	8.8%	20.6%
1995	$26.38	17.2%	$1.78	7.9%	25.1%
1996	$34.50	30.8%	$1.82	6.9%	37.7%

CHAPTER SEVEN

Retail
Properties

SHOPPING CENTERS HAVE TRADITIONALLY been classified by the market area they serve, region, community, or neighborhood; however, as a result of recent trends in the industry toward greater specialization, many shopping centers are now classified by the type of shopping offered in the center. Specialty centers, for instance, offer high fashion, while outlet centers offer an array of discount stores.

The super regional mall represents the largest concentration of retail shops. It is normally anchored by 3 or more major department stores and contains over 100 small retail stores selling a wide range of items including men's, women's, and children's clothing; sporting goods; specialty gifts; luggage; electronics; books; artwork; and jewelry. Super regional malls range in size from 750,000 to more than one million square feet and generally serve a market area with a population of 200,000 or more.

The design of the super regional mall is critical to the success of small tenants. Major anchors are placed at opposite ends of the mall so that consumers traveling from one anchor to another pass by the smaller shops in between. These centers usually also contain restaurants and movie theaters that can serve as separate destination stops for customers.

The regional center is normally very similar in layout and has many of the same tenants as super regional malls. The primary difference is size. The regional malls range in size from 300,000 to

750,000 square feet and generally include one or more regional or major department stores, each with at least 100,000 square feet of space. These stores will be complemented by up to 100 smaller shops and restaurants.

A community center is usually built around a junior department store, discount store, or variety store. It normally includes shops that sell clothing, as well as hard-line products such as appliances and hardwares, and may also include a supermarket. Community centers range in size from 100,000 to 300,000 square feet and may be either enclosed, open-air, or set up as a strip center (a center with a single line of tenants or a single-side design). They have usually been associated with super-discount stores such as Kmart, Wal-Mart, or Target because the advertising, low prices, and reputation of these retailers help generate traffic for these centers.

Community centers generally require trade areas with populations exceeding 100,000; however, these centers are often found in smaller, rural locations and serve a wider area than would be the case with similar retail properties located in population centers.

The fourth type of center, the neighborhood center, is usually a strip center of 100,000 square feet or less, built around a supermarket or drug store. It will include stores that sell convenience goods such as food, drugs, and sundries, as well as shops that provide personal services such as a hair salon, dry cleaners, and travel agency.

Specialty shopping centers generally are smaller in size, about 50,000 square feet, and usually contain only local retailers. Most feature restaurants and stores that sell high-fashion clothing, books, or specialty items. These centers are normally located in business areas and convention locations, and generate most of their sales during the business day. Thus, even more so than the other types of shopping centers, location is key to their success. Most of these centers cater to convenience or impulse shopping.

Another type of center that is relatively new to the industry is the "power center." Typically, power centers comprise three or more category killer retailers in "big box" buildings that range in size from 25,000 to a 150,000 square feet. (Category killers are retailers that specialize in a single kind of merchandise.) The attraction of these stores include their wide range of selections and the value pricing they offer for goods such as toys, electronics, computers, home furnishings, and hardware.[1]

Regardless of its size, the success of any shopping center is dependent on the scope of its trade area, the quality of its market, and the competitive position of the center. From the owner's perspective, the keys to a successful center are major tenants that will draw consumers to the center, the right mix of tenants (providing for one stop shopping for consumers), lease terms that enable the owner to maximize rental income, and provisions under which the tenants pay for much of the center's operating expenses.[2]

Rental terms for individual tenants in a shopping center will vary depending on the size and the reputation of the tenant. Major tenants normally have the most favorable leases because they are the stores that generate much of the customer traffic. Sometimes, the landlord will lose money on these leases; however, because major tenants usually sign long term leases, they provide a measure of stability to the shopping center's operations.

The lease terms for small shops, meanwhile, depend on their reputation and the length of their rental agreement. Stores with high name recognition will obtain more favorable leases because the landlord will also view their presence as drawing more consumers to the center, as well as providing the center with greater prestige.

Landlords tend to enter into short-term leases with the smaller tenants (i.e., 3 to 6 years), because this affords them the opportunity to increase rental rates more frequently (the smaller tenants usually end up generating most of the rental income in a shopping center) and replace those shops that are not meeting sales expectations.

Sales are important to the landlord because it will dictate how much the tenant is able to pay in base rent and it also will determine the revenue the landlord receives from another source of income, percentage rent. When negotiating leases, a landlord usually seeks to secure three sources of revenue from a tenant:[3]

- A base rental payment, normally calculated on a square foot basis.

- Percentage rental payments, which are tied to the tenant's total sales. This rental payment is usually calculated on any sales in excess of a "floor" amount agreed on between the landlord and the tenant.

- Expense reimbursements, requiring the tenant to share in the costs of operating the shopping center.

Regardless of the lease terms entered into by a landlord, a shopping center will only be profitable over the long term if it is successful in attaining and retaining a competitive position in its marketplace. Mall REITs, for instance, publish information comparing sales per square foot recorded in their center from year to year. Annual sales results that compare favorably to the competition are a good indication that the center is maintaining its competitive position in a given market area. Positive operating results also enable a landlord to increase rents more aggressively, because tenants in a successful center will generally be able to afford higher rental increases.

Attaining year-to-year sales increases is becoming more difficult, however, because of the abundance of retail properties. The general consensus in both the retail and real estate industries is that the United States today has far too many stores. Retail space in the United States totals approximately 20 square feet per person, more than 3 times that of Europe.[4] Despite this fact, up until very recently a number of retailers have been expanding without any regard to the relationship between the amount of retail space in the country and the population growth or disposable income.[5]

At the same time that there are more choices available than ever before, the public seems to have less interest in shopping. Growth in retail sales in the 1990s has slowed considerably from last decade, leading to ever-increasing competition for the consumers' business.[6] This has resulted in a difficult retail environment and a need for shopping center landlords to distinguish their centers from the competition. Steps being undertaken by many retail REITs (especially mall REITs) is the upgrading of their properties both in terms of the physical appearance as well as their tenant base.

Most retail REITs have been allocating a significant percentage of their resources toward the re-development and renovation of their properties. These re-development efforts have involved the addition of anchors and specialty store space, or, in some instances, have comprised a complete makeover for the centers. Some large scale renovations have included a realigning of a center's merchandising mix, thus generating a new public perception of the center and a new competitive position in the marketplace. The reality is that shoppers prefer newer and fresher looking facilities to older, worn-out centers. By renovating or re-developing their properties,

78

shopping center owners can gain market share and help their tenants boost sales at the same time.

Shopping center owners must also stay abreast of developments in the retail trade. That's because the retail industry has been undergoing evolutionary changes in the 1990s. Some long-standing retailers have experienced significant financial difficulties in recent years; many have gone out of business. Consolidation has been prevalent because retailers have had to reduce their costs in order to survive in today's market. These developments have caused shopping center owners to pay closer attention to the financial well-being of both current and prospective tenants.

In order to maintain the loyalty of consumers, shopping centers must be concerned with drawing tenants whose product lines and/or retailing concepts are the most popular. In the 1980s, high-fashion was in vogue.[7] In the 1990s, consumers have turned their attention more toward value. This trend has led to the emergence of factory outlet malls and "big box" discount retailers as significant players in the industry.

The task of keeping their centers looking "fresh" with the newest concepts requires that landlords proactively recruit new retailers, restaurateurs, and entertainment operations that can maintain, and even increase, traffic to their centers. Taubman Centers, for instance, has a special group of professional shoppers who tour the country looking for new and promising concepts to add to the company's malls. This is part of Taubman's effort to stay ahead of the curve and monitor the newest shopping trends.

In the late 1980s, Taubman detected a declining interest in apparel on the part of its female customers and an increased interest in home-related goods and children's apparel on the part of baby boomers who were starting families. As a result, the company recruited companies such as Domain, which sold pricey, yet fashionable furniture, and The Right Start, which sold higher end children's toys and accessories. These steps helped Taubman increase its same 1995 store sales by 7 percent, versus 4.5 percent for the industry.[8]

Other shopping center companies maintain a strong consumer and market research effort by managing not only their own properties but those of third parties. By managing centers in different regions, these companies are able to monitor retailing trends developing in various markets throughout the country. One of these trends has been the increasing prominence of value retailing. Value retailing is the sale of branded or quality merchandise at less than department store prices. It is a description that applies to various retailing organizations, including category killers, outlet stores, and discount retailers. The category killers have been able to take significant market share away from department stores and general merchandise stores because they offer the consumer greater variety and generally lower prices.[9]

Outlet store operations, which were initially set up by manufacturers close to their plants to sell both overstock from the previous season and defective items, have evolved into significant shopping attractions located near major cities and resorts. It is not uncommon for an outlet mall to contain 100 or more stores, including such names as Tommy Hilfiger, Ann Taylor, Levis, Nike, and Bass. Many companies in this sector now manufacture items specifically for sale through their outlet stores.

One company that has taken the outlet concept a step further is the Mills Corporation (NYSE:MLS). This REIT specializes in building mega-malls, what the company calls "Mills", which are fully enclosed shopping centers containing more than one million square feet of selling space. The malls combine manufacturers' outlets, department store outlets, specialty retail store outlets, supersavings stores, off-price retailers, catalog outlets, and category dominant stores under one roof. Mills' centers are strategically located near major metropolitan areas and serve larger geographical areas than even super regional shopping malls.

The popularity of this concept is substantiated by the fact that the company's Potomac Mills mall has become the #1 tourist attraction in Virginia and its Sawgrass Mills property in Florida is that state's #2 tourist attraction, second only to Disney World. The Mills Corporation is proceeding full speed with development of a number of new mega-malls, some of which are now being developed as part of joint ventures with Simon DeBartolo Property Group and Taubman Centers.[10]

Although retail REITs often invest in different types of properties, they usually focus in one of three segments: (1) malls (2) neighbor, community, or power centers, or (3) factory outlet centers. Therefore, I have divided the retail REIT sector into these three segments.

MALL REITs

All of the publicly-owned mall REITs are relatively new to the REIT business. Taubman Centers was the first to go public in 1992. Eight of the other nine mall REITs entered the fray in either 1993 or 1994.

All of the mall REITs except for one, The Macerich Company, trace their origins to a time when their primary focus was development. Back in the 1970s and 1980s, the "malling" of America took place and all of these companies played significant roles in developing some of America's largest and most prominent regional malls and super regional malls. Because all of these REITs had accumulated sizable retail portfolios as a result of these development operations, most were formed as UPREITs.

Now that the development of regional and super regional malls has been scaled back, these REITs have turned their attention toward management activities. All of the mall REITs manage most or all of their properties (some malls are owned by joint ventures and therefore management responsibilities are either shared or undertaken by the joint venture partner). Many of them are also actively engaged in managing malls and shopping centers owned by third parties. Such activities have made three REIT organizations, General Growth Properties, Simon DeBartolo Group and Urban Shopping Centers, Inc., the largest managers of retail properties in the United States today.[11]

The competitive landscape in this segment of the retail sector is different from other sectors because many malls located in second tier markets (smaller trade areas) are the only game in town. This gives them a monopoly in their market area; however, it is a monopoly they cannot take for granted. This is because consumers in these trade areas still have other alternatives, including shopping by catalog, cable TV, and the Internet, and traveling to malls in other trade areas.

Super regional and regional malls that are located in major markets will usually face competition; therefore, it is important that they develop a strategy for gaining and retaining a competitive advantage. They can gain this edge by capturing a certain segment of the marketplace, either a geographical area or a particular group of shoppers.

A mall can become the dominant shopping attraction in its trade area by providing consumers with enough alternatives so there is no need for them to visit any other malls in the marketplace. Most of the mall REITs seek to achieve this position within their respective market areas. A mall can also cater to a specific segment of the market, upscale shoppers, for instance, by leasing space to retailers who target the same consumer segment. Taubman Centers and Urban Shopping Centers employ this strategy to gain a competitive advantage.

One of the unique aspects of mall leases is that landlords usually sign coveted anchor tenants to non-compete agreements, which prohibit the retailer from opening a store in another mall within the same market area. If consumers want to shop at this retailer's store, they must travel to the mall where it is located. This provides the given mall with an advantage in the marketplace and limits the overdevelopment of malls.

Securing prominent anchor tenants is a key to developing a successful mall. If major retailers are already committed to other malls in a particular market area, it may be difficult, if not impossible, for a developer to build a new mall that will prosper. Additionally, other potential anchor tenants will agree to lease space in a new mall only if their independent research concludes there is a sufficient demand in the marketplace to support another center. This adds another level of research to the development plans.

While other malls might be constructed in the marketplace, they will usually not have the same anchor tenants. This will differentiate one mall from another and, depending upon the appeal of their respective anchor tenants, may provide for an ongoing competitive advantage.

The existing mall REITs seek to enhance their profits through one or more of the following means: developing new malls, expanding and/or renovating existing centers, increasing rental rates on lease renewals and on the execution of leases with new tenants, and through their participation in the increasing revenues of tenants.

Most of the mall REITs are still very active in developing new malls, targeting primarily high growth markets. These REITs do not limit themselves geographically because building successful malls is a specialty that relatively few firms possess. It demands not only superior technical skills in developing a property with up to a million square feet of space and more than 100 individual stores, but polished political skills in obtaining the necessary approvals to build such a major project in a given community. The company must also have excellent contacts within the retail trade.

Securing prominent tenants is the key to success for any shopping center; however, for a mall being constructed in a marketplace where there is already competition, as is the case most of the time, it is essential.

Expanding and renovating shopping malls today is also a key to staying successful. In Englewood, Colorado, a suburb of Denver, the Cinderella City Mall opened with great fanfare in 1968. It contained everything you would want in a mall—prominent anchor tenants and close to 100 specialty shops. It was the largest mall west of the Mississippi River at the time. By the end of 1995, however, it was virtually closed, with only one major anchor and a few specialty shops left. What killed the Cinderella City Mall was the construction of a new mall within the trade area with a more contemporary look, anchor tenants with greater drawing power, and more appealing specialty stores.

This is why the mall REITs spend considerable time and resources updating their properties and expanding them to accommodate new tenants. By doing so, they are able to maintain their market share and dissuade potential competition from entering their respective trade areas.

One REIT that neglected to allocate enough resources to renovation and expansion activities paid for it. Crown American Realty Trust, whose predecessor had been engaged in the development of retail properties since 1950, owns malls located primarily in second tier markets. While these malls were generally the dominant centers in their areas, they were losing occupancy and were in need of upgrading. Therefore, in 1995, Crown American decided to cut its annual dividend by more than 42 percent to provide the necessary funds for renovations. As a result, its stock dropped by almost the same percentage that year.

Beside their ownership of shopping malls, most of the REITs in this segment of the industry also own and operate a substantial number of community shopping centers. There are several reasons for this.

One reason is that some markets are not big enough to support a regional mall. Therefore, in order to more fully utilize the expertise of their personnel and their contacts in the retail industry, these REITs have elected to operate community shopping centers as well. The fact is that the skills necessary to running a successful mall, selecting the right mix of tenants, marketing the center in the given trade area, and maintaining an attractive and efficient facility, are the same skills needed to manage a profitable community center. Additionally, many of the tenants that lease space in a REIT's regional malls are also candidates to rent space in their community centers.

Another reason mall REITs operate community centers is because these centers are often located adjacent to their malls. Regional malls usually draw large numbers of shoppers within a given trade area. This is why other smaller centers are usually located nearby; they are looking to benefit from the drawing power of the regional mall. It is logical that if an adjacent community center benefits from a given mall's operations, then the owner of the mall might as well own the community center.

A third reason why mall REITs own various types of shopping centers is to help insulate them from shifts in the marketplace. As noted previously, there has been a rather significant change over the last decade in consumer buying habits. From the quality orientation of the 1980s, the consumers of today are more value conscious. This has worked to the advantage of community shopping centers that generally lease space to discount retailers or category killers.

While increased competition from outlet store operations, category killer retailers, and discounters have impacted the dominance of malls in the retail trade, quality malls are still considered a solid investment. This is partially due to the fact that mall operators have become increasingly more aggressive in changing their tenant mix, renovating and expanding their properties, and trying new concepts to draw customers to their centers.

The reality is that because of the variety they offer under one roof, the fact that some of the most popular retailers are located in their facilities, and their properties are so well maintained, high-quality malls will remain dominant players in the industry. Alternatively, those malls that have not been maintained, have been unsuccessful in attracting the right mix of tenants, and have outdated layouts, will likely lose their appeal over time and become extinct.

Mall REITs

CBL & Associates Properties Inc.
One Park Place
6148 Lee Highway
Chattanooga, TN 37421
(423) 855-0001

Exchange: New York (CBL)
Initial Public Offering: November 3, 1993
Initial Offering Price: $19.50
Geographical Focus: Southeast and Northeast
Competitive Strategies: Acquires existing centers whose cash flow can be enhanced through improved leasing efforts, re-development, and expansion; third party management operations; new property development capabilities; targets high growth second-tier markets where it can achieve its goal of being the dominant retail center.
Special Notes: Successor to a business operation founded in 1978. Owns both malls as well as community and neighborhood shopping centers.
Investment Performance:

	Close	Gain/Loss	Dividend	% Yield	Annual Return
1993	$18.13	—	$0.24	—	—
1994	$20.63	13.8%	$1.50	8.3%	22.1%
1995	$21.75	5.5%	$1.59	7.7%	13.2%
1996	$25.88	19.0%	$1.68	7.7%	26.7%

Crown American Realty Trust
Pasquerilla Plaza
Johnstown, PA 15901
(814) 536-4441
(http://www.crownam.com)

Exchange: New York (CWN)
Initial Public Offering: August 17, 1993
Initial Offering Price: $17.25
Geographical Focus: Pennsylvania

Competitive Strategies: Targets second tier markets where its malls are the only major shopping center in the trade areas or the most dominant center; refurbishing and re-tenanting its malls to maintain its competitive edge in their respective marketplaces.

Special Notes: Successor to a company founded in 1950. The company's stock declined by 42 percent in 1995 after the firm announced plans to cut its quarterly dividend from $.35 to $.20.

Investment Performance:

	Close	Gain/Loss	Dividend	% Yield	Annual Return
1993	$15.00	—	$0.17	—	—
1994	$13.50	(10.0)%	$1.40	9.3%	(0.7)%
1995	$ 7.88	(41.7)%	$1.10	8.1%	(33.6)%
1996	$ 7.50	(4.8)%	$0.80	10.2%	5.4%

General Growth Properties, Inc.
55 West Monroe, Suite 3100
Chicago, IL 60603-5060
(312) 551-5000
(http://www.ggpi.com)

Exchange: New York (GGP)
Initial Public Offering: April 15, 1993
Initial Offering Price: $22.00
Geographical Focus: National
Competitive Strategies: Owns properties in second tier markets where they have strong competitive positions as a result of being the only enclosed shopping center or the largest shopping center in the marketplace; new property development capability; third party management operations (it is the largest manager of shopping centers in the United States).

Special Notes: Since its IPO, General Growth has made two major acquisitions. In February, 1994, the REIT acquired a 40 percent interest in Centermark Properties (31 total properties) from the Prudential Insurance Company of America. It subsequently sold this interest in 1996 at a substantial profit. In December 1995, General Growth acquired a 38.2% interest in Homart Development Company from Sears, Roebuck and Company (28 properties).

Investment Performance:

	Close	Gain/Loss	Dividend	% Yield	Annual Return
1993	$21.50	—	$1.05	—	—
1994	$22.63	5.3%	$1.58	7.4%	12.7%
1995	$20.75	(8.3)%	$1.72	7.6%	(0.7)%
1996	$32.25	55.4%	$1.72	8.3%	63.7%

JP Realty, Inc.
35 Century Park-Way
Salt Lake City, UT 84115
(801) 486-3911
(http://www.jprealty.com)

Exchange: New York (JPR)
Initial Public Offering: January 21, 1994
Initial Offering Price: $17.50
Geographical Focus: Intermountian Region (Utah, Idaho, Wyoming)
Competitive Strategies: Geographically focused in the Intermountain Region; the company's regional malls are generally the dominant and, in some cases, the only mall within their respective trade areas: new property development capabilities.
Special Notes: Successor to a development business founded more than 35 years ago by John Price. The REIT owns interests in a variety of properties, including enclosed regional malls, community shopping centers, free-standing retail properties, and mixed use commercial/business properties
Investment Performance:

	Close	Gain/Loss	Dividend	% Yield	Annual Return
1994	$21.00	—	$1.53	—	—
1995	$21.88	4.2%	$1.64	8.0%	12.2%
1996	$25.88	18.3%	$1.70	7.8%	26.1%

The Macerich Company
233 Wilshire Blvd., Suite 700
Santa Monica, CA 90401
(310) 394-6911
(http://www.macerich.com)

Exchange: New York (MAC)
Initial Public Offering: March 10, 1994
Initial Offering Price: $19.00
Geographical Focus: National
Competitive Strategies: Seeks to acquire existing properties that offer the potential for revenue growth through rental rate increases, more aggressive management of costs, the addition of satellite stores, and the reformulation of the tenant mix; the company also re-develops and/or expands its centers when necessary to maintain their standing in their respective trade areas.
Special Notes: Successor to an organization founded in 1965. It is the only mall REIT that is not engaged in new property development.
Investment Performance:

	Close	Gain/Loss	Dividend	% Yield	Annual Return
1994	$21.38	—	$0.87	—	—
1995	$20.00	(6.4)%	$1.66	7.8%	1.4%
1996	$26.13	30.7%	$1.70	8.5%	39.2%

The Mills Corporation
1300 Wilson Blvd., Suite 400
Arlington, VA 22209
(703) 526-5000
(http://www.potomac-mills.com)

Exchange: New York (MLS)
Initial Public Offering: April 21, 1994
Initial Offering Price: $23.50
Geographical Focus: National
Competitive Strategies: The company develops and manages super regional, value-oriented malls called "Mills", that are approximately 1.5 million square feet in size and combine the features of super regional malls, factory outlets, big box/power centers, and entertainment venues.
Special Notes: Successor to a business founded in 1967. Most of The Mills Corporation's mega-malls are part of joint ventures with other institutional investors. In October 1996, announced a joint venture with Cambridge Shopping Centres to develop malls in major Canadian cities such as Toronto, Vancouver, Montreal, and Cal-

gary. Prior to 1986, the company was known as Western Development Corporation and engaged in the development and management of community shopping centers. It still owns and operates a number of such centers throughout the country.
Investment Performance:

	Close	Gain/Loss	Dividend	% Yield	Annual Return
1994	$18.13	—	$1.31	—	—
1995	$17.00	(4.2)%	$1.89	10.4%	6.2%
1996	$23.88	40.4%	$1.89	11.1%	51.5%

Simon DeBartolo Group, Inc.
115 W. Washington Street
Indianapolis, IN 46204
(317) 636-1600

Exchange: New York (SPG)
Initial Public Offering: December 20, 1993
Initial Offering Price: $22.25
Geographical Focus: National
Competitive Strategies: It is the largest REIT in the country and owns twice the retail space as the next retail company; third party management operations (it is the second largest manager of retail properties in the nation); new property development capabilities.
Special Notes: The REIT is the result of a 1996 merger of Simon Property Group with DeBartolo Realty. Simon Property Group was the successor to a shopping center business founded in 1960 by brothers Mel and Herb Simon. DeBartolo Realty continued the shopping center development and management business founded in the mid-1940s by the late Edward DeBartolo. At the time of the merger, the company was operated by his son, Edward J. DeBartolo, Jr., who also owns the San Francisco 49ers NFL team.
Investment Performance:

	Close	Gain/Loss	Dividend	% Yield	Annual Return
1993	$22.63	—	$—	—	—
1994	$24.25	7.2%	$1.90	8.4%	15.6%
1995	$24.38	0.5%	$1.97	8.0%	8.6%
1996	$31.00	27.2%	$1.63	6.7%	33.5%

Taubman Centers Inc.
200 East Long Lake Road, Suite 300
Bloomfield, MI 48304
(810) 258-6800
(http://www.taubman.com)

Exchange: New York (TCO)
Initial Public Offering: November 1992
Initial Offering Price: $10.00
Geographical Focus: National
Competitive Strategies: Targets more affluent markets (66 of the nation's 100 wealthiest zip codes are within a 20 mile radius of the company's centers); new property development and expansion of existing shopping centers; active in retenanting malls with new and more contemporary concepts.
Special Notes: In response to declining apparel store sales, Taubman has increased its emphasis on "lifestyle" retail stores catering to the home, leisure activities, health, children, and entertainment.
Investment Performance:

	Close	Gain/Loss	Dividend	% Yield	Annual Return
1992	$11.63	—	$0.07	—	—
1993	$11.63	0.0%	$0.88	7.6%	7.6%
1994	$ 9.75	(16.2)%	$0.88	7.6%	(8.6)%
1995	$10.00	2.6%	$0.88	9.0%	11.6%
1996	$12.88	28.8%	$0.89	8.9%	37.7%

Urban Shopping Centers, Inc.
900 N. Michigan Avenue, Suite 1500
Chicago, IL 60611
(312) 915-2000

Exchange: New York (URB)
Initial Public Offering: October 14, 1993
Initial Offering Price: $23.50
Geographical Focus: National
Competitive Strategies: New property development capability; third party management operations (it is the third largest manager of retail properties in the country); renovation and/or expansion of

mall properties to maintain a competitive status in their respective market areas.

Special Notes: Formed to continue the shopping center business of JMB Realty Corporation, a Chicago-based real estate investment firm that had been in the business of owning and managing regional malls for more than 25 years. Through predecessor companies, Urban Retail has produced some of the most prominent shopping centers and mixed-use properties in the United States including Water Tower Place and 900 North Michigan in Chicago and Copley Place in Boston.

Investment Performance:

	Close	Gain/Loss	Dividend	% Yield	Annual Return
1993	$22.00	—	—	—	—
1994	$19.88	(9.6)%	$1.82	8.3%	(1.3)%
1995	$21.38	7.5%	$1.94	9.8%	17.3%
1996	$29.00	35.7%	$1.98	9.3%	45.0%

Westfield America, Inc.
11601 Wilshire Blvd., 12th Floor
Los Angeles, CA 90025
(310) 478-4456

Exchange: New York (WEA)
Initial Public Offering: May 16, 1997
Initial Offering Price: $15.00
Geographical Focus: National
Competitive Strategies: Acquire existing regional and super regional malls and reposition them through extensive property renovations and new anchor tenants; focus on specific major metropolitan areas where it can acquire multiple properties, thereby gaining economies of scale; development capabilities.

Special Notes: The company's properties are managed under a contract with a subsidiary of Westfield Holdings, Inc., an Australian company which contributed the initial portfolio of properties to Westfield America. Westfield Holdings' investments in U.S. retail properties date back to 1977. It also owns property in Australia, New Zealand, and Malaysia. At the time of the IPO, Westfield Holdings owned a 32% interest in the REIT.

SHOPPING CENTERS

Shopping center REITs consist of neighborhood, community, and power centers. The neighborhood and community centers are usually anchored by a supermarket and/or drug store. The community centers also usually include a discounter such as Wal-Mart or Kmart. The power centers, meanwhile, are normally anchored by "big box" category killers such as Home Depot, Toys Я' Us, or CompUSA.

The investment appeal of neighborhood, community and power centers is that they are less expensive to build and depend on smaller market areas than regional malls. However, these features also present risks. Because they are not as expensive to build, there is the risk that too many will be built in a given metropolitan area. Construction of such centers is often rampant during good economic times; however, when the economy slows, there may be insufficient business to support all of these centers.

Another risk is the lack of covenants precluding anchor tenants from abandoning their locations and building bigger facilities nearby. While these anchors are contractually obligated to continue making rental payments on the unexpired leases for their abandoned stores, the lack of an anchor tenant in a center negatively impacts the business of the other stores which are left behind.

Many of the neighborhood shopping center REITs claim their assets have limited downside risk because their primary tenants sell basic goods, that is goods we all need for everyday living. While this is true, it is also true that consumers in a given market area usually have a number of centers they can travel to in order to obtain such necessities.

The key to being competitive in a marketplace is for a shopping center to be the most appealing one in its trade area. This means they must copy the operating strategy of successful malls: attract the most popular tenants and have the newest look. For many owners, it has meant expanding their facilities to add tenants who will give area consumers another reason to travel to their center as opposed to a competing center.

Most of the shopping center REITs are geographically focused. In order to be successful in this segment, it is important to have a solid understanding of your markets: their growth patterns, the nature of the competition, and consumer habits. This is especially important when you are engaged in new property development, as are about half of the REITs in this sector of the industry. In most cases, this is where the firm's expertise was prior to forming the REIT; they have simply carried these activities over to the REIT's operations.

By focusing their activities in specific geographical areas, these REITs are in a better position to secure the most coveted sites for future development. Because a good location is what every retailer seeks when opening a new store, this positioning provides the regionally focused REITs with a competitive advantage within their markets.

Some shopping center REITs stay clear of new development, preferring to acquire existing centers and, if warranted, renovate and/or expand such facilities. Federal Realty, for instance, has implemented a "Main Street" strategy under which it acquires older properties located along main streets in major metropolitan areas, renovates the properties, and leases them to well-known retailers. The Trust believes that such facilities offer great potential, due to their convenient location and their novelty.[12]

Other REITs such Burnham Pacific Properties, HRE Properties, Mid-Atlantic Realty Trust, Saul Centers, and Vornado Realty Trust, look to buy properties in established areas where there are few sites available for new retail property development. This provides them with a measure of safety that is difficult to attain in the retail trade.

The shopping center REITs generally invest in two types of properties: single tenant retail facilities and multitenant centers. Most REITs acquire multitenant facilities primarily because they possess less risk than single tenant properties. A number of shopping center REITs that have gone public in the 1990s initially owned portfolios that consisted primarily of triple net leased assets, that is properties which were leased to a single tenant such as Kmart or Wal-Mart on a long-term basis under terms that required the tenants to pay all of the costs associated with the operation of their store, including insurance, taxes, and maintenance.

As a result of the financial difficulties retailers such as Kmart experienced in the mid-1990s, however, these REITs have generally sought to diversify their portfolios to multitenanted shopping centers where the leases are shorter-term, operating leases (that require the landlord to pay for the operation of the center).

Shopping center REITs are also investing in larger scale properties as well. An examination of acquisitions which have been made over the years by some long-standing REITs shed light on the trend toward larger shopping centers. New Plan Realty is one such REIT. It initially went public in 1962, converted to REIT status in 1972, and in 1988 became the first listed REIT to become self-administered and self-managed.

Since 1990, the size of the shopping center properties New Plan has acquired has increased substantially. The supermarket properties it has purchased since 1989 have averaged 42,000 square feet; 14,000 square feet more than those it acquired before 1990. Its post-1989 shopping center acquisitions have been approximately 35,000 square feet larger than the properties it bought in previous decades.[13]

These numbers highlight the fact that in today's retail industry, bigger is usually better. This is largely due to the fact that the increasing number of working couples simply have less time to shop. When these couples do shop, they want convenience. This translates into a need for shopping centers to offer consumers the opportunity to do one stop shopping. A neighborhood center should have a grocery store, drug store, dry cleaners, liquor store, and video rental shop on site so that the two income earning couple can take care of most of their daily needs in one location. The need for convenience has also enhanced the popularity of category killers that offer a wide selection of merchandise at everyday low prices, which reduces the need for consumers to do comparison shopping.[14]

Shopping Center REITs

Agree Realty Corporation
31850 Northwestern Highway
Farmington Hills, MI 48334
(810) 737-4190

Exchange: New York (ADC)
Initial Public Offering: April 22, 1994
Initial Offering Price: $19.50
Geographical Focus: Midwest
Competitive Strategies: New property development capability; focuses on acquiring centers that have national and prominent regional tenants as anchors; ownership of single tenant, triple net leased properties that provide a steady stream of income.

Special Notes: Successor to Agree Realty Group, which was founded in 1971 to develop shopping centers.
Investment Performance:

	Close	Gain/Loss	Dividend	% Yield	Annual Return
1994	$15.50	—	$1.25	—	—
1995	$14.63	(5.5)%	$1.80	11.6%	6.0%
1996	$21.38	46.2%	$1.80	12.3%	58.5%

Alexander Haagan Properties, Inc.
3500 Sepulveda Blvd.
Manhattan Beach, CA 90266
(310) 546-4520

Exchange: American (ACH)
Initial Public Offering: December 27, 1993
Initial Offering Price: $18.00
Geographical Focus: West Coast
Competitive Strategies: New property development; national or prominent regional anchor tenants at its neighborhood shopping centers.
Special Notes: Successor to a company that had been engaged in the development of retail properties for more than 25 years; portfolio includes neighborhood shopping centers, single tenant centers, promotional/power centers, and regional malls.
Investment Performance:

	Close	Gain/Loss	Dividend	% Yield	Annual Return
1993	$17.75	—	$0.36	—	—
1994	$15.88	(10.5)%	$1.44	8.1%	(2.4)%
1995	$12.25	(22.8)%	$1.44	9.1%	(13.7)%
1996	$14.75	20.4%	$1.44	11.8%	32.2%

Bradley Real Estate, Inc.
40 Skokie Blvd., Suite 600
Northbrook, IL 60062
(847) 272–9800

Exchange: New York (BTR)
Initial Public Offering: 1961
Geographical Focus: Midwest and New England

Competitive Strategies: Focuses on grocery-anchored neighborhood retail facilities and community shopping centers anchored by discounters such as Kmart or Wal-Mart; enhances portfolio value through renovation, expansion, and leasing strategies.

Special Notes: One of the nation's oldest existing REITs, having been established in 1961. In 1996, the company completed the acquisition of Tucker Properties Corporation (NYSE:TUC), resulting in a doubling of Bradley's real estate portfolio.

Investment Performance:

	Close	Gain/Loss	Dividend	% Yield	Annual Return
1991	$12.50	13.6%	$1.20	10.9%	24.5%
1992	$15.75	26.0%	$1.20	9.6%	35.6%
1993	$18.50	17.5%	$1.22	7.8%	25.3%
1994	$15.25	(17.6)%	$1.29	7.0%	(10.6)%
1995	$13.50	(11.5)%	$1.32	8.7%	(2.8)%
1996	$18.00	33.3%	$1.32	9.8%	43.1%

Burnham Pacific Properties
610 W. Ash Street, Suite 1600
San Diego, CA 92101
(619) 652-4700
(800) 568-2722
(http://www.burnhampacific.com)

Exchange: New York (BPP)
Initial Public Offering: 1987
Initial Offering Price: $17.50
Geographical Focus: California

Competitive Strategies: To become the dominant retail REIT on the West Coast by targeting in-fill retail properties located in major metropolitan areas in California where there are barriers to entry and where market demand is proven; focuses on three types of properties: anchored grocery/drug centers, promotional centers (anchored by discount retailers), and entertainment centers; new property development.

Special Notes: Successor to an organization founded in 1963. In 1995, changed its strategy of investing in a diversified portfolio of real estate to a more focused strategy of investing in only retail properties.

Investment Performance:

	Close	Gain/Loss	Dividend	% Yield	Annual Return
1991	$14.88	32.3%	$1.36	12.1%	44.3%
1992	$15.88	6.7%	$1.36	9.1%	15.8%
1993	$17.13	7.9%	$1.39	8.8%	16.7%
1994	$12.75	(25.6)%	$1.42	8.3%	(17.3)%
1995	$ 9.63	(24.5)%	$1.33	10.4%	(14.1)%
1996	$15.00	55.8%	$1.00	10.4%	66.2%

Developers Diversified Realty Corporation
34555 Chagrin Blvd.
Moreland Hills, OH 44022
(216) 247-4700

Exchange: New York (DDR) ✓
Initial Public Offering: February 9, 1993
Initial Offering Price: $22.00
Geographical Focus: National
Competitive Strategies: New property development capability; focuses on acquiring community shopping centers and power centers with major national or regional retailers as the anchor tenants.
Special Notes: Formed to continue the business operations of an organization founded in 1965. Entered into a joint venture in 1996 with the Ohio State Teachers Retirement System to buy and manage more than $50 million in shopping centers.
Investment Performance:

	Close	Gain/Loss	Dividend	% Yield	Annual Return
1993	$29.25	—	$1.42	—	—
1994	$31.25	6.8%	$1.92	6.6%	13.4%
1995	$30.00	(4.0)%	$2.16	6.9%	2.9%
1996	$37.13	23.8%	$2.40	8.0%	31.8%

Excel Realty Trust, Inc.
16955 Via Del Campo, Suite 110
San Diego, CA 92127
(619) 485-9400

Exchange: New York (XEL)
Initial Public Offering: August 4, 1993
Initial Offering Price: $19.75
Geographical Focus: National
Competitive Strategies: Focuses on acquiring community shopping centers with national or regional tenants such as Kmart, Wal-Mart, J.C. Penney, or major supermarket/drug store chains; preference for multitenant facilities.
Special Notes: Purchased 59 properties from the Ohio State Teachers Retirement System (OTR) shortly after its 1993 IPO. Maintains regional office operations in Arizona, Florida, Georgia, Kentucky, North Carolina, Tennessee, and Utah to manage its national portfolio of properties.
Investment Performance:

	Close	Gain/Loss	Dividend	% Yield	Annual Return
1993	$18.25	—	$0.65	—	—
1994	$16.50	(9.6)%	$1.70	9.3%	(0.3)%
1995	$20.50	24.2%	$1.77	10.8%	35.0%
1996	$25.38	23.8%	$1.84	9.0%	32.8%

Federal Realty Investment Trust
1626 East Jefferson Street
Rockville, MD 20852-4041
(301) 998-8100
(800) 658-8980

Exchange: New York (FRT)
Initial Public Offering: 1962
Geographical Focus: East and West Coasts, Chicago
Competitive Strategies: Focuses on major metropolitan markets with high household densities and above average median incomes; implementation of a "Main Street" retail strategy that involves the acquisition and refurbishment of small retail properties on established main street shopping areas in major cities, bringing stores

closer to consumers; acquisition of older, well-located shopping centers and enhancement of their revenue potential through a program of renovation, re-leasing, and re-merchandising.

Special Notes: Through 1996, the Trust had paid a dividend to its shareholders every year since its inception and had increased the dividend rate each of the prior 29 years. From 1984 through 1996, Federal Realty's real estate portfolio increased in size from $185 million to more than $1 billion.

Investment Performance:

	Close	Gain/Loss	Dividend	% Yield	Annual Return
1991	$18.88	31.3%	$1.50	10.4%	41.7%
1992	$25.00	32.4%	$1.53	8.1%	40.5%
1993	$25.00	0.0%	$1.55	6.2%	6.2%
1994	$20.63	(17.5)%	$1.57	6.3%	(11.2)%
1995	$22.25	10.3%	$1.60	7.8%	18.1%
1996	$27.13	19.2%	$1.65	7.3%	26.5%

First Washington Realty Trust
4350 East-West Highway, Suite 400
Bethesda, MD 20814
(301) 907-7800

Exchange: New York (FRW)
Initial Public Offering: June, 1994
Initial Offering Price: $19.50
Geographical Focus: Mid-Atlantic states
Competitive Strategies: Acquisition of supermarket-anchored neighborhood shopping centers that are located in densely populated areas, have high visibility and the potential to increase in value through expansion and/or renovation; anchor tenants consist primarily of prominant national or regional tenants, which management believes help generate regular consumer traffic and provide economic stability.
Special Notes: Formed in June 1994 as a private REIT through the consolidatioin of 16 individual limited partnerships; became a public REIT in December 1994.
Investment Performance:

	Close	Gain/Loss	Dividend	% Yield	Annual Return
1994	$15.00	—	—	—	—
1995	$18.13	20.9%	$0.98	6.5%	27.4%
1996	$23.50	29.7%	$1.95	10.8%	40.5%

Glimcher Realty Trust
20 South Third Street
Columbus, OH 43215
(614) 621-9000

Exchange: New York (GRT)
Initial Public Offering: January 26, 1994
Initial Offering Price: $20.25
Geographical Focus: Eastern United States
Competitive Strategies: To help insulate it from shifts in the marketplace, the company employs a "Tri-Focus" business strategy, investing in three distinctive lines of retail properties: regional malls, community shopping centers, and value-oriented super regional malls; new property development capability.
Special Notes: Successor to the Glimcher Company of Columbus, Ohio, which was founded in 1959.
Investment Performance:

	Close	Gain/Loss	Dividend	% Yield	Annual Return
1994	$21.88	—	$1.74	—	—
1995	$17.25	(21.1)%	$1.91	8.7%	(12.4)%
1996	$22.00	27.5%	$1.92	11.1%	38.6%

HRE Properties
321 Railroad Avenue
Greenwich, CT 06830
(203) 863-8200

Exchange: New York (HRE)
Initial Public Offering: 1969
Geographical Focus: Northeast
Competitive Strategies: Geographical focus in the Northeast; acquisition of shopping center properties in established areas.
Special Notes: Founded in 1969 as Hubbard Real Estate Invest-

ments by mortgage bankers John C. and George M. Hubbard, the Trust's initial focus was mortgage investments. In 1989, HRE shifted from a diversified REIT to one focused on retail properties.
Investment Performance:

	Close	Gain/Loss	Dividend	% Yield	Annual Return
1991	$11.50	4.5%	$1.40	12.7%	17.2%
1992	$11.63	1.1%	$1.16	10.1%	11.2%
1993	$14.25	22.6%	$1.08	9.3%	31.9%
1994	$13.75	(3.5)%	$1.10	7.7%	4.2%
1995	$13.13	(4.5)%	$1.14	8.3%	3.8%
1996	$18.00	37.1%	$1.22	9.3%	46.4%

IRT Property Company
200 Galleria Parkway, Suite 1400
Atlanta, GA 30339
(770) 955-4406

Exchange: New York (IRT)
Initial Public Offering: 1969
Geographical Focus: Southeast
Competitive Strategies: Focuses in markets that possess a diverse economic base and above-average population and employment growth; renovation and/or expansion of properties to accommodate both existing as well as new tenants and to maintain a competitive position.
Special Notes: Founded in 1969 as Investors Realty Trust, a Tennessee business trust investing in real estate. Maintains regional offices in Atlanta, Charlotte, Orlando, and New Orleans.
Investment Performance:

	Close	Gain/Loss	Dividend	% Yield	Annual Return
1991	$ 9.50	24.6%	$0.80	10.5%	35.1%
1992	$12.25	28.9%	$0.81	8.5%	37.4%
1993	$10.75	(12.2)%	$0.84	6.9%	(5.3)%
1994	$10.25	(4.7)%	$0.84	7.8%	3.1%
1995	$ 9.25	(9.8)%	$0.89	8.7%	(1.1)%
1996	$11.50	24.3%	$0.90	9.7%	34.0%

JDN Realty Corporation
3340 Peachtree Road, NE, Suite 1530
Atlanta, GA 30326
(404) 262-3252
(http://www.irinfo.com/jdn)

Exchange: New York (JDN)
Initial Public Offering: March 29, 1994
Initial Offering Price: $22.00
Geographical Focus: Southeast
Competitive Strategies: Has been and continues to be a major developer of Wal-Mart stores; new property development capabilities; focuses on centers that are in need of renovation, refurbishment, or expansion, that are well located, and that are anchored by major creditworthy tenants.
Special Notes: Formed to continue the real estate business started in 1978 by J. Donald Nichols, JDN's Chairman. JDN achieved the highest return of all retail-oriented REITs in 1995 with a 20.9 percent overall return.
Investment Performance:

	Close	Gain/Loss	Dividend	% Yield	Annual Return
1994	$20.00	—	$1.33	—	—
1995	$22.38	11.9%	$1.80	9.0%	20.9%
1996	$27.63	23.5%	$1.90	8.5%	32.0%

Kimco Realty Corporation
3333 New Hyde Park Road, Suite 100
New Hyde Park, NY 11042
(526) 869-9000
(http://www.centernet.com/kimco.htm)

Exchange: New York (KIM)
Initial Public Offering: November, 1991
Initial Offering Price: $13.33
Geographical Focus: Eastern half of the United States
Competitive Strategies: It is the owner and operator of the largest publicly traded portfolio of neighborhood and community shop-

ping centers in the United States; focuses on properties whose cash flow and value can be enhanced through renovation, expansion, re-tenanting, and rollover of below market rents; third party management services; the "de-malling" of small malls to make their configuration more convenient to shoppers.

Special Notes: In 1995, obtained from Woolworths leases on some 5.4 million square feet of space previously occupied by Woolco Department Stores. In 1996, it bought the real estate assets of the Clover division of Strawbridge and Clothier.

Investment Performance:

	Close	Gain/Loss	Dividend	% Yield	Annual Return
1991	$14.33	—	$—	—	—
1992	$20.67	44.2%	$0.99	6.9%	51.1%
1993	$23.42	13.3%	$1.25	6.1%	19.4%
1994	$25.25	7.8%	$1.33	5.7%	13.5%
1995	$27.25	7.9%	$1.44	5.7%	13.6%
1996	$34.88	28.0%	$1.56	5.7%	33.7%

* In 1995, Kimco's stock split 3 for 2.

Kranzco Realty Trust
128 Fayette Street
Conshohocken, PA 19428
(610) 941-9292
(http://www.krt.com)

Exchange: New York (KRT)
Initial Public Offering: November 19, 1992
Initial Offering Price: $20.00
Geographical Focus: Mid-Atlantic and Northeast
Competitive Strategies: Focuses on acquiring properties anchored by "big box" retailers or supermarkets and properties in need of renovation and more intensive management; seeks to generate revenue increases through a mix of property renovation and expansion, tenant replacement, and percentage rent increases.
Investment Performance:

	Close	Gain/Loss	Dividend	% Yield	Annual Return
1992	$21.38	—	$0.22	—	—
1993	$21.38	0.0%	$1.84	8.6%	8.6%
1994	$19.00	(11.1)%	$1.90	8.9%	(2.2)%
1995	$14.75	(22.4)%	$1.92	10.1%	(12.3)%
1996	$16.88	14.4%	$1.92	13.0%	27.4%

Malan Realty Investors, Inc.
30200 Telegraph Road, Suite 105
Birmingham, MI 48025
(810) 644-7110

Exchange: New York (MAL)
Initial Public Offering: June 24, 1994
Initial Offering Price: $17.00
Geographical Focus: Midwest
Competitive Strategies: Targets small to medium-size towns in the Midwest; acquires centers that are leading centers in their trade areas and are anchored by national and regional credit tenants with long term leases.
Special Notes: Succeeded the operations of Malan Construction Company, which, from 1966 until the company's IPO in 1984, developed or re-developed approximately 14 million square feet of retail property throughout the United States. At the time of Malan's IPO, Kmart represented 60 percent of its total revenues. Since then, the company has expended considerable efforts to diversifying its portfolio with other anchor tenants.
Investment Performance:

	Close	Gain/Loss	Dividend	% Yield	Annual Return
1994	$13.38	—	$0.85	—	—
1995	$12.38	(7.5)%	$1.70	12.7%	5.2%
1996	$16.25	31.3%	$1.70	13.7%	45.0%

Mark Centers Trust
600 Third Avenue
Kingston, PA 18704-1679
(717) 288-4581

Exchange: New York (MCT)
Initial Public Offering: June 1, 1993
Initial Offering Price: $19.50
Geographical Focus: Northeast and Southeast
Competitive Strategies: Focuses on centers located primarily in secondary markets where they dominate their respective trade areas; new property development capability.
Special Notes: Successor to an organization founded in 1960.
Investment Performance:

	Close	Gain/Loss	Dividend	% Yield	Annual Return
1993	$14.50	—	$0.36	—	—
1994	$13.00	(10.3)%	$1.44	9.9%	(0.4)%
1995	$11.38	(12.5)%	$1.44	11.1%	(1.4)%
1996	$10.13	11.0%	$1.44	12.7%	1.7%

Mid-America Realty Investments, Inc.
11506 Nicholas Street, Suite 100
Omaha, NE 68154
(402) 496-3300

Exchange: New York (MDI)
Initial Public Offering: October 1986
Geographical Focus: Midwest
Competitive Strategies: Focuses on properties that are anchored primarily by discount operations such as Wal-Mart, Kmart, or Target, or by a regional supermarket , and that are the dominant centers in their trade areas; geographically focused in the Midwest.
Special Notes: Was incorporated as Dial REIT in 1986 and changed its name to Mid-America Realty in 1984 to more clearly identify the REIT with its strategy of investing in properties in "Mid-America."
Investment Performance:

	Close	Gain/Loss	Dividend	% Yield	Annual Return
1991	$12.88	21.2%	$1.58	14.9%	36.1%
1992	$ 9.13	(29.1)%	$1.18	9.2%	(19.9)%
1993	$ 9.63	5.5%	$0.88	9.6%	15.1%
1994	$ 7.25	(24.7)%	$0.88	9.1%	(15.6)%
1995	$ 7.75	6.9%	$0.88	12.1%	19.0%
1996	$ 9.50	22.6%	$0.88	11.4%	34.0%

Mid-Atlantic Realty Trust
170 W. Ridgely Road, Suite 300
Lutherville, MD 21093
(410) 684-2000

Exchange: American Exchange (MRR)
Initial Public Offering: September 11, 1993
Initial Offering Price: $10.50
Geographical Focus: Mid-Atlantic states
Competitive Strategies: New property development capabilities; specializes in renovating older retail properties located in well-established areas.
Special Notes: In recent years, the Trust has sold assets that are not located in the Mid-Atlantic region and focused its acquisition and development efforts in this region.
Investment Performance:

	Close	Gain/Loss	Dividend	% Yield	Annual Return
1993	$ 9.13	—	$0.05	—	—
1994	$ 8.25	(9.6)%	$0.85	9.3%	(0.3)%
1995	$ 8.63	4.5%	$0.89	10.8%	15.3%
1996	$11.25	30.4%	$0.93	10.8%	41.2%

New Plan Realty Trust
1120 Avenue of the Americas
New York, NY 10036
(212) 869-3000

Exchange: New York (NPR)
Initial Public Offering: 1962
Geographical Focus: Eastern half of the U.S.
Competitive Strategies: One of the largest REITs in the country; A+ rating from Standard & Poor's and A2 from Moody's enables the company to gain access to low cost debt.
Special Notes: Origins date back to 1926 when Morris Newman opened an office in New York City as a CPA and real estate broker; by 1942, he was selling investments in real estate syndications to small investors. The company went public in 1962, became a REIT in 1972, and in 1988, became the first listed REIT to become self-

administered and self-managed. At year-end 1996, its portfolio consisted primarily of shopping centers (61%), apartment properties (18%), and factory outlet centers (15%).

Investment Performance:

	Close	Gain/Loss	Dividend	% Yield	Annual Return
1991	$23.63	38.0%	$1.13	6.6%	44.6%
1992	$23.88	1.1%	$1.21	5.1%	6.2%
1993	$22.25	(6.8)%	$1.27	5.3%	(1.5)%
1994	$19.50	(12.4)%	$1.32	5.9%	(6.5)%
1995	$21.75	11.5%	$1.36	7.0%	18.5%
1996	$25.38	16.7%	$1.43	6.6%	23.3%

Price REIT, Inc.
7979 Ivanhoe Avenue, Suite 524
LaJolla, CA 92037
(619) 551-2320
(http://www.pricereit.com)

Exchange: New York (RET)
Initial Public Offering: December 3, 1991
Initial Offering Price: $25.00
Geographical Focus: National
Competitive Strategies: New property development capability; focuses on centers anchored by national "big box" retailers.
Special Notes: Formed in 1991 as a spin-off of The Price Club, a wholesale membership club started in the 1970s.
Investment Performance:

	Close	Gain/Loss	Dividend	% Yield	Annual Return
1991	$27.25	—	$0.19	—	—
1992	$29.00	6.4%	$2.26	8.3%	14.7%
1993	$29.75	4.3%	$2.38	8.2%	12.5%
1994	$31.00	6.0%	$2.56	8.6%	14.6%
1995	$27.75	(10.5)%	$2.67	8.6%	(1.9)%
1996	$38.50	38.7%	$2.80	10.1%	48.8%

Ramco-Gershenson Properties Trust
2700 Northwestern Highway, Suite 200
Southfield, MI 48034
(810) 350-9900

Exchange: New York (RPT)
Formation Date: 1988
Geographical Focus: East Coast and Central states
Competitive Strategies: New property development capabilities; selective expansion and re-development of existing properties.
Special Notes: Formed as a result of the May 1996, merger between Ramco-Gershenson, and RPS Realty Trust. Ramso-Gershenson was previously a private company engaged in the acquisition, development, and management of neighborhood and community shopping centers. RPS Realty was a public REIT engaged in mortgage lending on commercial properties. It was formed in 1988 as a result of the consolidation of four separate finite-life trusts which were engaged in mortgage lending activities.
Investment Performance:

	Close	Gain/Loss	Dividend	% Yield	Annual Return
1991	$19.50	(9.3)%	$2.80	13.0%	4.3%
1992	$20.00	2.6%	$2.40	12.3%	14.9%
1993	$15.50	(22.5)%	$1.28	6.4%	(16.1)%
1994	$17.50	12.9%	$1.28	8.3%	21.2%
1995	$18.50	5.7%	$1.28	7.3%	13.0%
1996	$16.88	(8.8)%	$1.68	9.7%	0.3%

Regency Realty Corporation
121 West Forsythe Street, Suite 200
Jacksonville, FL 32202
(904) 356-7000

Exchange: New York (REG)
Initial Public Offering: November 5, 1993
Initial Offering Price: $19.25
Geographical Focus: Southeast
Competitive Strategies: New property development capability; third party management operations; focuses on community and neighborhood shopping centers.

Special Notes: Succeeded to substantially all of the commercial real estate business of The Regency Group, an organization that had been engaged in the development, ownership and management of commercial properties in the Southeast United States for three decades. In 1996, Security Capital U.S. Realty agreed to invest $130 million in exchange for special Class B shares.

Investment Performance:

	Close	Gain/Loss	Dividend	% Yield	Annual Return
1993	$16.63	—	—	—	—
1994	$16.75	0.8%	$1.38	8.3%	9.1%
1995	$17.25	3.0%	$1.58	9.4%	12.4%
1996	$26.25	52.2%	$1.62	9.4%	61.6%

Saul Centers, Inc.
8401 Connecticut Avenue
Chevy Chase, MD 20815
(301) 986-6000

Exchange: New York (BFS)
Initial Public Offering: August 26, 1993
Initial Offering Price: $20.00
Geographical Focus: Washington D.C./Baltimore area
Competitive Strategies: Focuses on properties located in well-established, densely populated, middle and upper income market areas; highly focused geographically.
Special Notes: Besides its investments in community and neighborhood shopping centers, the REIT also owns an office building, an office/retail property, and a research park, all of which are located in the Washington D.C. metro area.
Investment Performance:

	Close	Gain/Loss	Dividend	% Yield	Annual Return
1993	$19.25	—	$0.54	—	—
1994	$14.75	(23.4)%	$1.56	8.1%	(15.3)%
1995	$13.63	(7.6)%	$1.56	10.6%	3.0%
1996	$15.88	16.5%	$1.56	11.5%	28.0%

Vornado Realty Trust
Park 80 West, Plaza II
Saddle Brook, NJ 07663
(201) 587-1000

Exchange: New York (VNO)
Initial Public Offering: May 21, 1993
Initial Offering Price: $35.50
Geographical Focus: Mid-Atlantic and Northeast
Competitive Strategies: Ownership of properties located in well-established East Coast cities; third party management operations; special situations—acquisition of interests in the real estate assets of failed retailers.
Special Notes: Built its portfolio by acquiring New Jersey's failing Two Guys Department stores in 1980 and converting them to strip centers anchored by supermarkets and discount stores. In 1995, Vornado acquired 29.3 percent of the common stock of Alexander's Inc, which owns eight properties in the greater New York metropolitan area. Alexander's was a New York-based retail chain that closed its store operations in the early 1990s and reorganized as a REIT with its previous store locations as its primary assets. In April 1997, Vornado merged with the Mendik Company, owner of a $650 million portfolio of office buildings located in New York City.
Investment Performance:

	Close	Gain/Loss	Dividend	% Yield	Annual Return
1993	$33.50	—	—	—	—
1994	$35.88	7.1%	$2.00	6.0%	13.1%
1995	$37.50	4.5%	$2.24	6.2%	10.7%
1996	$52.50	40.0%	$2.44	6.5%	46.5%

Weingarten Realty Investors
2600 Citadel Plaza Drive
P.O. Box 924133
Houston, TX 77292-4133
(713) 866-6000
(http://www.weingarten.com)

Exchange: New York (WRI)
Initial Public Offering: 1985
Geographical Focus: Texas
Competitive Strategies: New property development capability; focuses on neighborhood and community centers; geographically focused.
Special Notes: Founded in 1948 and restructured as a REIT in 1985. Through 1996, the Trust had increased its dividend every year of its existence and had provided shareholders with an impressive 14.7 percent compounded annual return.
Investment Performance:

	Close	Gain/Loss	Dividend	% Yield	Annual Return
1991	$32.88	32.8%	$1.88	7.6%	40.4%
1992	$36.63	11.4%	$2.04	6.2%	17.6%
1993	$37.50	2.4%	$2.16	5.9%	8.3%
1994	$37.88	1.0%	$2.28	6.1%	7.1%
1995	$38.00	0.3%	$2.40	6.3%	6.6%
1996	$40.63	6.9%	$2.48	6.1%	13.0%

Western Investment Real Estate Trust
3450 California Street
San Francisco, CA 94118
(415) 929-0211

Exchange: American (WIR)
Initial Public Offering: 1962
Geographical Focus: Northern California and Nevada
Competitive Strategies: Highly focused geographically in second tier markets where the competition for investment property is less; most of its properties are leased on a triple net basis.
Special Notes: One of the older REITs still operating. It was founded in 1962 and, from its inception through 1996, continuously paid quarterly dividends. California's economic downturn in the early 1990s negatively impacted its performance during those years.
Investment Performance:

	Close	Gain/Loss	Dividend	% Yield	Annual Return
1991	$11.38	(21.6)%	$1.29	8.9%	(12.7)%
1992	$12.38	8.8%	$1.12	9.8%	18.6%
1993	$12.88	4.0%	$1.12	9.0%	13.0%
1994	$12.88	0.0%	$1.12	8.7%	8.7%
1995	$10.75	(16.5)%	$1.12	8.7%	(7.8)%
1996	$13.00	20.9%	$1.12	10.4%	31.3%

FACTORY OUTLET CENTERS

Factory outlet centers have gone through a metamorphosis over the years. Originally, they were small, "bare bones" facilities where manufacturers sold imperfect or excess merchandise, factory overruns, and the prior season's styles. These centers were first located adjacent to a manufacturer's plants, then they became part of a cluster of such stores in mill towns and selected tourist areas in New England.

Today, factory outlet centers are large, modern looking and architecturally appealing properties. Many are located within 20 miles of major metropolitan areas and in popular vacation spots. Irregular and damaged merchandise, which once comprised most of the outlets' merchandise, account for less than 20 percent of such wares today. The vast majority of merchandise sold by current factory outlet shops is first quality, in-season goods.[15]

Name manufacturers and retailers such as Ann Taylor, Brooks Brothers, Tommy Hilfiger, Nike, Corning/Revere, OshKosh B'Gosh, London Fog, The Gap, and Casual Corner have entered the outlet store business. For these companies, such stores represent more than just a venue in which to sell overruns and out of season merchandise. Instead, they have emerged as another means of distribution.

Some of these companies actually produce certain merchandise for sale exclusively in their outlet stores. While much of this merchandise has the same look as the more expensive items sold in their regular retail stores or in department stores, it is sometimes made of inferior fabric or is manufactured in a less expensive manner.

The factory outlet store business has grown exponentially over the past decade, in large measure due to the consumer shift toward value shopping. The number of factory outlet centers in the United States increased from 108 in 1988 to 350 by the end of 1996. Additionally, the number of companies operating outlet stores grew from 261 in 1988 to more than 535 in 1996 and industry sales increased from $6.3 billion in 1990 to more than $13 billion in 1996.[16]

The REITs that focus in this segment of the industry have been heavily involved in the growth of factory outlets and today operate some of the most successful outlets in the United States. The keys to success for these REITs is to identify locations that are ripe for outlet stores and to attract to these centers prominent manufacturers who will draw customers.

Because each market area can only support a limited number of outlet centers, the factory outlet REITs are national in scope. This enables them to maximize their expertise in developing such properties and their contacts with major manufacturers who are in the outlet business.

Despite the impressive growth of outlet operations and the role the factory outlet REITs have played in this growth, the shares of these REITs have underperformed the industry by a wide margin since they went public in 1993 and 1994. This has been partially due to concern over potential overbuilding in the industry, as well as the ability of outlet centers to compete against more aggressive pricing strategies being implemented by department stores.[17]

Van Husen Corporation, which has been one of the largest players in the outlet store business, decided in 1996 to close almost 300 of its outlet stores nationwide due to poor sales. Additionally, same store sales for outlet centers in recent years have been flat, causing some of the factory outlet REITs to reconsider their expansion plans and focus more of their attention on existing properties.

One factory outlet REIT, FAC Realty, is shifting its strategy away from the outlet industry. It has plans to reduce its exposure to outlet stores to 50% of its portfolio, with the rest made up of conventional retail operations such as strip shopping centers.

Other outlet center operators are recognizing that they may

have to become more creative in providing reasons for the consumer to travel to their centers instead of staying closer to home and seeking out special sales at the local shopping malls. One strategy that has been implemented by Prime Retail is the introduction of The Sports Court at some of its locations. The Sports Court features clustered stores selling sports apparel, equipment, and footwear. It includes interactive facilities where customers can test various equipment before making a purchase. The company has targeted this concept to companies that have not traditionally distributed their products through factory outlets.

Prime Retail is considering this same concept for other merchandise, including home electronics and furnishings. If such concepts are successful, they may provide outlet malls with a new competitive advantage in the crowded retail marketplace.

Factory Outlet REITs

Chelsea GCA Realty Inc.
103 Eisenhower Parkway
Roseland, NJ 07068
(201) 228-6111
(http://www.chelseagca.com)

Exchange: New York (CCG)
Initial Public Offering: November 2, 1993
Initial Offering Price: $27.50
Geographical Focus: Western and Northeastern United States
Competitive Strategies: New property development capabilities; seeks to provide each of its centers with an architecturally distinctive design that is compatible with its environment; heavily promotes some of its centers to international tourists.
Special Notes: The company is engaged in the development and management of upscale and fashion-oriented manufacturer's outlet centers located in major metropolitan areas and near major tourist destinations. Two of the REIT's facilities, Woodbury Commons in Central Valley, New York and Desert Hills in Cabazon, California, are among the most successful outlet malls in the country.
Investment Performance:

	Close	Gain/Loss	Dividend	% Yield	Annual Return
1993	$27.13	—	$0.30	—	—
1994	$27.25	0.5%	$1.90	7.0%	7.5%
1995	$30.00	10.1%	$2.14	7.9%	18.0%
1996	$34.63	15.4%	$2.36	7.9%	23.3%

FAC Realty Trust
11000 Regency Parkway, Suite 300
Cary, NC 27511
(919) 462-8787
(http://www.facrealty.com)

Exchange: New York (FAC)
Initial Public Offering: June 10, 1993
Initial Offering Price: $25.00
Geographical Focus: National
Competitive Strategies: Expansion of successful outlet malls; new property development
Special Notes: Concurrent with its IPO, the company acquired 21 factory outlet centers owned by VF Corporation, a major manufacturer of apparel, including Lee and Wrangler jeans, Jantzen, Vanity Fair, and Health-Tex. VF remains a major tenant in these centers. The company suffered a significant decline in its 1995 operating performance due to higher interest costs, increased operating expenses, and a dividend payout ratio that exceeded 100 percent. It subsequently reduced its dividend in 1996, which caused its stock to decline in value. In early 1997, it acquired six community shopping centers in North Carolina as part of a strategy to diversify its retail property holdings.
Investment Performance:

	Close	Gain/Loss	Dividend	% Yield	Annual Return
1993	$25.00	—	$1.00	—	—
1994	$21.63	(13.5)%	$1.89	7.6%	(5.9)%
1995	$13.13	(39.3)%	$2.01	9.3%	(30.0)%
1996	$ 6.50	(49.5)%	$0.75	5.7%	(43.8)%

Horizon Group
5000 Hakes Drive
Norton Shores, MI 49441
(616) 798-9100

Exchange: New York (HGI)
Initial Public Offering: November 8, 1993
Initial Offering Price: $24.00
Geographical Focus: National
Competitive Strategies: New property development capability; expansion of existing facilities.
Special Notes: Formed on July 14, 1995, as a result of the acquisition of the McArthur/Glen Realty Corporation by Horizon Outlet Centers. At the end of 1996, it was the largest owner of factory outlets properties in the country.
Investment Performance:

	Close	Gain/Loss	Dividend	% Yield	Annual Return
1993	$23.00	—	$0.25	—	—
1994	$26.13	13.6%	$1.76	7.7%	21.3%
1995	$22.88	(12.4)%	$2.13	8.2%	(4.2)%
1996	$19.88	(13.1)%	$2.10	9.2%	(3.9)%

Prime Retail, Inc.
100 East Pratt Street
Baltimore, MD 21202
(410) 234-0782
(http://www.primeretail.com)

Exchange: NASDAQ (PRME)
Initial Public Offering: March 22, 1994
Initial Offering Price: $19.00
Geographical Focus: National
Competitive Strategies: The company's centers are generally larger than the industry's average, providing it with a "critical mass" that protects the centers' competitive position in their respective trade areas; develops its properties with amenities such as food courts, playgrounds, and attractive village settings, all designed to increase the customers' "length-of-stay"; the company is experimenting with

new concepts designed to increase customer traffic including The Sports Court, a collection of factory-direct shops that will offer value-priced apparel, equipment, and footwear from leading sporting goods manufacturers not currently operating in the outlet industry. Special Notes: Formed from a division of The Prime Group, which, from its founding in 1981 until 1994, was involved in the development and management of more than 20 million square feet of income producing property, including retail centers.
Investment Performance:

	Close	Gain/Loss	Dividend	% Yield	Annual Return
1994	$13.25	—	$0.92	—	—
1995	$11.88	(10.4)%	$1.18	8.9%	(1.5)%
1996	$12.50	5.3%	$1.33*	11.2%	16.5%

* includes a special distribution

Tanger Factory Outlet Centers
1400 W. Northwood Street
Greensboro, NC 27408
(910) 274-1666
(hhtp://www.tangeroutlet.com)

Exchange: New York (SKT)
Initial Public Offering: June 4, 1993
Initial Offering Price: $22.50
Geographical Focus: National
Competitive Strategies: New property development capabilities; expansion of existing outlet centers; guarantees customers get the lowest prices at its centers through its "Relax—It's Guaranteed" program.
Special Notes: Stanley Tanger entered the factory outlet business in 1981 after building and managing a family-owned apparel manufacturing business. In 1993, Mr. Tanger contributed 15 operating factory outlet centers to Tanger Properties Limited Partnership in conjunction with the formation of this REIT. Since its initial public offering in June 1993, Tanger Factory Outlet Centers has more than doubled in size.
Investment Performance:

Retail Properties

	Close	Gain/Loss	Dividend	% Yield	Annual Return
1993	$28.75	—	$0.54	—	—
1994	$23.50	(18.3)%	$1.80	6.3%	(12.0)%
1995	$25.00	6.4%	$1.96	8.3%	14.7%
1996	$27.25	9.0%	$2.06	8.2%	17.2%

CHAPTER EIGHT

Office/Industrial Properties

OFFICE BUILDING REITs and industrial REITs are classified as a single segment in the industry because a significant number of REITs invest in both types of properties. Their customers tend to be businesses in need of office and industrial space, sometimes all under one roof. The REITs that do invest in both office and industrial properties tend to focus on suburban office properties as opposed to downtown office buildings because this is generally where their customers want to be. Additionally, many REITs specialize in developing and owning both business parks and industrial parks. Such efforts effectively provide them with a monopoly within selected markets.

While the office and industrial sectors are classified as one in the REIT industry, we will review them as two different segments. Their histories are quite different, as are the dynamics of each sector.

OFFICE BUILDINGS

The office market was the hardest hit of all real estate sectors from the overbuilding of the 1980s. As a result, it was the last to recover; but when it did, it was quite a recovery. In 1995, equity REITs focusing on office building investments recorded a spectacular 38.8 percent return versus a 15.3 percent total return for all equity REITs. In 1996, office building equity REITs did even better, registering a

119

51.8 percent total return versus a 35.3 percent return for all equity REITs. These high returns enabled publicly-registered office REITs to become a favorite on Wall Street. Despite being one of the smaller sectors (at least in terms of the number of companies), office REITs experienced an influx of capital during 1995 and 1996. This enabled five office REITs to finish 1996 with stock market values in excess of $1 billion.[1]

What propelled the office REITs into the spotlight was the turnaround in office markets throughout the country. In the late 1980s and early 1990s, the office sector was in shambles; vacancy levels were high, rents were on the decline, and office building owners were scrambling to salvage their investments.[2] This was a complete turnaround from the situation that existed in the early and mid-1980s. At that time, office properties were a favorite of investors. Institutional real estate buyers and limited partnership sponsors loved those mega-office properties that populated so many central cities. For the institutions, it gave them prestige; for partnership sponsors, it meant that their offerings would be a hit in the marketplace.

Office buildings had a good story behind them as well. In the four year period leading into the 1980s (1978 to 1981), office properties produced a rather hefty 22 percent average annual return for their owners. Additionally, office buildings were also experiencing high occupancy levels. In 1982, for instance, the national vacancy rate for downtown office properties was less than 5 percent.[3]

Future demand was also predicted to be strong, with projections that the surge of white collar employment in the fast growing U.S. service sector would result in record level demand for office space throughout the decade. The net result was that developers started the construction cranes in the mid-1980s and did not stop until 1989 when they had added an unprecedented amount of new space to the market.

While demand for this space also increased at a rapid pace, it could not possibly keep up with the new supply. As a result, vacancy levels soared. Just when it was thought they had peaked, they rose even more. By 1986, the amount of empty office space in suburban office markets nationwide had jumped to just under 25 percent. Even after the supply of new space had started to decline in the late 1980s, vacancy rates still exceeded the 25 percent mark in a number of major cities including, Dallas, Denver, Houston, and Phoenix (Exhibit 8-1).[4]

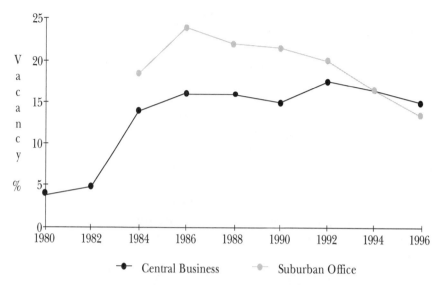

Exhibit 8-1   U.S. Office Vacancy Rates (1980–1996) SOURCE: Coldwell Banker

Today, conditions have improved substantially. This is because there was a dearth of new construction in the office sector in the early 1990s, enabling demand to catch up with the available supply. Even with these more promising market conditions, however, the office sector is not one for novice real estate investors.

First of all, not all markets have improved at the same rate. Minneapolis, for instance, saw its office vacancy rate drop from 18 percent in 1992 to under 8 percent by the end of 1996. As a result, rents were projected to increase there by 18 percent in both 1997 and 1998 and the acquisition cost of Class A office space, which had been $118 per square foot in 1995, increased to $144 per square foot in 1996.[5]

In Boston, office property vacancies dropped from 15 percent to less than 7 percent during the three year period ending in 1996. The result: rents rose by more than 20 percent over that time frame and Class A space increased in value from $189 per square foot to almost $205 per square foot.[6]

On the other end of the spectrum, rents in Honolulu were expected to decline by more than 6 percent a year in both 1997 and 1998 due to a depressed economy. In downtown New York City, rental rates were projected to drop by almost 7 percent in 1997 as companies continued to flee the city for less expensive space in New Jersey and Connecticut.[7]

The increased use of technology by businesses is also having a significant impact on the demand for office space, as is their effort to reduce overhead expenses. While demand has been on the rise, tenants have been much more selective in their choice of space. They are taking a closer look at their actual needs and their cost parameters and matching those variables with what's available in the marketplace. Gone are the days when companies sought the most prestigious space. Instead, they are now more concerned with what is practical, both from a financial standpoint as well as in terms of the productivity of their workforce. This has resulted in more companies leasing space in suburban office locations where rents are lower and locations are generally more convenient for their employees.[8]

When evaluating office markets, an investor must distinguish between the two primary markets: the central business district (CBD) and the suburban office market. Within these markets there are certain sub-markets. In major cities such as New York, the office market is divided into various sub-markets, such as midtown and downtown, while in newer cities like Dallas, Denver, and Houston, there are various suburban office markets that have been developed in proximity to particular areas of residential housing.

The central business district (CBD) normally consists of high rise buildings that serve as the national or regional headquarters of major industrial, technological, health care, and financial services companies. Other firms that have extensive dealings with these businesses or with government agencies, such as lawyers, accountants, and trade groups, also tend to locate their offices in the central city.

Suburban office properties are located on the outskirts of a city, usually near major highways, shopping centers, and restaurants. In major metropolitan areas, there are usually a number of office developments. This provides greater convenience for workers, who generally prefer to limit their commuting time. It also reduces traffic congestion in these cities.

While the central city and suburban office markets are usually evaluated separately, there are instances when they do impact each other. For instance, if due to high vacancy levels rents in a central business district decline precipitously, then some suburban tenants seeking to "move up" may elect to relocate to the central city. In a more stable marketplace, however, the functional use of office space usually dictates the location and the quality of the building a business selects in leasing space. Major corporations and professionals such as attorneys and accountants, generally prefer prestigious office space to support the upscale image they are looking to present to their clients.

The next level is general office space. While it is still considered quality space, its location is not as prominent and its physical features are not as impressive as the more prestigious office space.

The last category of functional use is supportive office space, where offices are combined with retail, warehousing, or technical operations. This type of space tends to be more "bare bones" in appearance and its location is generally not as accessible as other office types.[9]

The quality of office properties will usually vary by their age as well as the overall physical condition of the property. Office properties are generally classified as follows:

Class A—An excellent location and access; in good to excellent condition; is able to charge rents that are competitive with those for newly constructed properties.

Class B—A good location; generally good physical condition; suffers from some functional obsolescence and physical deterioration.

Class C—Older buildings that suffer from physical deterioration and functional obsolescence.

The market for office space users can be segmented among those that serve a local market, such as doctors, dentists, lawyers, and accountants and those users that serve a non-local market, such as the regional offices of major corporations. For the first group of users, proximity to their customer base is critical in selecting an office location. The latter group, meanwhile, is more concerned with proximity to the airport, freeways, or needed business services.[10]

In evaluating the demand for office space in a given market area, a REIT must focus on the current level and projected growth of white collar employment. This total, combined with the number of tenants seeking to move up to higher quality space, will determine the need for a particular level of office space, whether it is Class A, B, or C.

The REIT's analysis will include an evaluation of the number of businesses being formed in the local marketplace, the number of firms that are expanding (and are candidates for new or additional space), plus firms relocating to the area. Subtracted from this total is the number of firms that are downsizing, ceasing business, or leaving the market. The final steps in this phase of analysis is a calculation of how many employees will be added and the amount of new space that will be needed for each new worker (Exhibit 8-2).

The other phase in the analytical process involves an evaluation of supply, both current and future. This includes gathering information on current vacancy levels as well as new stock that is being added to the market.

As with other asset types, there are a number of sub-markets in the office sector. This impacts the investment evaluation. While a particular suburban market might be overbuilt, another suburban office area within the same marketplace might be under-supplied. The REIT must look beyond market-wide vacancy numbers in evaluating a metropolitan area.

Businesses being formed
+
Local firms expanding
+
Companies moving to the area
Less
Local firms which are downsizing,
ceasing business,
and leaving the market
Equals
Net Business Additions (Subtractions)
×
Square Feet Required/Employee
Equals
Office Space Demand

Exhibit 8-2 Local Office Demand Analysis

Office space is constructed on both a non-speculative and speculative basis. Non-speculative space is usually designed and build for occupancy by one tenant, a headquarters building for a major corporation, for instance. While such properties are generally not factored into the office/supply picture for a local market (because it is space that is not available for lease), they do have an impact on market conditions. This is because corporations that build their own office buildings usually relinquish space in the local office market. The net result is that this space is added to the available supply.

Alternatively, if a corporation scales back its operations, it will often decide that it no longer needs its own headquarters building. It will then consolidate operations within the building and lease out the remaining space, or it will relocate to another location and either sell its building or lease the space to other businesses.[11]

After the market analysis is complete, the REIT must then turn its focus to individual properties within its selected market or markets. In analyzing potential acquisitions, it will examine such factors as:

- The current tenant base and the terms of their leases (length, rental rate, renewal options),
- The physical condition of the property and any major capital improvements required,
- The competitiveness of the property in the marketplace (its amenity package, location, visibility, and functional characteristics).

Because office property leases normally run three to five years, an analysis of a building's leases is important in determining an acquisition price. If market rates have changed considerably since many of the property's leases were signed, the buyer can expect to realize either a significant increase or decrease in revenues when such leases come up for renewal.

Office building leases can vary considerably. Their terms and conditions will depend on which party has the bargaining power at the time negotiations take place. In the late 1980s and early 1990s, when vacancy levels were high and absorption levels low in most major markets, the tenants possessed the leverage. This enabled them to obtain concessions from office building owners on their base rental rate, rental rates increases, the assumption of pro-rata operating expenses, build-out expenses (the cost of preparing the office space for the new tenant), and the length of the lease. In markets which were especially soft, prospective tenants were sometimes able to convince their new landlords to pay for their relocation expenses as well.[12]

In a healthy office market, the bargaining power is usually held by the landlord. This means the prospective tenant will receive few if any concessions, and the terms of the lease will largely mirror those offered by the landlord.

Regardless of market conditions, the cost of leasing office space can be substantial. Many office building owners rely on independent leasing brokers to rent out their vacant space. These leasing agents receive healthy commission checks for their efforts. Additionally, depending upon the tenant's needs, the owner may incur substantial build-out expenses in preparing space for a new lessee. This may involve reconfiguring the office space by adding or eliminating individual offices. New carpeting and freshly painted walls may also be required.

Improved real estate market conditions in the mid-to-late 1990s have made life a little easier for office building owners because of improved demand and a considerable drop-off in new development. After a five year period at the close of the 1980s when an average of 98 million square feet was added each year (as shown in Exhibit 8-3), completions dropped by half in 1991, and then by another 50 percent a year later. By 1993, new office construction was almost non-existent.

The absorption of space, which had trailed supply throughout much of the 1980s, was able to outpace new construction in both 1993 and 1994 by a factor of almost 12 to 1. While this was positive, the fact is that the level of absorption was still well below the levels recorded in the mid-to-late 1980s. Absorption is not likely to reach that level again; at least not in the near term.

A major reason for the high level of demand in the 1980s was due to demographics. The peak of the baby boomers (children born between 1957 and 1961) moved into the workforce. Moreover, women entered the market in larger numbers, expanding their participation in the work force from 38 percent to 44 percent from 1970 to 1985. White collar employment grew from about 45 million in 1975 to nearly 60 million by the end of 1985.[13]

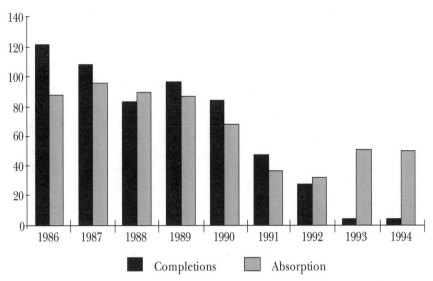

Exhibit 8-3 U.S. Office Construction & Absorption (in million sq. ft.) SOURCE: Coldwell Banker

In the 1990s, conditions are much different. The influx of baby boomers into the economy is essentially complete. Corporate America, meanwhile, has been cutting costs—that means people and space. There will be even fewer employees doing the work in the future as automation becomes more prevalent. Those doing the work will likely have to perform their tasks in more confined quarters. This means that competition in the office building sector will continue to be substantial.[14]

The increased use of technology has reduced the need for companies to maintain centrally located business operations. This has resulted in many back-office operations being relocated to markets where both office space and labor expenses are lower. In the late-1990s, traveling salespeople do not have to step foot in their company's offices. Instead, their employers are providing them with their own computers, fax machines, and multi-line telephones, and having them work out of their home when they are not on the road. The increased use of computers and other high tech equipment (automated phone systems, for instance) have made newer buildings more appealing because they can provide adequate power sources, accommodate complex wiring needs, and offer flexible office configurations.[15]

While many older, well-maintained structures still have an aura about them, for many companies they are no longer practical. Instead, in the future, they will likely be occupied by firms whose technological needs are limited. Thus, in the long term, Class A and B buildings appear safe, but Class C properties could be in for a rough ride.

Another change that has taken place in the office sector is the shift in demand from the central business district to the suburban market. Throughout the 1980s, central city office markets maintained significantly higher occupancy levels than suburban markets; however, as a result of increased traffic congestion in many metropolitan areas, as well as the desire of workers to be closer to their places of work, central business districts have become less desirable for many companies in the 1990s. This has resulted in greater demand for suburban office space and a more rapid recovery for the suburban office markets.

This is why many of the office sector REITs focus on the suburban markets. Cali Realty, Highwoods Properties, Parkway Properties, Arden Realty, and Koger Equity all specialize in suburban office park investments in specific regions of the country. Cali Realty focuses its activities in the Northeast, Highwoods Properties and Parkway Properties in the Southeast, Arden Realty in Southern California, and Koger Equity in the Southeast and Southwest. Carr-America, meanwhile, invests in suburban properties in major markets throughout the United States.

Cali Realty has been an aggressive buyer of office properties since going public in late 1994, first in New Jersey, then in New York and Philadelphia. Highwoods Properties has expanded primarily through the acquisition of other real estate firms, including Crocker Realty Trust, another public REIT that specialized in office investments.

Parkway Properties began as Texas First Mortgage REIT in 1971 and dropped its trust status in the mid-1970s after running into financial difficulties. It continued as a public company over the years, assembling a diversified portfolio of direct real estate investments. In 1997, Parkway converted back to a REIT and is now focused exclusively on the acquisition and management of multistory suburban properties located in first and second tier markets in the Sunbelt region.

Arden Realty, which went public in late 1996, has traditionally fo-

128

cused its operations in Southern California. It made it through California's economic downturn in the early 1990s and is now poised to expand its portfolio of Class A suburban office properties in its home market.

The road to prosperity has been a little different for Koger Equity. It was formed in 1988 to invest in office buildings developed by a sister company, Koger Properties. After Koger Properties went bankrupt in the early 1990s, Koger Equity acquired Koger Properties' assets under terms that required it to allocate future profits to reducing debt on the acquired properties. As a result, Koger Equity has focused its efforts in recent years on improving the operating performance of its portfolio as opposed to expanding its operations like the other office REITs.

CarrAmerica Realty Corporation traditionally focused on downtown office buildings in one marketplace: Washington, D.C. However, as a result of a strategic alliance the company entered into with Security Capital U.S. Realty in early 1996, CarrAmerica has changed its focus to investing in suburban office buildings in high growth markets throughout the United States.

Cornerstone Properties, which went public in April 1997, invests in Class A properties located in both central business districts and suburban markets in major metropolitan areas throughout the United States. When it went public, the company's portfolio included primarily CBD office properties located in seven cities: Boston, Chicago, Denver, Minneapolis, New York, Pittsburgh, and Seattle.

Boston Properties also went public in 1997 with a portfolio of urban and suburban properties. The company was founded in Boston in 1970 by publishing magnate Mortimer Zuckerman and Edward Linde. They have largely focused their efforts on developing properties in Boston, midtown New York City, and the Washington D.C. metropolitan area. At the time of its initial offering, Boston Properties owned 75 properties, including 63 office buildings, 9 industrial facilities, 2 hotels, and 1 parking garage.

The other major office REITs have been more active in the acquisition and/or development of downtown office buildings.

Beacon Properties initially focused its acquisitions in its home city of Boston, where market conditions have improved substantially in the mid-1990s after an economic downturn at the outset of the decade. In late 1996, Beacon expanded its horizons in a significant way through the acquisition of the 32 building, 3.3 million square foot Perimeter Center portfolio in Atlanta, Georgia. It also had holdings in Washington, D.C., Chicago, San Francisco, Los Angeles, and Philadelphia.

Crescent Real Estate Equities owns a diversified portfolio of real estate, with a primary focus on office buildings. Despite the lackluster comeback of central business districts, Crescent has been one of the few REITs that has not been shy about acquiring downtown office structures.

The reason why office REITs have been so aggressive in expanding their portfolios is because office properties have generally been available for prices well below their replacement values. The overbuilding of the 1980s resulted in a substantial decline in rental rates, which equated to lower profits and decreased property values in this sector.

As market conditions continue to improve in most major markets, the office REITs will be the beneficiaries of increasing rental rates. The capital markets have anticipated this and have driven up the stock values of the office REITs accordingly.

Buying for less than replacement value has not been the only competitive strategy employed by office REITs. The REITs that focus on acquiring suburban office properties have generally sought to acquire entire business parks, providing them with a monopoly in certain sectors of specific real estate markets. Office REITs that have acquired downtown office properties have generally sought to acquire prominent properties, the type of buildings that stand out in a city because of their tenant base, architecture, and/or location.

Office Building REITs

Arden Realty Inc.
9100 Wilshire Blvd., Suite 700E
Beverly Hills, CA 90212
(310) 271-8600

Exchange: New York (ARI)
Initial Public Offering: October 4, 1996
Initial Offering Price: $20.00
Geographical Focus: Southern California

Competitive Strategies: Purchase and renovate underperforming suburban office properties and Class A suburban buildings with stable cash flows for less than replacement value; highly focused geographically; acquire properties located in submarkets where rent growth is expected to be above average due to positive employment trends, declining vacancy rates, and limited new construction; third party property management.

Special Notes: Successor to a company that acquired over four million square feet of commercial office space in Los Angeles and Orange County in the 1980s.

Investment Performance:

	Close	Gain/Loss	Dividend	% Yield	Annual Return
1996	$26.50	—	$ —	—	—

Beacon Properties Corporation
50 Rowes Wharf
Boston, MA 02110
(617) 330-1400
(http://www.beaconproperties.com)

Exchange: New York (BCN)
Initial Public Offering: May 26, 1994
Initial Offering Price: $17.00
Geographical Focus: East Coast
Competitive Strategies: Third party management operations; purchase properties for less than replacement value; target strong office markets such as Boston, Atlanta, Washington, D.C., Chicago, Los Angeles, and San Francisco.
Special Notes: Successor to a company that was founded in 1946 to provide general contracting services on development projects and which, in the 1960s, started developing properties for its own account. In February 1996, acquired the 32 building, 3.3 million square foot, Perimeter Center portfolio in Atlanta, Georgia. In September 1996, it expanded its operations to Chicago with the purchase of six office properties in that city. The company owns some of Boston's premier properties, including Rowes Wharf, 75-101 Federal Street, One Post Office Square, South Station, and Center Plaza.
Investment Performance:

	Close	Gain/Loss	Dividend	% Yield	Annual Return
1994	$19.00	—	$0.56	—	—
1995	$23.00	21.1%	$1.64	8.6%	29.7%
1996	$36.63	59.2%	$1.77	7.7%	66.9%

Boston Properties, Inc.
8 Arlington Street
Boston, MA 02116
(617) 859-2600

Exchange: New York (BXP)
Initial Public Offering: June 23, 1997
Initial Share Price: $25.00
Geographical Focus: Boston, New York, Washington, D.C.
Competitive Strategies: Acquire and manage a diversified portfolio of Class A urban and suburban office properties in major metropolitan areas for less than replacement value; focus in certain select markets where it can assemble a portfolio of properties, thereby gaining economies of scale in the management of such properties; new property development capabilities.
Special Notes: Formed by Mortimer Zuckerman and Edward Linde. Most of its properties were developed by a firm founded by both men in Boston in 1970. Zuckerman also owns *Atlantic Monthly* magazine, *U.S. News & World Report,* and the *New York Daily News.* At the time of the IPO, Zuckerman, and Linde owned 27% of the operating Partnership (under the UPREIT format) and 8% of Boston Properties' shares.

Cali Realty Corporation
11 Commerce Drive
Cranford, NJ 07016
(908) 272-8000
(http://www.calirealty.com)

Exchange: New York (CLI)
Initial Public Offering: August 31, 1994
Initial Offering Price: $17.25
Geographical Focus: Northeast

Competitive Strategies: Focuses on Class A suburban office properties, most of which are located in business parks; concentrates on buying properties in sub-markets where it is or can become a significant and preferred owner and operator.

Special Notes: Successor to an organization founded in 1949 to manage partnerships investing in office properties in the state of New Jersey.

Investment Performance:

	Close	Gain/Loss	Dividend	% Yield	Annual Return
1994	$16.00	—	$0.56	—	—
1995	$21.88	36.7%	$1.66	10.4%	47.1%
1996	$30.88	41.1%	$1.75	8.0%	49.1%

CarrAmerica Realty Corporation

1700 Pennsylvania Street N.W.
Washington, D.C. 20006
(202) 624-7500
(http://www.carramerica.com)

Exchange: New York (CRE)
Initial Public Offering: 1993
Initial Offering Price: $20.00
Geographical Focus: National
Competitive Strategies: Third party management operations; focuses on acquiring and developing properties in high growth suburban markets throughout the United States with a principal focus on Washington, D.C.

Special Notes: Since November 1995, Security Capital U.S. Realty has invested more than $500 million in the company as part of a strategic alliance with CarrAmerica.

Investment Performance:

	Close	Gain/Loss	Dividend	% Yield	Annual Return
1993	$23.00	—	$1.06	—	—
1994	$18.00	(21.7)%	$1.75	7.6%	14.1%
1995	$24.38	35.4%	$1.75	9.7%	45.1%
1996	$29.25	20.0%	$1.75	7.2%	27.2%

Cornerstone Properties, Inc.
Tower 56
126 East 56th Street
New York, NY 10022
(212) 605-7100

Exchange: New York (CPP)
Initial Public Offering: April 15, 1997
Initial Offering Price: $14.00
Geographical Focus: National
Competitive Strategies: Acquisition of Class A office properties in the central business districts and suburban markets in major metropolitan areas for below replacement; Purchase of assets through stock-for-asset swaps with major institutional owners of property.
Special Notes: Formed in 1981 as AIRCO America Realestate Investment Company to provide individual German investors the opportunity to invest in U.S. commercial real estate. In September 1995, the company completed a reorganization in which it was renamed Cornerstone Properties, and adopted a plan to increase the size of its portfolio and broaden its shareholder base. In November 1996, it completed a private placement of $166.5 million of preferred stock with the New York State Teachers Retirement System.

Crescent Real Estate Equities, Inc.
900 Third Avenue, 18th Floor
New York, NY 10022
(212) 603-6800
(http://www.cei-crescent.com)

Exchange: New York (CEI)
Initial Public Offering: May 5, 1994
Initial Offering Price: $25.00
Geographical Focus: National
Competitive Strategies: Acquisition of Class A office buildings in markets that are benefiting from internal growth as well as the immigration of new businesses; purchases assets that are gaining occupancy and achieving rental rates increases at prices well below their replacement cost; opportunistic joint venture investments in luxury hotels/resorts and residential land developments with experienced

co-investors who have the ability to effectively identify and manage such assets.

Special Notes: Formed to continue the real estate investment and operating businesses affiliated with Richard Rainwater and The Rosewood Corporation. In its first year and a half in existence, the company acquired more than $580 million in real estate investments. In May 1997, created Crescent Operating Inc., which was spunoff to existing shareholders and which will manage about 90 behavioral health care facilities which Crescent previously acquired from Magellan Health Services Inc.

Investment Performance:

	Close	Gain/Loss	Dividend	% Yield	Annual Return
1994	$27.13	—	$0.79	—	—
1995	$34.13	25.8%	$2.10	7.7%	33.5%
1996	$52.75	54.6%	$2.44	7.2%	61.8%

Highwoods Properties
3100 Smoketree Court, Suite 600
Raleigh, NC 27604
(919) 872-4924

Exchange: New York (HIW)
Initial Public Offering: June 14, 1994
Initial Offering Price: $21.00
Geographical Focus: Southeast
Competitive Strategies: Third party management services; focus on suburban office properties; aggressive growth strategy achieved primarily through mergers with other public and private real estate companies and the acquisition of portfolios from other real estate firms; new property development capability.
Special Notes: Is the successor to the operations of the Highwoods Group, a firm that was founded in 1978. It is the largest developer and operator of office buildings in North Carolina. In 1996, Highwood acquired another REIT, Crocker Realty (ASE:CKT), which resulted in the addition of 70 Class A office buildings and 235 acres of undeveloped land to its portfolio.
Investment Performance:

	Close	Gain/Loss	Dividend	% Yield	Annual Return
1994	$21.63	—	$0.93	—	—
1995	$28.25	30.6%	$1.78	8.2%	38.8%
1996	$33.75	19.5%	$1.92	6.8%	26.3%

Koger Equity, Inc.
3986 Boulevard Center Drive, Suite 101
Jacksonville, FL 32207
(904) 398-3403
(http://www.koger.com)

Exchange: American (KE)
Initial Public Offering: June 21, 1988
Geographical Focus: Southeast and Southwest
Competitive Strategies: Third party management operations; the development and acquisition of business parks (called Koger Centers) that provide the company with both name recognition within its markets as well complete control of its office parks.
Special Notes: Initial portfolio was acquired from Koger Properties, both before and after Koger Properties' bankruptcy filing in 1991. The properties acquired after the bankruptcy filing were obtained through a merger of the entities. The merger agreement required that, for a specified period of time, Koger Equity allocate all operating profits and property sale proceeds to the reduction of debt. This is why there were no distributions from 1992 through 1995.
Investment Performance:

	Close	Gain/Loss	Dividend	% Yield	Annual Return
1991	$ 4.00	(49.2)%	$0.77	0.0%	(49.2)%
1992	$ 4.63	15.6%	$0.00	0.0%	15.6%
1993	$ 8.50	83.8%	$0.00	0.0%	83.8%
1994	$ 7.25	(14.7)%	$0.00	0.0%	(14.7)%
1995	$10.63	46.6%	$0.00	0.0%	46.6%
1996	$18.75	76.5%	$0.05	0.5%	77.0%

Parkway Properties, Inc.
One Jackson Place, Suite 1000
Jackson, MS 39201
(601) 948-4091
(800) 748-1667
(http://www.parkwayco.com)

Exchange: New York (PKY)
Conversion Date: January 1, 1997
Conversion Price: $26.00
Geographical Focus: Southeast and Texas
Competitive Strategies: Acquisition of well-located Class A, A-, or B+ multi-story office buildings for below replacement cost; focus on high growth markets; third party management operations.
Special Notes: Began as Texas First Mortgage REIT in 1971. The company terminated its REIT status in the mid-1970s after it experienced financial problems, converting to a C-corporation; it changed to a Texas corporation in 1981, and then back to a REIT in 1997. Up until mid-1995, it maintained a diversified portfolio of real estate investments, at which time it elected to focus in the office building sector. Formerly part of the Eastover Group, which all spun off another public REIT, Eastgroup Properties.

INDUSTRIAL PROPERTIES

The industrial property sector is one that has gained in popularity in the 1990s primarily due to the fact that this segment of the real estate industry managed to avoid the overbuilding that occurred in so many other sectors last decade. The net result has been that occupancy levels for industrial properties in the United States have generally been higher than those for other types of commercial property. This has meant more stable and predictable cash flows for their owners.

Nationally, industrial property vacancy levels have normally averaged about 5 percent and, even during recessionary periods when demand normally declines, they have rarely exceeded 10 percent. Investment yields, meanwhile, have usually averaged 8 to 10 percent and annual total returns generally a few percentage points higher (for the eight year period 1983 through 1990, annual returns were between 8.6 percent and 12 percent) (Exhibit 8-4).[16]

137

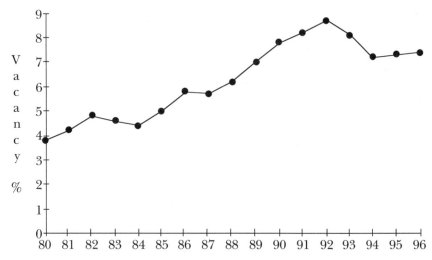

Exhibit 8-4 Industrial Vacancy Rates 1980–1996 SOURCE: CB Commercial

The absence of overbuilding in the industrial property sector has been largely due to the lack of speculative building. Most new properties are developed to meet the demands of a specific tenant or group of tenants. Because industrial properties generally require a comparatively short development period, there is little need to engage in speculative development in order to meet future tenant needs.

Demand for industrial space is on the rise as large companies continue to consolidate their operations and smaller companies become an increasingly more potent force in the economy. For larger companies, industrial properties that combine office and distribution/warehouse space in a more economical setting offer a means to trim real estate expenses. For smaller companies that do not have the capital to provide separate facilities for their administrative, sales, research and development, production, and distribution operations, industrial properties that contain office space provide the flexibility they are seeking.

Another reason for the increased demand for industrial properties and warehouses is the role these facilities are playing in the ever-changing distribution chain. As retailers and manufacturers continue to focus their efforts on the "just-in-time" delivery of goods to store shelves (saving retailers the cost of having to maintain large inventories), they have become more dependent on warehouses to store goods closer to their final destination. Warehouses in growing markets and in cities located along the path of goods (i.e., major highways) are experiencing an increase in demand and use.

In years past, most warehouses were multistory structures located in urban areas. As urban planning came into vogue, however, industrial properties were shifted to developments within communities which, while close to transportation routes, were clear of residential areas and office buildings. This negated the need for multi-level buildings and led to the creation of more practical single-story industrial warehouse buildings involving relatively uncomplicated construction techniques.

There are three types of industrial properties in the marketplace today: bulk warehouse, light industrial, and business service buildings.

Bulk warehouse properties are used for the storage of materials and manufactured goods. They have dock facilities for tractor trailer trucks as well as loading areas for lighter vehicles and vans. Bulk warehouses are usually 18 to 30 feet in height, which provides sufficient stackable space for lift trucks to store and retrieve goods; and most have some office space. These facilities are generally located near interstate highways and in areas away from the center city where land is less expensive.

Light industrial properties combine the utility of a warehouse with the attributes of a corporate office. They are used for the design, assembly, packaging, and distribution of goods and often house a small company's headquarters, sales offices, and research and development operations. These properties generally have lower ceiling heights than bulk warehouses (14 to 22 feet is common) and most have dock facilities as well. Glass fronts provide for windowed offices for executives, salespeople and/or engineers, with such space accounting for 10 percent to as much as 50 percent of a light industrial facility.

Business service buildings (also called business parks) are structures that contain primarily office space, but also have warehouse space that can be utilized for storage or as showrooms. The warehouse space is usually located in the rear of the building and opens to an area with loading facilities. The front of the buildings include storefront windows and paved areas for automobile parking.

Business service buildings provide for a more visible location, a higher image, and more conventional office space than light industrial properties. While their rents are higher than other types of industrial properties, they are typically about 25 percent less than for comparable suburban office buildings. Like suburban office properties, however, they tend to be located close to shopping centers, restaurants, and housing developments.

Besides their generally positive demand/supply picture, industrial properties compare favorably to other commercial real estate investments for a number of reasons, including:[17]

1. **High Tenant Retention**—Unlike office, retail and multifamily properties, most industrial facilities are occupied by a single tenant. Since these tenants normally invest significant capital in specific site improvements, relocation tends to be costly. Most industrial property tenants stay put once they settle upon a location.

2. **Less Management Responsibility**—Individual industrial properties are usually leased to one tenant or a few tenants who enter into leases ranging in length from three to five years. Many industrial property owners rely on independent leasing agents to market their properties. Additionally, there are usually minimal tenant improvements required to lease a facility. The management requirements for industrial properties are usually far less than that for multifamily properties, office buildings, and many retail facilities.

3. **Less Physical Depreciation**—Because most warehouses are simply shells without much internal building improvements, they tend to require less maintenance and capital improvement expenditures.

4. **Lower Capital Expenditures**—Most industrial properties are located in outlying areas and/or in industrial parks, where land costs are usually less than for office buildings, retail facilities, and apartment properties. This fact, combined with the lower cost of building such properties, results in a lower price tag for industrial facilities.

5. **Lease Arrangements**—Most industrial space leases are written for terms of three to five years and provide for periodic rental increases that are either fixed or based on changes in

the Consumer Price Index. The leases are also generally triple net leases, requiring the tenants to pay directly, or reimburse the landlord, for virtually all costs of occupancy, including property taxes, utilities, insurance, and maintenance.

Most buyers of industrial facilities seek properties that have multiple purposes and can be re-leased to a new tenant without the major capital renovations that are usually required in converting highly specialized facilities. Other factors that industrial property REITs consider in analyzing potential acquisitions include:

- the type of property: bulk warehouse, light industrial, or business service building,
- the location, construction quality, condition, and design of the property,
- its potential for capital appreciation,
- the opportunity for increasing the property's value through renovations,
- the terms of current tenant leases,
- the potential for expanding the property and the amount of adjacent land available for such expansion, and
- the demand/supply outlook in the market area.

Location within a metropolitan area is of critical importance from a business perspective. Facilities should be situated away from residential areas (to avoid complaints from the community regarding truck traffic), but should be accessible to trucks, employees, customers, and salespeople. It is also important that such facilities be close to major transportation routes, such as interstate highways, and that they be located on level sites, making it easier for delivery trucks to maneuver. Many industrial parks are situated near airports, since air transportation has become increasingly important in an economy where many firms maintain just-in-time inventory operations.

As a result of their higher occupancy levels, competitive cash-on-cash returns, and fairly predictable appreciation patterns, industrial properties have emerged as an ideal investment for REITs. The REITs that focus in the industrial sector generally concentrate their investments in major metropolitan areas because such areas usually generate sufficient demand to keep most facilities substantially to fully occupied.

In the past, industrial properties were situated in cities that were important to companies for their proximity to a firm's (1) end-product markets, (2) raw material supplies, or (3) labor supply. As a result of a shift in much of the United States' manufacturing base to foreign nations, however, proximity to raw materials has largely been replaced as a criteria by the proximity to import and export markets. Export/import markets are cities that are positioned to benefit from the growth in trade with the Pacific Rim, Mexico, and Europe. Pacific Coast cities such as Los Angeles, San Francisco, and Seattle are examples of such markets.

The end-product markets are cities that are strategically situated along major transportation routes (air, water, rail, or highway) and close to major population centers. Atlanta, Cincinnati, and Kansas City are examples of such cities.

Location to labor supply these days usually translates into low cost manufacturing markets, specifically lower cost labor markets. The maquiladora (the United States/Mexico twin plant) program is one example of targeting lower cost labor supply. This program promotes the manufacture and assembly of products close to the Mexican border. It has made the city of El Paso, Texas, an attractive market for industrial properties.

Within the industrial sector of the REIT industry, there are companies that are national in scope and REITs that concentrate their investments in a specific region or regions of the country.

Security Capital and Meridian Industrial Trust have properties throughout the nation. Security Capital is the largest firm in this sector. It has focused on three primary markets: export/import growth markets, low cost manufacturing markets, and growth distribution markets. Within these cities, it has primarily acquired and developed bulk warehouse space. Security Capital has also sought to distinguish itself through the development of master-planned, full-service distribution parks that offer both bulk warehouse and light industrial space, as well as such extras as conference/meeting facilities, exercise facilities, and trailer storage. Meridian Industrial Trust targets markets it believes will experience increased demand for warehouse/industrial space due to population growth or because of their strategic location along the nation's path of goods.

First Industrial, CenterPoint Properties, and Weeks Corporation are the other industrial REITs. Their geographical focus is more targeted. First Industrial concentrates its efforts in the Midwest. Key markets for it include Detroit, Grand Rapids, Minneapolis/St. Paul, Chicago, St. Louis, and central Pennsylvania. The company believes these areas are and will remain important manufacturing bases and distribution centers because of the excellent roadway, rail, and water transportation infrastructures that exist in most of these markets. CenterPoint Properties and the Weeks Corporation are focused on specific cities: CenterPoint in Chicago and Weeks in Atlanta. While both companies are highly concentrated geographically, they are diversified by the type of industrial properties they acquire. This is because they seek to meet all of their tenants' needs; whether it is bulk warehousing, light industrial, or combination office/industrial space. Both firms also develop properties for specific tenants and manage properties for third party owners.

Industrial Property REITs

CenterPoint Properties
401 North Michigan Avenue, 30th Floor
Chicago, IL 60611
(312) 346-5600

Exchange: New York (CNT)
Initial Public Offering: December 10, 1993
Initial Offering Share Price: $18.25
Geographical Focus: Greater Chicago
Competitive Strategies: Geographical concentration—it is the largest owner and developer of industrial facilities in the Chicago metropolitan area; by focusing its efforts in one market area, the company believes it is better equipped to meet the needs of tenants seeking to expand within the market as well as prospective tenants looking to enter the area; Focuses its acquisitions on warehouse/industrial properties in the $3 million to $6 million range, a marketplace where there is less competition from other buyers; it is also attracted to properties in need of re-development because most industrial property buyers are not interested in taking on such projects.

Special Notes: Based upon research from two national organizations, the Greater Chicago area (defined as the area within a 150-mile radius of Chicago, including Milwaukee, Wisconsin and South Bend, Indiana) is the largest warehouse/industrial market in the United States with approximately 1.1 billion square feet of space.
Investment Performance:

	Close	Gain/Loss	Dividend	% Yield	Annual Return
1993	$18.38	—	$0.09	—	—
1994	$19.50	6.1%	$1.50	8.2%	14.3%
1995	$23.13	18.6%	$1.56	8.0%	26.6%
1996	$32.75	41.6%	$1.62	7.0%	48.6%

First Industrial Realty Trust Inc.
311 South Wacker Drive, Suite 4000
Chicago, IL 60606
(312) 344-4300
(http://www.firstindustrial.com)

Exchange: New York (FR)
Initial Public Offering: June 23, 1994
Initial Offering Price: $23.50
Geographical Focus: Midwest
Competitive Strategies: To develop or acquire a critical mass of sites in its target markets; focuses on cities that are well-positioned for long-term growth because of the extensive roadway, rail, and water transportation and infrastructure that interconnect them to other key market areas.
Special Notes: Formed to continue and expand the Midwestern property business of The Shidler Group, a national organization with over 20 years of experience as an industrial property owner and manager.
Investment Performance:

	Close	Gain/Loss	Dividend	% Yield	Annual Return
1994	$19.50	—	$0.95	—	—
1995	$22.50	15.4%	$1.95	10.0%	25.4%
1996	$30.38	35.0%	$2.02	9.0%	44.0%

Meridian Industrial Trust, Inc.
455 Market Street, 17th Floor
San Francisco, CA 94105
(415) 281-3900
(http://www.mit-reit.com)

Exchange: New York (MDN)
Conversion Date: February, 1996
Initial Conversion Price: $15.00
Geographical Focus: National
Competitive Strategies: Target industrial/warehouse properties
which sell for between $1 million and $7 million, because competition in this price range is generally less than for higher-priced industrial assets; focuses on markets that are expected to experience increased populations or that are located strategically along the path of goods.
Special Notes: Formed through the merger of ASE-listed Meridian Point Realty Trust IV, VI, and VII, and the purchase of nine properties from NASDAQ-listed Meridian Point Realty Trust '83. As part of the merger, Meridian Industrial received investments from several major investment groups, including Hunt Realty Acquisitions, USAA Real Estate Company, Ameritech, investment entities managed by J.P. Morgan Investment Management, and The Ohio State Teachers Retirement System.
Investment Performance:

	Close	Gain/Loss	Dividend	% Yield	Annual Return
1996	$21.00	—	$1.16	—	—

Security Capital Industrial Trust
14100 East 35th Place
Aurora, CO 80011
(800) 820-0181

Exchange: New York (SCN)
Initial Public Offering: October 4, 1994
Initial Offering Price: $15.75
Geographical Focus: National
Competitive Strategies: It is the largest industrial REIT in the nation and one of the largest REITs in the industry; the Trust has sought to

distinguish itself as the only true national operating company fulfilling the distribution space needs of corporate America; it accomplishes this task through its "National Operating System," in which a national service group, development team, and marketing division work together to address the needs of existing and prospective tenants; its investment strategy is to acquire generic bulk distribution and light industrial facilities and to develop full-service, master-planned distribution parks in metropolitan areas that demonstrate strong demographic growth and positive real estate fundamentals and in which the company can achieve a dominant market position. Special Notes: Focuses on three types of industrial investment markets: those that serve as key ports for imports and/or exports; those that possess cost and quality labor advantages for both domestic and foreign manufacturers; and those that are highly accessible to major transportation networks.
Investment Performance:

	Close	Gain/Loss	Dividend	% Yield	Annual Return
1994	$17.00	—	$0.21	—	—
1995	$17.50	2.9%	$0.94	5.5%	8.4%
1996	$21.38	22.1%	$1.01	5.8%	27.9%

Weeks Corporation
4497 Park Drive
Norcross, GA 30093
(404) 923-4076

Exchange: New York (WKS)
Initial Public Offering: August 24, 1994
Initial Offering Price: $19.25
Geographical Focus: Atlanta
Competitive Strategies: Highly focused geographically; new property development capabilities; third party management operations.
Special Notes: Successor to a firm which was founded in 1965. Before going public in 1994, it had developed 112 properties with a total of 8.7 million square feet. Metropolitan Atlanta is the largest industrial market in the Southeastern United States. From 1992 through 1995, it also experienced the highest job growth in the nation.
Investment Performance:

	Close	Gain/Loss	Dividend	% Yield	Annual Return
1994	$21.88	—	$0.52	—	—
1995	$25.13	14.9%	$1.53	7.0%	21.9%
1996	$33.25	32.3%	$1.60	6.4%	38.7%

OFFICE/INDUSTRIAL PROPERTIES

The category of mixed office/industrial REITs was created by the industry's association, the National Association of Real Estate Investment Trusts, in 1996 because of the increasing number of companies that invest in both office and industrial properties, with no special orientation toward either category.

Most of the REITs in this sector are development-oriented companies that focus their operations in specific regions of the country. They generally purchase and develop Class A suburban office buildings and industrial properties, usually in business park settings. By acquiring multiple properties in individual business parks, these REITs are better equipped to meet the needs of existing tenants looking for additional space as well as prospective tenants seeking to locate in one of the company's office or industrial properties. This is because the more properties a company controls in a market, the better equipped it is to find space that will meet a given tenant or prospective tenant's needs.

Liberty Property Trust has traditionally met the needs of its tenants by building properties for them. Its predecessor, Rouse and Associates, developed 25 million square feet of commercial space in the 22 years prior to its conversion to a REIT in 1994. More recently, Liberty has spent time buying existing properties in its targeted regions of the Mid-Atlantic and Southeast.

Reckson Associates Realty Corporation succeeded The Reckson Group, a company founded in 1959. From its beginnings, Reckson concentrated on the development and re-development of Class A office and industrial properties on Long Island. Since its 1995 IPO, the company has been actively acquiring properties, especially office properties, in several markets throughout the Northeast.

Spieker Properties was also the successor to a company that was heavily engaged in new property development. That company,

Speiker Partners, was once part of the Trammel Crow organization, a major developer of commercial properties in the United States during the 1980s. Spieker focuses its activities along the West Coast: California, Oregon, and Washington. While its expertise has been in new property development, the company has also been aggressively acquiring office and industrial properties since it went public in 1993. The recession in California provided some excellent buying opportunities for companies like Spieker.[18]

Prentiss Properties also took advantage of the real estate downturn in the early 1990s to acquire office and industrial properties for bargain prices. It financed the acquisitions through a joint venture with four major pension plans: American Airlines, Exxon Corporation, Ameritech, and the Public Employees Retirement System of Idaho. Prentiss Properties also has a substantial third party management operation, which provides the company with many of its acquisitions, as well as a new property development division.

The two remaining office/industrial REITs both focus their activities on the West Coast. The Kilroy Corporation, which went public in 1997, concentrates its efforts in Southern California. Its specialty has also been developing commercial office and industrial properties, something it has done since its founding in 1947.

Bedford Property Investors' past is quite different. It was founded in 1985 as ICM Property Investors, a REIT that invested in suburban office properties through mortgage loans and joint ventures. The overbuilding of the late 1980s wreaked havoc on ICM's portfolio, causing it to suspend dividends in 1990. In 1992, it devised a new strategy of investing directly in suburban office and industrial properties in the western United States. This strategy has been met with a favorable reception in the capital markets, as Bedford's stock recorded an average annual return of better than 35 percent in the four years ending in 1996.

Office/Industrial REITs

Bedford Property Investors, Inc.
270 Lafayette Circle
Lafayette, CA 94549
(510) 283-8910

Exchange: New York (BED)
Initial Public Offering: 1985
Geographical Focus: Western United States
Competitive Strategies: Focuses on markets that are experiencing economic growth and that are subject to limitations on new property development; the acquisition of general purpose industrial properties that are suitable for a diverse spectrum of tenants ranging from small firms to large corporations engaged in various businesses, rather than highly improved properties that cater to a limited number of tenants based on use and size.
Special Notes: The successor to ICM Property Investors, a New York-based REIT founded in 1985 to invest in suburban office buildings, primarily through secondary mortgage loans and joint venture partnerships. The overbuilding in the suburban office sector in the late 1980s caused ICM to suffer operating losses on its investments and to suspend dividends in 1990. In 1992, Peter Bedford was named chairman and developed a new strategic business plan focusing on equity investments in industrial and suburban office properties.
Investment Performance:

	Close	Gain/Loss	Dividend	% Yield	Annual Return
1991	$ 5.00	(31.0)%	$0.00	0.0%	(31.0)%
1992	$ 6.25	25.0%	$0.00	0.0%	25.0%
1993	$ 9.75	56.0%	$0.36	5.8%	61.8%
1994	$11.00	12.8%	$0.71	7.3%	20.1%
1995	$14.25	30.0%	$0.82	7.5%	37.5%
1996	$17.50	22.8%	$1.00	7.0%	29.8%

1 for 2 stock split in March, 1996

Kilroy Realty Corporation
2250 East Imperial Highway
El Segundo, CA 90245
(213) 772-1193

Exchange: New York (KRC)
Initial Public Offering: January 28, 1997
Initial Offering Price: $23.00
Geographical Focus: Southern California

Competitive Strategies: New property development; highly focused geographically on suburban office and industrial properties in Southern California.

Special Notes: Successor to an organization founded in 1947 by John Kilroy Sr., the REIT's chairman. The company's long-standing track record, its geographical focus, and its portfolio of suburban office and industrial properties made it one of the most sought after REIT IPOs since 1994.

Liberty Property Trust
Great Valley Corporate Center
65 Valley Stream Parkway
Suite 100
Malvern, PA 19355
(610) 648-1700

Exchange: New York (LRY)
Initial Public Offering: June 23, 1994
Initial Offering Price: $20.00
Geographical Focus: Southeast and Mid-Atlantic states
Competitive Strategies: New property development capabilities with a focus on build-to-suit opportunities and inventory buildings that meet identified demand.
Special Notes: Formed in 1994 to continue the business operations of Rouse and Associates, a real estate firm founded in 1972, that focused on the development of suburban industrial and office properties. From inception through the time of its IPO, the company developed 25 million square feet of commercial real estate.
Investment Performance:

	Close	Gain/Loss	Dividend	% Yield	Annual Return
1994	$19.63	—	$0.83	—	—
1995	$20.75	5.7%	$1.60	8.2%	13.9%
1996	$25.75	24.1%	$1.62	7.8%	31.9%

Prentiss Properties Trust
3890 West Northwest Highway, Suite 400
Dallas, TX 75220
(214) 654-0886

Exchange: New York (PP)
Initial Public Offering: October 17, 1996
Initial Offering Price: $20.00
Geographical Focus: National
Competitive Strategies: Acquire properties in high growth markets; A national organization with regional headquarters in five cities and a presence in 21 markets throughout the United States; significant third party management operations which provide the company with potential property acquisitions; new property development capability.
Special Notes: The Operating Partnership in which Prentiss Properties holds an interest was formed in 1991 through a joint venture with The American Airlines, Inc. Master Fixed Benefit Trust, the Ameritech Pension Trust, the Public Employees Retirement System of Idaho, and the Exxon Corporation. All of these pension plans have continued as investors except for Exxon Corporation which had previously decided to reduce its investments in real estate.
Investment Performance:

	Close	Gain/Loss	Dividend	% Yield	Annual Return
1996	$25.00	—	$0.31	—	—

Reckson Associates Realty Corporation
225 Broadhollow Road
Melville, NY 11747-0983
(516) 694-6900

Exchange: New York (RA)
Initial Public Offering: June 2, 1995
Initial Offering Price: $24.25
Geographical Focus: Northeast
Competitive Strategies: New property development capabilities; highly focused geographically; achieves operating efficiencies through the acquisition of office properties and industrial facilities in parks where the company has other holdings.
Special Notes: Successor to the Reckson Group which was engaged in the development and re-development of Class A office and industrial properties throughout Long Island, New York since its founding in 1959. Reckson's IPO timing was excellent as it went

public when office and industrial REITs were in high demand. As a result, the company's offering was the first successful IPO in the market in almost a year.
Investment Performance:

	Close	Gain/Loss	Dividend	% Yield	Annual Return
1995	$29.38	—	$1.34	—	—
1996	$42.25	6.1%	$2.38	8.1%	51.9%

Spieker Properties, Inc.
2180 Sand Hill Road, Suite 200
Menlo Park, CA 94025
(415) 854-5600
(http://www.spieker.com)

Exchange: New York (SPK)
Initial Public Offering: November 18, 1993
Initial Offering Price: $20.50
Geographical Focus: California and the Northwest
Competitive Strategies: Ownership of a diversified portfolio of industrial facilities and suburban office properties in a geographically focused area; new property development capabilities.
Special Notes: Successor to Speiker Partners, which was founded in 1987 as a spin-off of the Trammel Crow Company, a nationwide real estate development and management firm. In early 1997, acquired the real estate assets of another public REIT, Mission West Properties (ASE:MSW).
Investment Performance:

	Close	Gain/Loss	Dividend	% Yield	Annual Return
1993	$18.63	—	—	—	—
1994	$20.38	9.4%	$1.60	8.6%	18.0%
1995	$25.13	23.3%	$1.68	8.2%	31.5%
1996	$36.00	43.3%	$1.72	6.9%	50.2%

CHAPTER NINE

Triple Net
Lease
Investments

THE TRIPLE NET LEASE investment sector of the REIT industry is not a separate property segment, but rather a different type of real estate investment. In a net lease transaction, the burden of managing a property is transferred from the property owner to the lessee. Net leases are generally classified as financing transactions; however, unlike a mortgage transaction where the tenant/owner retains ownership of the property, in a net lease transaction property ownership is transferred by the tenant.

Under net leases, the tenant is responsible for not only paying rent to the property owner, but also for covering all of the operating expenses associated with the property including real estate taxes, maintenance, utilities, and insurance. In most net leases, the tenant is also required to pay periodic rent increases that take the form of inflation-mandated adjustments or percentage rent.

Net lease transactions are a fairly common method employed in the leasing of single tenant commercial properties such as small office buildings, industrial facilities, restaurants, child care centers, health care facilities, and retail stores. They are often the result of a sale/leaseback transaction under which the REIT acquires a property from the tenant and leases it back to the same tenant under a long term lease agreement.

In such a transaction, the REIT realizes the benefits of ownership: property appreciation potential, current cash flow from rental payments, depreciation deductions, and avoids most of the burdens normally associated with property ownership: maintaining the facility, leasing the property, and meeting operating expenses.

The primary benefit to a tenant in a sale/leaseback is the opportunity to free up equity in the property for use in its business operations. The costs of acquiring real estate to house a firm's operations can consume a significant amount of cash; cash that can often be used more productively in the business rather than in real estate holdings.

Sale/leaseback financing is a common vehicle used by retail chains to finance the expansion of their retail outlets. Businesses that often utilize this form of financing are fast food restaurants, child care centers, auto parts stores, auto service centers, grocery stores, and drug stores.

Real estate investment trusts that focus in this sector generally seek to do business with companies that are in a growth mode, because this opens the possibility of multiple leases with the same lessee. The lessee could be either the franchiser or a franchisee. Increasingly, franchisees are sizable business organizations that operate a number of retail facilities, often with different franchisers.

Triple net lease real estate investments generally provide their investors with a high level of current income and modest dividend growth through mandated rent increases or percentage rent agreements. The primary risks of the investment are credit risk and interest rate risk. Because triple net lease properties are usually leased to a single tenant, if the tenant should go bankrupt and abandon the site, the occupancy level of the subject property will decline from 100 percent to 0 percent overnight. Depending upon the location of the property and its configuration, it could take a considerable period of time to find a new tenant.

If the tenant should declare bankruptcy but continue in business, it will often seek to renegotiate its lease. If the property is one that has a highly specialized use (i.e., a fast food restaurant with limited seating capacity), the landlord's most appealing option might be to renegotiate the lease (usually for a lower rental rate) rather than seek a new tenant. In either event, it is critical that REITs that specialize in net lease investments carefully examine the creditworthiness of their lessees before entering into any agreements.

The other primary risk, interest rate risk, is comparable to the risk that all REITs face. Because triple net leases are usually long term in duration and rental rate increases limited, the risk of increasing interest rates will generally have a greater impact on the share price of triple net lease REITs. Despite this risk, however, for an investor seeking a stable and predictable dividend with some modest growth potential, triple net lease REITs are an alternative that should be considered.

A number of the REITs in this segment of the industry were formed as a result of the consolidation of public limited partnerships that had invested in net lease properties. These programs were ideal candidates for the REIT format because they were primarily yield-oriented investment vehicles with little or no debt. By converting to the REIT structure, these entities provided their investors with several new benefits, including increased liquidity and diversification.

The liquidity was an especially appealing benefit because, unlike many other real estate partnerships formed in the 1980s, the net lease programs were designed to have very long lives—generally 12 to 15 years. As a result of converting to a REIT, the net lease partnerships provided investors with the benefit of deciding when to terminate their interest in the portfolio.

In the net lease REIT sector, the investment focus of companies varies. Some invest exclusively in chain restaurants, other invest primarily in retail properties, and some have diversified holdings. Lexington Corporate Properties leases distribution centers and office buildings to well-known, high creditworthy clients. TriNet Realty has followed a similar investment strategy, but also has investments in retail properties. Commercial Net Lease Realty initially focused its investments in the restaurant industry, but has expanded its operations over the years to incorporate a host of retail properties including book stores, drug stores, and auto supply shops. Franchise Finance, the largest independent chain restaurant finance company in the United States, is exclusively engaged in providing financing for chain restaurants such as Burger King, Arby's, and Hardees. Realty Income Corporation (RIC) has focused much of its investments in child care centers. Other portfolio holdings include chain restaurants and automotive centers.

Triple Net Lease REITs

Commercial Net Lease Realty, Inc.
400 E. South Street, Suite 500
Orlando, FL 32801
(407) 422-1574
(http://www.nnnreit.com)

Exchange: New York (NNN)
Initial Public Offering: 1984
Geographical Focus: South and Southeast
Competitive Strategies: Targets retailers that the company views as leaders in their respective market segments and that have the financial strength to compete effectively; focuses its investments on properties that are located within major traffic corridors near other shopping areas, business developments, and major thoroughfares.
Special Notes: Formed in 1984 for the purpose of investing in commercial properties that were net leased to their tenants. Since its inception, the company has gone through two name changes. First called Golden Corral Realty, the REIT changed its name to CNL Realty Investors, and then to its current name.
Investment Performance:

	Close	Gain/Loss	Dividend	% Yield	Annual Return
1991	$ 9.75	14.7%	$1.03	12.1%	26.8%
1992	$12.13	24.4%	$1.08	11.1%	35.5%
1993	$13.75	13.4%	$1.10	9.1%	22.5%
1994	$12.25	(10.9)%	$1.14	8.3%	(2.6)%
1995	$12.75	4.1%	$1.16	9.5%	13.6%
1996	$15.88	24.5%	$1.18	9.3%	33.8%

Franchise Finance Corporation of America
17207 North Perimeter Drive
Scottsdale, AZ 85255
(602) 585-4500
(http://www.ffca.com)

Exchange: New York (FFA)
Conversion Date: June 1, 1994
Conversion Price: $20.00
Geographical Focus: National
Competitive Strategies: The largest independent chain restaurant finance company in the United States; focuses on fast food restaurants affiliated with national or regional chains.
Special Notes: Formed in 1980 as a real estate finance company and from its inception through 1993, sponsored 11 public limited partnerships that provided financing for chain restaurant operators. In 1994, the company consolidated these partnerships into an infinite-life REIT.
Investment Performance:

	Close	Gain/Loss	Dividend	% Yield	Annual Return
1994	$17.38	—	$1.05	—	—
1995	$22.63	30.2%	$1.80	10.4%	40.6%
1996	$27.63	22.1%	$1.80	8.0%	30.1%

Lexington Corporate Properties, Inc.
355 Lexington Avenue, 14th Floor
New York, NY 10017
(212) 692-7260
(http://www.lxp.com)

Exchange: New York (LXP)
Conversion Date: October 12, 1993
Conversion Price: $10.00
Geographical Focus: National
Competitive Strategies: Portfolio diversification is central to its investment strategy as the company has sought to structure a portfolio that is insulated from regional recessions, industry specific downturns and price fluctuations in property type.
Special Notes: Formed to continue the business of two limited partnerships, Lepercq Corporate Income Fund I and Lepercq Income Fund II.

Investment Performance:

	Close	Gain/Loss	Dividend	% Yield	Annual Return
1993	$10.13	—	—	—	—
1994	$ 9.00	(11.1)%	$1.08	10.7%	(0.4)%
1995	$11.25	25.0%	$1.08	12.0%	37.0%
1996	$14.63	30.0%	$1.10	9.8%	39.8%

Realty Income Corporation
220 West Crest Street
Escondido, CA 92025-1725
(800) 375-6700

Exchange: New York (O)
Conversion Date: August 15, 1994
Conversion Price: $16.00
Geographical Focus: National
Competitive Strategies: Focuses on chains with a replicable concept, a proven operating history, a critical mass for further expansion, and a desire to utilize sale/leaseback capital to finance growth.
Special Notes: Formed as a result of the merger in August 1994, of 10 private and 15 public limited partnerships previously sponsored by the company. In August 1995, the shareholders approved the merger of the company's advisor, R.I.C. Advisor, into Realty Income Corporation, enabling the company to become a fully integrated, self-managed and self-administered REIT.
Investment Performance:

	Close	Gain/Loss	Dividend	% Yield	Annual Return
1994	$17.13	—	$0.75	—	—
1995	$22.50	31.4%	$1.86	10.9%	42.3%
1996	$27.88	6.1%	$1.89	8.4%	14.5%

TriNet Corporate Realty Trust, Inc.
Four Embarcadero Center, Suite 3150
San Francisco, CA 94111

(415) 391-4300
(http://www.tricorp.com)

Exchange: New York (TRI)
Initial Public Offering: June 3, 1993
Initial Offering Price: $24.25
Geographical Focus: National
Competitive Strategies: The largest publicly-owned REIT focused on acquiring predominantly office and industrial properties that are net leased to major corporations; seeks properties that are important to a lessee's operations and that can be acquired for less than replacement cost.
Special Notes: Formed to succeed the net lease business operations of The Shidler Group, which was founded in 1985. (The Shidler Group was also responsible for the formation of another REIT in 1993, First Industrial). Tenants at TriNet's properties include such companies as Unisys, Nike, Microsoft, TRW, PepsiCo, AT&T, Sears, and Volkswagen AG.
Investment Performance:

	Close	Gain/Loss	Dividend	% Yield	Annual Return
1993	$27.63	—	$1.27	—	—
1994	$29.25	5.9%	$2.38	8.6%	14.5%
1995	$27.25	(6.8)%	$2.45	8.4%	1.6%
1996	$35.50	30.3%	$2.49	9.1%	39.4%

CHAPTER TEN

Self-Storage Centers

THE SELF-STORAGE SEGMENT is much like the industrial real estate sector; not very glamorous, but a fairly consistent money maker.

The target customer is, of course, different. Self-storage facilities generally cater to small businesses and households that are looking for low-cost, accessible storage for their inventory and excess possessions. Self-storage properties are also more management intensive because they have multiple tenants, fairly high turnover, and are generally open for business seven days a week.

The origins of the self-storage industry date back to the early 1960s when these facilities were built in the Southwest to accommodate the needs of transient military personnel. Since that time, the need for and supply of self-storage space has developed throughout the country due at least in part to the following factors:

- the increased mobility of Americans,
- the prevalence of condominiums and townhomes,
- the construction of homes in the Sunbelt without basements, and
- the higher consumption of recreational vehicles and equipment in the United States.

Self-storage facilities are generally built along major thoroughfares, providing easy access and visibility. In high density areas where the construction of new self-storage properties is not economical or where there is a lack of available space, older, multilevel buildings have often been converted to self-storage facilities. Otherwise, self-storage properties are usually single story structures that house a wide size range of individual storage units.

The market area for a self-storage property is usually a three to five mile radius around the site. Therefore, it is imperative that the location be selected with great care. Ideally, operators should situate their properties on main thoroughfares where there are not only a significant number of small businesses, but also a large residential base from which to draw. This type of location provides the operator with two different potential users: commercial and residential. The customer base of a typical self storage center is usually comprised of 75 percent residential customers and 25 percent business customers.

The primary factors that dictate success among competitors within a particular market area are location, rental rates, the quality of the property, the level of security at the facility, accessibility, and the availability of suitable rental space. The ability of individual facilities to accommodate special tenant needs (i.e., climate-controlled units) can also provide a competitive advantage.

Self-storage customers rent fully enclosed storage units for their exclusive use. They have the flexibility to enter their units during business hours, and control access to their units by furnishing their own locks. Most facilities are lighted, fenced, and equipped with computer-controlled gates that provide certain tenants with 24-hour access to their storage units.

The self-storage business is highly fragmented, with facilities owned and operated by individuals, small businesses, REITs, limited partnerships, and corporations. Due to their lack of curb appeal and their relatively low cost, these assets have traditionally not held much appeal among institutional investors.

Competition within this segment of the real estate industry can be substantial. That's because entry into the business through the acquisition of existing facilities is relatively easy for parties that possess the necessary capital. Development of new storage properties is usually more difficult due to zoning and regulatory requirements.

It is estimated that there are more than 23,000 self-storage facilities throughout the United States. Approximately 10 percent of these facilities are controlled by the five major public REITs.[1]

One of the primary challenges for self-storage REITs is to become a recognized leader in their respective markets. This first requires the acquisition and/or development of a critical mass of sites, enabling the operator to become one of the top providers of storage space in a given market. The second phase of the process involves promoting the company's name in the marketplace, thereby creating a brand awareness.

Back in the late 1980s, one of the self-storage REIT operators, Public Storage, started advertising on television as a way to develop brand awareness within its markets. Other methods that are employed include advertising in the local Yellow Pages and newspapers, and promoting facilities through direct mail and sales calls to area business owners.

Another self-storage REIT, Shurgard Storage Centers, has attempted to develop an identity in its communities through the construction of a lighthouse at the entrance to its newly developed properties. Such a structure is, of course, designed to bring attention to the facility and make it stand out in the area.

The largest operator of self-storage properties in the United States is Public Storage, Inc. This Glendale, California-based firm has been engaged in the ownership and management of storage facilities since the early 1970s. In the late 1970s and the 1980s, the company was one of the largest syndicators of public real estate programs in the United States, raising hundreds of millions of dollars for various partnership offerings. It sponsored several different types of investment programs, including: Public Storage Properties, which developed new self-storage properties; PS Partners and Storage Equities, which acquired existing storage facilities; and PS Business Parks, which invested in business parks.

Like many other limited partnership sponsors, Public Storage converted its various partnerships to REITs in the early 1990s; however, unlike other sponsors, it converted each into a separate REIT, as opposed to merging all of them into one large REIT. The rationale for this was the company's desire to avoid the turmoil that normally resulted when a sponsor attempted to place a value on individual partnerships for the purpose of a proposed consolidation. (Often, such efforts simply resulted in a host of investor lawsuits.)

Public Storage allowed the market to value these entities before it attempted to consolidate them. This strategy also enabled the company to complete development and lease-up of properties owned by some of the more recently formed Properties partnerships. As a result, these partnerships were able to achieve a fully operational status and receive an appropriate valuation from the capital markets before being merged.

All of Public Storage's partnerships were initially converted to REITs at a conversion price of $20 per share. They immediately dropped in price, many to less than 25 percent of their conversion price. This was largely the result of the pent-up interest many investors had in selling their partnership interests.

The early stock performance of the Public Storage REITs was largely a reflection of the general dissatisfaction many investors had with the performance of limited partnerships formed in the 1980s, as well as the fact that a number of the Public Storage partnerships formed in the mid to late 1980s fell short of expectations. The net result was that when investors in these partnerships had the opportunity to sell their interests, they did so. As a consequence, the share prices for the Public Storage REITs were driven down excessively.

Public Storage took advantage of these low stock prices to buy back shares in the market. This action, combined with a recognition in the marketplace that the shares were indeed undervalued, helped the stock values of Public Storage's REITs rebound rather significantly throughout 1995 and 1996. Public Storage has been gradually consolidating its various REITs into one infinite life REIT, Public Storage, Incorporated. Once completed, it will be one of the largest REITs in the country. (That is why I have listed only one of Public Storage's REITs, Public Storage, Incorporated, in the listing of self storage REITs at the end of the chapter.)

The other four publicly-owned REITs focusing in the self storage industry are: Shurgard Storage Centers, Sovran Self Storage, Storage Trust Realty, and Storage USA.

Shurgard was also involved in the syndication of public limited partnerships in the 1980s. In 1994, it consolidated the operations of 17 of its partnerships; however, unlike Public Storage, Shurgard converted all of these entities into one REIT. At the end of 1996, the company was the third largest self storage REIT in the nation. Since becoming a REIT, Shurgard has been expanding its asset base at a modest pace through a combination of acquisitions, development, and joint ventures.

The remaining three REITs have not been in the self-storage business as long as either Public Storage or Shurgard; therefore, when they went public, their portfolios were not as large or diverse as their competitors. This has meant they have had some catching up to do, and they have done it in a big way.

Storage USA has been the most aggressive. It went public in March, 1994 with a portfolio of 31 self storage facilities. By the end of 1996, it was the second largest REIT in this segment of the industry with a portfolio of 219 facilities. Storage Trust Realty has also been active in the marketplace since its IPO in mid-1994. At the time, the company owned interests in 69 properties. By the end of 1996, its portfolio had more than doubled to 165 self storage facilities.

Sovran Self Storage is the newest self storage REIT, having gone public in mid-1995. At the end of 1996, it owned 111 facilities located in 14 states in the eastern half of the country. Twenty of these properties were acquired in the company's initial five months in business. Most of Sovran's properties are operated under the name "Uncle Bob's."

Like other REITs, self-storage trusts have their benefits and risks. The potential benefits of investing in one or more self-storage REITs include fairly predictable dividends that are likely to increase during positive economic periods. Because most tenants lease their units on a month-to-month basis, self-storage operators are usually able to implement rent increases more frequently than owners of most other property types.

The risk of self-storage REITs is that these properties are comparatively inexpensive to develop and/or acquire; therefore, overbuilding is always a concern. In recent years, however, the lack of available financing for real estate projects has resulted in a decline in the construction of new storage properties.

Self Storage REITs

Public Storage, Inc.
701 Western Avenue
Glendale, CA 91201
(818) 244-8080
(http://www.publicstorage.com)

Exchange: New York (PSA)
Initial Offering: July 1980
Geographical Focus: National
Competitive Strategies: It is the largest REIT in this industry segment; advertises its properties on television in selected markets.

Special Notes: Public Storage is the successor to Storage Equities, a REIT started by Public Storage, Inc. in 1980. In November 1995, Storage Equities merged with its adviser, Public Storage Advisors, and acquired substantially all of the real estate assets of its adviser's parent, Public Storage, Inc., including two subsidiaries, Public Storage Management, Inc. and Public Storage Commercial Properties Group. In April 1997, announced a $220 million joint venture with a major public pension fund to develop 50 to 60 self-storage sites throughout the nation.

Investment Performance:

	Close	Gain/Loss	Dividend	% Yield	Annual Return
1991	$ 8.25	24.5%	$ 0.82	12.4%	36.9%
1992	$ 8.88	7.6%	$ 0.84	10.2%	17.8%
1993	$14.25	60.6%	$ 0.84	9.5%	70.1%
1994	$14.38	0.9%	$ 0.85	6.0%	6.9%
1995	$19.00	32.2%	$ 0.88	6.1%	38.3%
1996	$31.00	63.2%	$ 0.88	4.6%	67.8%

Shurgard Storage Centers
1201 Third Avenue, Suite 2200
Seattle, WA 98101
(800) 955-2235
(206) 624-8100
(http://www.shurgard.com)

Exchange: New York (SHU)
Conversion Date: March 1, 1994
Conversion Price: $18.90
Geographical Focus: National
Competitive Strategies: Locates in high density areas with relatively few competitors, growing populations, and strong economies; individually designs each property to conform with construction designs in communities, thus enabling it to build in areas that were reticent to approve such facilities; seeks to own at least 15 properties in each market in order to realize operating and marketing efficiencies and increase brand awareness.

Special Notes: Formed in 1994 as a result of the consolidation of 17 limited partnerships previously sponsored by Shurgard. Became a self-managed REIT in 1995 through a merger with Shurgard, Inc. Operates a national call center which fields calls from properties when on-site employees are not available. Employees at the national call center are able to market and sell rental space at the company location nearest to the caller.

Investment Performance:

	Close	Gain/Loss	Dividend	% Yield	Annual Return
1994	$20.75	—	$ 1.02	—	—
1995	$27.00	30.1%	$ 1.84	9.0%	39.1%
1996	$29.63	9.7%	$ 1.88	7.0%	16.7%

Sovran Self Storage, Inc.
5166 Main Street
Williamsville, NY 14221
(716) 633-1850

Exchange: New York (SSS)
Initial Offering: June 26, 1995
Initial Offering Price: $23.00
Geographical Focus: Eastern United States
Competitive Strategies: Focuses on markets with populations in excess of 250,000 where the company believes it can achieve significant market penetration through the purchase of a number of properties; this "clustering" strategy enables the company to achieve certain economies of scale in its operations.
Special Notes: Began its operations in the mid-1980s. Most of the properties are operated under the name "Uncle Bob's."
Investment Performance:

	Close	Gain/Loss	Dividend	% Yield	Annual Return
1995	$26.50	—	$ 1.04	—	—
1996	$31.25	17.9%	$ 2.08	7.9%	25.8%

Storage Trust Realty
2407 Rangeline Street
Columbia, MO 65202
(573) 499-4799
(http://www.storagetrust.com)

Exchange: New York (SEA)
Initial Offering: November 1994
Initial Offering Price: $17.50
Geographical Focus: Southeast
Competitive Strategies: Maintains a decentralized operation, with its regional managers overseeing five geographic regions and its property managers trained at its "Storage Trust University."
Special Notes: In 1996, acquired 25 self-storage facilities from the Balcor/Colonial Storage Income Fund-86 partnership.
Investment Performance:

	Close	Gain/Loss	Dividend	% Yield	Annual Return
1994	$17.88	—	—	—	—
1995	$22.75	27.3%	$ 1.57	8.8%	36.1%
1996	$27.00	18.7%	$ 1.67	7.3%	26.0%

Storage USA
10440 Little Patuxent Parkway, Suite 1100
Columbia, MD 21044
(410) 730-9500
(http://www.sus.com)

Exchange: New York (SUS)
Initial Offering: March 23, 1994
Initial Offering Price: $21.75
Geographical Focus: National
Competitive Strategies: The company has a program called "Total Storage Satisfaction Guaranteed", that empowers property managers to take care of customer needs; focuses on acquiring underperforming facilities that offer upside potential due to low occupancy levels or non-premium pricing.
Special Notes: Formed in 1985 and, through 1992, focused most of

its efforts on the development of self-storage facilities. Security Capital U.S. Realty invested $220 million in Storage USA in 1996. Investment Performance:

	Close	Gain/Loss	Dividend	% Yield	Annual Return
1994	$27.50	—	$ 1.41	—	—
1995	$32.63	18.6%	$ 2.04	7.4%	26.0%
1996	$37.63	15.3%	$ 2.25	6.9%	22.2%

CHAPTER ELEVEN

Health Care

THE HEALTH CARE SERVICES industry is one of the largest in the United States, representing almost 16 percent of annual personal consumption, which equates to almost $1 trillion yearly. With the country's aging population and advances in medical technology and treatment, the health care industry will only get larger.[1]

Because health care providers are under increasing pressure to reduce their costs, it is expected that more health care facilities will be put on the market as operators seek to separate their real estate holdings from their health care services. By leasing instead of owning their facilities, these operators will be able to access capital to invest in new equipment and services that will enable them to provide the desired quality of care to their patients.[2]

For REITs that specialize in this segment, that means opportunity. While health care REITs had a stock market capitalization of more than $11 billion at the end of 1996, it was estimated that they financed only 1 percent of the properties used in the delivery of health care services.[3] Potential competition, savings and loans, banks and insurance companies, have generally been reluctant to provide significant financing to the health care industry because of the changes taking place within the industry and the uncertainty these changes have caused. This leaves REITs as key players in the leasing and financing of properties in this sector.

The opportunities will be there, but REITs that focus in this segment will still have to tread carefully. In recent years, national legislation has been introduced that would significantly impact the delivery and cost of health care in the country. While many of these initiatives have failed to pass, these measures, combined with pri-

171

vate efforts to curb skyrocketing health care costs, have resulted in a health care industry revolution.

Major consolidations, strategic alliances, and mergers have been commonplace. In 1994 and 1995 it was estimated that industry-wide mergers and consolidations totaled $125 billion. This trend is likely to continue in the near term as health care providers seek to remove the industry's excess capacity and duplication of services.

Health care REITs will have to be selective in the type of properties they acquire and finance and the operators with whom they deal. Unlike most other sectors of the REIT industry, health care REITs do not manage the majority of properties they acquire (the exception is for medical office buildings). This is because much of the revenues derived from the operation of these properties is not from the real estate but rather from the services provided. This income would preclude a company from qualifying as a REIT. Therefore, in the health care sector, REITs either lease facilities to health care operators or provide mortgage financing to operators that own and operate their own properties.

The primary objective of health care REITs is to become proficient in identifying competent, capable, and financially sound operators and then to either acquire well-located and well-maintained properties for them to manage or provide financing for such properties. The type of health care properties which REITs acquire or provide financing for include:

1. **Acute Care Hospitals**—These hospitals provide services for patients whose average length of stay is less than 30 days. Services provided may include operations, obstetrics, radiology, intensive care, clinical labs, physical therapy, rehabilitation services, and outpatient care.

2. **Rehabilitation Hospitals**—These facilities provide inpatient and outpatient medical care to patients requiring physical, respiratory, neurological, orthopedic, and other treatments that will enable patients to achieve their maximum functional capacity.

3. **Alcohol and Substance Abuse Facilities**—These are centers that provide specialized service to individuals who are suffering from addiction to alcohol, drugs, or both.

4. **Psychiatric Facilities**—These health care operations pro-

vide diagnostic and treatment services to patients with mental or emotional disorders.

5. **Physician Clinics**—These clinics serve as outpatient treatment centers.

6. **Medical Office Buildings**—These office buildings are generally located near hospitals and are used by physicians and other health care professionals in providing services to their patients.

7. **Assisted Living Facilities**—These facilities are basically apartment properties for senior citizens. The residents of these properties are provided with all of their meals and usually have a range of social activities in which they can participate.

8. **Congregate Care Facilities**—Congregate care facilities are the next step up from assisted living in terms of the level of care provided. They are geared toward senior citizens who are not as independent as those residing in assisted living projects. Specialized services include medication supervision, bathing assistance, and limited therapeutic programs.

9. **Alzheimer's Care Facilities**—These facilities are relatively new to the industry and are designed to care for individuals afflicted with Alzheimer's who are unable to be cared for in a home environment.

10. **Long Term Care Facilities**—Traditionally called nursing homes, these facilities provide a range of services including skilled nursing care, subacute care, rehabilitation therapy, and other specialized services to the elderly and other patients with medical needs that cannot be properly addressed in a home environment, but that are not serious enough to be admitted to an acute care hospital.

These are the investment choices for the health care REITs. Their evaluation of which property type or types to invest in will be swayed by the reforms and changes taking place in the health care industry.

One of the more significant changes taking place is the trend toward managed health programs. The result is that more and more doctors are providing their services through such programs. It has also resulted in an increasing number of medical providers merging their operations to reduce overhead expenses and meet the demands being placed on them by managed health care programs to provide high quality care at the lowest possible cost.

Recent trends in the industry are toward shorter hospitals stays, greater reliance on outpatient services, and increased demand for delivery of services at fixed prices. Both government and third party payers are implementing new policies that limit the scope of reimbursable services and restrict increases in the rates charged for medical services.[4]

Outpatient services are playing a much larger role in the health care delivery system now due to the cost containment efforts. In the early 1970s, outpatient revenues were about three percent of total hospital revenues; today, they are almost 36 percent, and they are projected to approach 50 percent by the Year 2000. Advances in medical technologies, as well as the lower costs associated with such services, have resulted in more and more patients being directed to outpatient care.[5]

All of these changes have caused health care REITs to take another look at their strategies and, in some cases, make significant changes. In the past, most REITs in this sector invested primarily in long-term care facilities. These properties were appealing because occupancy levels were strong and the supply of new facilities was tightly controlled by state governments. The changing landscape of the health care industry, however, combined with efforts to reduce Medicaid expenditures (which pays for most long term care) and attempts to require a universal, higher level of care by nursing home operators, has led most health care REITs to diversify their portfolios beyond long term care facilities.

Many of the REITs are expanding into assisted living facilities as well as congregate care properties. Both are expected to witness increased demand in the future as a result of the aging of the American population. People 75 or older represent the fastest growing segment of the American population, with their ranks expected to increase from 13 million in 1990 to 17 million by 2000.[6]

Senior citizens who want to retain their independence but desire companionship and some assistance with their daily needs, find assisted living to be an ideal arrangement. Residents of assisted living facilities are supplied with a room that includes its own kitchenette and bathroom. In addition, they are provided with three meals a day, transportation, daily activities, and housekeeping and laundry services. This increased demand for assisted living facilities is expected to result in more than 1.4 million such properties in the year 2000; double the number that existed at the end of 1995.[7]

The increased use of outpatient services has also led to greater demand for physician's clinics and rehabilitation hospitals. A number of health care REITs have jumped into these sectors to meet this growing demand.

The financing of these health care properties by REITs is usually conducted either in the form of a sale/leaseback or a mortgage. The option that is selected depends on whether the operator wants to retain ownership of the subject facility. The leases entered into by health care REITs are generally triple net, requiring the operator to pay rent and all additional charges incurred in the operation of the leased property. Most REITs obtain additional revenues from either annual CPI-based rent increases or from participation in the increasing revenues of the facility. Leases are generally written for an initial period of ten years, with one or more renewal options for five years each. Some of the agreements also provide the operator with an option to purchase the subject property after the lease expires for an amount equal to the greater of its cost or appraised value.

Permanent mortgage loans provided by health care REITs are generally 10-year term, fixed-rate loans that have an interest rate adjustment in the fifth year based on a specified benchmark (such as ten year Treasuries). They usually have an additional interest component that is based either on an increase in gross revenues or fixed interest rate hikes. Some trusts also negotiate equity participations in the appreciation of the underlying property.

Just like REITs that focus in certain sectors of the retail industry, geographical and tenant diversification are considered important for health care REITs because the health care industry, even though very much national in scope, is still local in focus. By investing in different areas of the country with different operators, the REITs are able to reduce the risks associated with regional economic downturns (which could impact government financing/reimbursement of health care facilities) and with potential financial problems of individual operators.

Other factors that are considered important in evaluating health care REITs include their property diversification, the credit quality of their operators, their access to low cost capital, and the experience and track record of the REIT's management.

Because of the significant changes taking place in the health care industry, REITs are making a concerted effort to diversify their property holdings into at least several different sectors. This enables them to reduce the risk associated with being in just one sector and it opens the door to more investment opportunities.

The increasing competition in the health care industry and the need to manage costs effectively means that operators must be financially solid and capable of exercising sound judgment in the operation of their facilities. This is why most health care REITs seek to develop relationships with publicly owned health care operators because these operators are subject to an additional level of scrutiny: the capital markets. This provides added protection for the REITs because financial information for these operators is more readily available and their strategies and operating skills are constantly reviewed by industry analysts.

Access to low cost capital is key to the profitability of health-care REITs because they make money on the spread between their return on capital and their cost of capital. Because the return on capital does not usually vary much from one health care REIT to another (because the marketplace largely dictates lease and mortgage rates), the difference in the profitability of individual REITs will be determined largely by their cost of obtaining capital.

Access to low cost capital is dependent on a health care REIT's debt rating which, in turn, is related to its size and prior performance. The more prominent health care REITs have stock market capitalizations in excess of $500 million and long, successful operating histories. This leads to investment grade debt ratings from the major rating services, and to the desired low cost capital.

Even though health-care REITs do not manage most of their holdings, management still plays a key role in the success or failure of these companies. Their knowledge of the industry, their relationships with a diversified group of high quality operators, and their ability to effectively evaluate the income potential of individual fa-

Index	Average Compound Annual Return
Health Care REITs	19.6%
Traditional Equity REITs	12.3%
S & P 500 Index	15.6%

Exhibit 11-1 Health Care REIT Returns Versus Equity REITs and the S & P 500

cilities, are essential to developing a sound portfolio of properties. The health care REIT sector is the only one that has a number of companies which have been around as REITs for a significant period of time. In fact, more than half of the REITs in this sector have been in existence since at least 1987.

In the 11 year period from the beginning of 1986 through the end of 1996, health care REITs outperformed both traditional equity REITs and the S&P 500, as shown in Exhibit 11-1.

Health Care REITs

American Health Properties, Inc.
6400 South Fiddlers Green Circle, Suite 1800
Englewood, CO 80111
(303) 796-9793

Exchange: New York (AHE)
Initial Public Offering: 1987
Geographical Focus: National
Competitive Strategies: Utilizes a nine-point evaluation system that focuses on whether a facility is part of an integrated health care network, where it is located, the demographics and economy of the market area, its competitive position, its range of services, the quality of management and the level of managed care participation, the creditworthiness of the operator, and the investment's potential rate of return; the company seeks to build relationships with experienced operators for whom it can provide financing on multiple properties.

Special Notes: Formed in 1987 with an original portfolio of seven hospitals managed by American Medical International. In 1995, the company separated the economic attributes of its portfolio into two separate components: psychiatric care represented by a special preferred stock (NASDAQ:AHEPZ) and its acute care, rehabilitation, and long-term care properties represented by regular common stock. This decision was the result of financial difficulties a number of the company's psychiatric facilities experienced in the early 1990s. Future dividends for the psychiatric group stock and the common stock will be based on the performance of the respective operating units.

Investment Performance:

	Close	Gain/Loss	Dividend	% Yield	Annual Return
1991	$34.25	39.1%	$ 2.62	10.6%	49.7%
1992	$19.63	(42.7)%	$ 2.64	7.7%	(35.0)%
1993	$25.00	27.4%	$ 2.25	11.5%	38.9%
1994	$19.50	(22.0)%	$ 2.30	9.2%	(12.8)%
1995	$21.50	10.3%	$ 1.98	10.2%	20.5%
1996	$23.88	11.1%	$ 2.02	9.4%	20.5%

Capstone Capital Corporation

1000 Urban Center Drive, Suite 630
Birmingham, AL 35242
(205) 967-2092

Exchange: New York (CCT)
Initial Public Offering: June 29, 1994
Initial Offering Price: $18.00
Geographical Focus: National
Competitive Strategies: Focuses on ancillary hospital facilities (properties that house physicians who work at and provide referrals to the hospitals to which such facilities are connected), outpatient, and other alternative-site facilities.
Special Notes: Started by Richard Scrushy, the Chief Executive Officer of Health South Rehabilitation Corporation, the largest operator in the rehabilitation industry, for the purpose of investing in ancillary hospital facilities.

Investment Performance:

	Close	Gain/Loss	Dividend	% Yield	Annual Return
1994	$15.63	—	$ .85	—	—
1995	$19.13	22.4%	$ 1.76	11.3%	33.7%
1996	$22.38	17.0%	$ 1.84	9.6%	26.6%

G&L Realty Corporation
439 N. Bedford Drive
Beverly Hills, CA 90210
(310) 273-9930

Exchange: New York (GLR)
Initial Offering: December 9, 1993
Initial Offering Price: $18.25
Geographical Focus: Southern California
Competitive Strategies: The only health care REIT primarily engaged in the development, ownership, and management of medical office buildings.
Special Notes: In 1995, the company expanded its operations to include a loan program to finance the sale of senior care facilities to not-for-profit organizations. In 1996, it entered into a joint venture agreement with Nomura Corporation to provide $200 million in financing for the senior care industry.
Investment Performance:

	Close	Gain/Loss	Dividend	% Yield	Annual Return
1993	$16.88	—	$ 0.07	—	—
1994	$13.00	(23.0%)	$ 1.64	9.7%	(13.3)%
1995	$10.38	(20.2%)	$ 1.24	9.5%	(10.7)%
1996	$17.00	63.9%	$ 1.36	13.1%	77.0%

Health and Retirement Properties Trust
400 Centre Street
Newton, MA 02158
(617) 332-3990

Exchange: New York (HRP)
Initial Public Offering: October 9, 1986
Geographical Focus: National
Competitive Strategies: Focuses on properties that are part of campuses that offer a combination of independent living, assisted living, and skilled nursing care in one setting.
Special Notes: Originally founded in 1986 as Health and Rehabilitation Properties, the company changed its name in 1994 to Health and Retirement Properties Trust (HRPT) to reflect its expansion into assisted living properties. In 1994, the company consummated a major transaction with the Marriott Corporation, acquiring 14 of the company's retirement communities for $320 million. These properties are net leased to Marriott through the year 2013.
Investment Performance:

	Close	Gain/Loss	Dividend	% Yield	Annual Return
1991	$14.38	71.7%	$ 0.99	11.8%	83.5%
1992	$12.38	(13.9)%	$ 1.26	8.8%	(5.1)%
1993	$14.75	19.2%	$ 1.30	10.5%	29.7%
1994	$13.38	(9.3)%	$ 1.33	9.0%	(0.3)%
1995	$16.25	21.5%	$ 1.38	10.3%	31.8%
1996	$19.25	18.5%	$ 1.42	8.7%	27.2%

Health Care Property Investors, Inc.
10990 Wilshire Blvd., Suite 1200
Los Angeles, CA 90024
(310) 473-1990
(http://www.hcpi.com)

Exchange: New York (HCP)
Initial Public Offering: March 1985
Geographical Focus: National
Competitive Strategies: Focuses on long term health care properties with other holdings in assisted living, acute care hospitals, rehabilitation hospitals, and medical office buildings; seeks relationships with major, publicly-held health care operators.
Special Notes: Spun out of National Medical Enterprises in 1985.

Investment Performance:

	Close	Gain/Loss	Dividend	% Yield	Annual Return
1991	$24.38	47.2%	$ 1.62	9.8%	57.0%
1992	$25.25	3.6%	$ 1.73	7.1%	10.7%
1993	$27.13	7.4%	$ 1.85	7.3%	14.7%
1994	$30.13	11.1%	$ 1.98	7.3%	18.4%
1995	$35.13	16.6%	$ 2.14	7.1%	23.7%
1996	$35.00	(0.4)%	$ 2.30	6.6%	6.2%

Healthcare Realty Trust Inc.
3310 West End Avenue, Suite 400
Nashville, TN 37203
(615) 269-8175
(http://www.healthcarerealty.com)

Exchange: New York (HR)
Initial Public Offering: June 3, 1993
Initial Share Price: $19.50
Geographical Focus: National
Competitive Strategies: The company has sought to distinguish itself from the other health care REITs by being the only full-service real estate company in this sector; it provides not only financing for health care facilities, but also property management, leasing and build-to-suit development services, and capital for the construction of new facilities.
Special Notes: One of the newer health care REITs, having gone public in 1993. The company is primarily engaged in leasing ancillary hospital facilities and medical office buildings to health care providers. Its holdings include ancillary hospital facilities, physician clinics, long-term care facilities, comprehensive ambulatory care centers, laboratories, ambulatory surgery centers, and medical office buildings.
Investment Performance:

	Close	Gain/Loss	Dividend	% Yield	Annual Return
1993	$22.50	—	$ 0.55	—	—
1994	$21.00	(6.7%)	$ 1.77	7.9%	1.2%
1995	$23.00	9.5%	$ 1.85	8.8%	18.3%
1996	$26.50	15.2%	$ 1.93	8.4%	23.6%

Health Care REIT
One SeaGate Suite1950
Toledo, OH 43604
(419) 247-2800

Exchange: New York (HCN)
Initial Public Offering: 1970
Geographical Focus: National
Competitive Strategies: Focuses on properties located in smaller communities, where competition is minimal, and on states where certificates of need are required before a new nursing home can be constructed, effectively limiting the development of new facilities.
Special Notes: The company has traditionally invested in nursing home properties. More recently, it has expanded its portfolio to include assisted living and retirement facilities and has shifted its investments from direct financing deals to the more traditional mortgage loan and operating lease arrangements which are preferred by most health care operators today. Its 1996 acquisitions increased its portfolio by 46 percent from a year earlier.
Investment Performance:

	Close	Gain/Loss	Dividend	% Yield	Annual Return
1991	$20.88	56.1%	$ 1.77	13.2%	69.3%
1992	$21.38	2.4%	$ 1.85	8.9%	11.3%
1993	$22.88	7.0%	$ 1.93	9.0%	16.0%
1994	$20.00	(12.6)%	$ 2.01	8.8%	(3.8)%
1995	$18.00	(10.0)%	$ 2.08	10.4%	0.4%
1996	$24.50	36.1%	$ 2.08	11.6%	47.7%

LTC Properties, Inc.
300 Esplanade Drive, Suite 1860
Oxnard, CA 93030
(805) 981-8665

Exchange: New York (LTC)
Initial Public Offering: August 25, 1992
Initial Share Price: $10.00
Geographical Focus: National
Competitive Strategies: Focuses on small and mid-size regional nursing home operators, as opposed to major, publicly owned companies.

Special Notes: Founded in 1992 by the former Chief Financial Officer of Beverly Enterprises and the former Vice President/Controller of Beverly. Beverly Enterprises is the largest operator of nursing homes in the United States. The company has traditionally maintained a conservative capital structure, with debt levels well below the average of health care REITs.

Investment Performance:

	Close	Gain/Loss	Dividend	% Yield	Annual Return
1992	$10.00	—	$ .35	—	—
1993	$12.88	28.8%	$ 1.02	10.2%	39.0%
1994	$13.25	2.9%	$ 1.10	8.5%	11.4%
1995	$15.00	13.2%	$ 1.21	9.1%	22.3%
1996	$18.50	23.3%	$ 1.34	8.9%	32.2%

Meditrust
197 First Avenue
Needham, MA 02194-9129
(617) 433-6000
(http://www.reit.com)

Exchange: New York (MT)
Initial Public Offering: October 9, 1985
Initial Offering Price: $13.33
Geographical Focus: National
Competitive Strategies: The nation's largest health care REIT; it has received investment grade ratings from Duff & Phelps, Moody's, and Standard & Poor's, enabling it to access the capital markets for low cost capital; use of a paired REIT structure to acquire and actively manage retirement communities.
Special Notes: From its inception through the end of 1996, increased its dividend every quarter and provided shareholders with an average annual return in excess of 20 percent. It has specialized in making investments in the long-term care and subacute sectors of the health care industry, but has recently expanded its focus to other properties, such as retirement communities, assisted living facilities, medical office buildings, and acute care hospitals. In 1997, the company acquired Santa Anita Cos. and its paired-share

REIT structure, which will enable Meditrust to both own and operate properties in the health care sector.

Investment Performance:

	Close	Gain/Loss	Dividend	% Yield	Annual Return
1991	$30.25	45.8%	$ 2.38	11.6%	57.4%
1992	$30.75	1.7%	$ 2.46	8.1%	9.8%
1993	$32.38	5.3%	$ 2.54	8.3%	13.6%
1994	$30.25	(6.6)%	$ 2.62	8.1%	1.5%
1995	$34.88	15.3%	$ 2.70	8.9%	24.2%
1996	$40.00	14.7%	$ 2.78	8.0%	22.7%

National Health Investors, Inc.

100 Vine Street, Suite 1402
Mufreesboro, TN 37130
(615) 890-9100

Exchange: New York (NHI)
Initial Public Offering: October 17, 1991
Initial Offering Price: $20.00
Geographical Focus: National
Competitive Strategies: Focuses on long-term care properties leased to well-capitalized, publicly held entities.
Special Notes: Formed in 1991 when it acquired 40 skilled long-term care facilities, three retirement centers, and four first mortgage notes from National HealthCare L.P. (NHC). The 43 properties were leased back to NHC under long term net lease agreements. NHC is a publicly traded limited partnership that operates approximately 100 retirement centers and four assisted living facilities in the Southeastern United States.
Investment Performance:

	Close	Gain/Loss	Dividend	% Yield	Annual Return
1991	$24.00	—	$ 0.42	—	—
1992	$22.88	(4.7)%	$ 2.04	8.5%	3.8%
1993	$27.75	21.3%	$ 2.18	9.5%	30.8%
1994	$26.13	(5.9)%	$ 2.38	8.6%	2.7%
1995	$33.13	26.8%	$ 2.61	10.0%	36.8%
1996	$37.88	14.3%	$ 2.84	8.6%	22.9%

Nationwide Health Properties Inc.
610 Newport Center Drive, Suite 1150
Newport Beach, CA 92660
(714) 718-4400

Exchange: New York (NHP)
Initial Public Offering: October 14, 1985
Geographical Focus: National
Competitive Strategies: Has specialized in acquiring and financing long-term care facilities; recently expanded its holdings to include assisted living facilities, especially those that are part of a "campus" that includes assisted living and a nursing home operation.
Special Notes: Commenced its operations in 1985. From 1991 through year-end 1996, provided shareholders with a compounded annual return of better than 26 percent.
Investment Performance:

	Close	Gain/Loss	Dividend	% Yield	Annual Return
1991	$13.63	55.7%	$ 1.03	11.8%	67.5%
1992	$16.25	19.3%	$ 1.12	8.2%	27.5%
1993	$17.75	9.2%	$ 1.21	7.5%	16.7%
1994	$17.88	0.7%	$ 1.32	7.4%	8.1%
1995	$21.00	17.5%	$ 1.41	7.9%	25.4%
1996	$24.25	15.5%	$ 1.48	7.1%	22.6%

2 for 1 stock split in March 1996

Omega Healthcare Investors Inc.
905 W. Eisenhower Circle, Suite 110
Ann Arbor, MI 48103
(313) 747-9790

Exchange: New York (OHI)
Initial Public Offering: August 14, 1992
Initial Offering Price: $21.00
Geographical Focus: National
Competitive Strategies: Focuses on long term care facilities

185

leased to middle-market firms that operate between 10 and 100 facilities and have revenues of between $20 million and $200 million.

Special Notes: In 1994, the company consummated the first merger in the health care REIT industry when it acquired Health Equity Properties (NYSE-EOP). The acquisition added $175 million in assets to Omega's portfolio and instantly made it one of the more substantial health care REITs in the industry. Besides its U.S. portfolio, Omega also manages and is a part owner of Principal Healthcare Finance, a company that owns and leases nursing home facilities located in the United Kingdom.

Investment Performance:

	Close	Gain/Loss	Dividend	% Yield	Annual Return
1992	$20.88	—	$ .26	—	—
1993	$25.25	21.0%	$ 2.04	9.8%	30.8%
1994	$24.13	(4.5)%	$ 2.20	8.7%	4.2%
1995	$26.63	10.4%	$ 2.36	9.8%	20.2%
1996	$33.25	24.9%	$ 2.48	9.3%	34.2%

Universal Health Realty Income Trust
Universal Corporate Center
367 South Gulph Road
King of Prussia, PA 19406
(610) 265-0688

Exchange: New York (UHT)
Initial Public Offering: December 24, 1986
Geographical Focus: National
Competitive Strategies: Focuses on acute care and rehabilitation hospitals.
Special Notes: Advised by UHS of Delaware. UHS of Delaware is a subsidiary of Universal Health Services, which leases eight facilities owned by the trust.
Investment Performance:

Health Care

	Close	Gain/Loss	Dividend	% Yield	Annual Return
1991	$18.00	65.5%	$ 1.54	14.2%	79.7%
1992	$15.25	(15.3)%	$ 1.63	9.0%	(6.3)%
1993	$16.63	9.0%	$ 1.66	10.9%	19.9%
1994	$16.38	(1.5)%	$ 1.67	10.0%	8.6%
1995	$17.88	9.2%	$ 1.68	10.3%	19.5%
1996	$20.50	14.7%	$ 1.70	9.5%	24.2%

CHAPTER TWELVE

The Lodging Industry

THE LODGING SEGMENT OF the real estate industry is perhaps the most susceptible to changing economic conditions. When the economy is sluggish, company travel budgets are cut back and families pare their vacation plans. These decisions significantly impact hotels and motels that rely on such travelers for much of their business. Alternatively, when the economy is strong, business travel accelerates and family vacations may include extensive travel. These developments enable lodging facilities to increase their daily rental rates, while at the same experiencing higher occupancy levels.

Within the last decade, we have witnessed one of these cycles in the lodging industry. A combination of overbuilding in the 1980s and an economic downturn in the early 1990s hit the industry hard. Hotels were a popular target of both limited partnership sponsors and institutional investors in the 1980s. As a result of such interest, development activity in this segment was strong—too strong in fact. Despite generally positive economic conditions during much of the decade, the oversupply of properties caused the lodging industry's average occupancy level to decline from 70.6 percent in 1980 to just under 62 percent by 1989.[1]

Conditions worsened in 1990 (Exhibit 12-1). Occupancy percentages dipped even further and the industry recorded a record $5.7 billion loss for the year. Although occupancy levels declined again the following year, to 60.9%, aggressive cost cutting measures helped reduce the industry's losses to $3 billion.[2]

Since 1992, the lodging industry's health has improved substantially. From 1992 through the end of 1996, room demand increased by more than 2.5 percent annually while the supply of new rooms

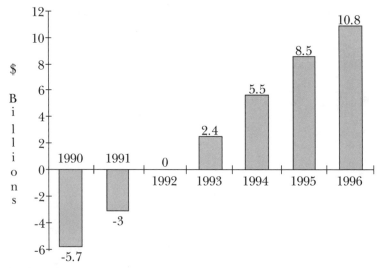

Exhibit 12-1   Hotel Industry Profitability SOURCE: Smith Travel Research

edged upward by about half that amount. The result was an average industry occupancy level of better than 66 percent in 1996 and record breaking profits of $10.8 billion.[3]

Hotel REITs have been the beneficiary of the industry's improving economics. In fact, in 1995 and 1996, they proved to be some of the most financially rewarding investments in the marketplace with returns of 30.9 percent and 49.2 percent, respectively.[4] Most of the public hotel REITs were fortunate in their timing. They were created after 1992 when the industry turnaround had already begun. This meant two things: they did not have any lingering financial problems to deal with after the last downturn; and, as a result, they had access to capital that enabled them to take advantage of some tremendous buying opportunities that existed in the marketplace.

One REIT that was around for the last cycle just barely made it through the bad times in tact. But that was only after it was rescued. Starwood Lodging, which went public in 1980 as Hotel Investors Trust, recorded nothing but losses for the four year period 1991 through 1994. It had suspended dividend payments and was on the verge of bankruptcy. Then in June 1994, a private hotel company, Starwood Capital stepped in and merged its operations with Hotel Investors Trust. Starwood renamed the company and infused some much needed capital into the REIT's operations. This helped Starwood Lodging to get back onto its feet financially and put it in a position where it was able to attract additional capital through Wall Street. The net result was that from 1994 through 1996, Starwood's asset base and stock price increased exponentially. In 1995 and 1996, Starwood Lodging's annual returns of 77.9 percent and 93.2 percent were the highest of all major equity REITs.[5]

The rags to riches story of Hotel Investors Trust/Starwood Lodging highlights the nature of the hotel industry. When times are good, they can be very good; and, when times are bad, they can be very bad. This is why the hotel sector of the REIT industry is one reserved for investors who understand and appreciate its highly cyclical nature.

The industry itself has become increasingly segmented over the years, as operators have sought to develop new products to meet the needs of specific customer niches. Hotels and motels fall into two broad categories: transient facilities and destination facilities. Transient facilities are generally located along major highways or at airports and depend on persons in transit from one location to another. Destination facilities are utilized by guests who are on vacation or attending a convention. Some of these destination facilities are located in resort cities, which can often result in conventioneers combining their business plans with vacation time. Within these two broad categories, there are at least five different customer segments that hotel operators target:[6]

1. **Luxury Hotels**—These hotels are generally of the "four star" variety, catering to the upscale traveler or business executive who is seeking the finest in accommodations. These hotels can be either small, independent, boutique facilities or part of larger specialty chains such as the Ritz Carlton or The Four Seasons.

2. **Corporate Style Hotels**—These facilities are also designed to satisfy the demands of the business traveler and the upscale leisure traveler; however, their price range is a step below that of the luxury hotel. Hotels in this category include: the Sheraton, Marriott, Westin, Hyatt, Hilton, Crown Plaza, and Ramada Renaissance. These facilities are located in mid-size to large cities and generally contain ample meeting rooms as well as restaurant and lounge facilities.

191

3. **Mid-market Hotels**—This segment includes the traditional center city or roadside full-service hotel, such as the Holiday Inn, Ramada, and Howard Johnson. They contain restaurant facilities on-site and sometimes have meeting rooms as well.

   Another category within this segment is the extended stay hotels. These properties contain fully equipped kitchens and usually provide daily newspaper delivery, a continental breakfast, wood-burning fireplaces, an evening hospitality hour, and in-room movies in facilities that are built to resemble apartment buildings. They are designed to appeal to business travelers such as consultants, engineers, attorneys, and accountants on extended stays for project-oriented work. They are also ideal for a family relocating to a new area. Most customers stay at one of these facilities between two and four weeks. Included in this category are the Residence Inn, Hampton Inn & Suites, and Homewood Suites.

   Another mid-market hotel type is the all-suite hotel. It offers many of the same amenities as the extended stay facilities, such as breakfast, cocktail hours, and pools/saunas. It is geared toward a shorter term guest who is seeking more space than that offered at a regular hotel. Chains such as the Embassy Suites and Clarion Suites dominate this sector.

4. **Limited Service Hotels**—This is the segment of the hotel industry that has been experiencing the highest rate of growth in recent years. The trend toward "value" on the part of consumers has led to a proliferation of mid-scale hotels offering clean and comfortable rooms at an affordable price. Chains such as the Hampton Inn, The Courtyard by Marriott, Holiday Inn Express, Fairfield Inn, and Ramada Inn have become the market leaders in this segment of the industry, which has become popular with both business and leisure travelers.

   These hotels are called limited service because they do not have any on-site restaurant facilities. Some offer a continental style breakfast and an afternoon cocktail hour during which beer, wine, and soft drinks are served.

5. **Economy Budget Hotels**—These lodging facilities are geared toward the consumer who is price sensitive. Chains

such as Econo Lodge, Super 8, Comfort Inn, and Rodeway Inns are significant players in this market segment.

Besides the increasing segmentation of the industry, another important development that has taken place over the years is the prominence of chain operations. Affiliation with a chain offers a number of benefits to hotel owners. It provides them with certain marketing advantages, such as centralized reservation systems and advertising, and it also helps them standardize their business practices. The net result is usually increased revenues and lower operating expenses. Chains also provide significant benefits to consumers. One benefit is the convenience of being able to make reservations through a centralized reservation service. Another benefit is being able to supply consumers with a level of standardization in their lodging selection.

The chain concept has proven to be so popular within the industry that a number of companies have developed chains in various segments of the industry. Clarion, for instance, has its upscale Clarion Hotels, its all-suite Clarion Suites, and its boutique inns called Clarion Inns. Holiday Inn has its Crowne Plazas, its full service Holiday Inn hotels and a limited service operation called Holiday Inn Express. The Marriott Corporation has its corporate style hotels, its extended stay Residence Inns, and its limited service hotels The Courtyard by Marriott and The Fairfield Inn.[7]

Chains that establish and strictly enforce standards at their facilities enable their hotel operators to gain a competitive advantage through the creation of a positive brand awareness. These standards apply to the physical appearance of the hotel properties as well as to guest amenities and services. It's no secret that an unpleasant experience at even one of the chain's facilities can destroy a customer's perception of the entire chain. Because of these standards, most hotel REITs focus on acquiring hotels that are affiliated with chains. Equity Inns, for instance, is the nation's largest owner of Hampton Inn hotels, while Felcor Suites is the largest owner of Embassy Suites hotels.

Chain standards are important to hotel REITs because most of them are not permitted to manage their own properties. Just like health care properties, a significant percentage of hotel revenues are usually derived from services other than room rentals. Under the Real Estate Trust Investment Act of 1960, this would disqualify a company from being a REIT.

There are a few exceptions to this rule, however. Two hotel REITs, Patriot American Hospitality and Starwood Lodging, enjoy a unique paired-share status. This status, which was banned by Congress in 1984, was grandfathered into law for just four REITs. It permits a company to have under its umbrella a REIT that owns property and an operating company that manages it. Patriot American Hospitality secured this status through its 1997 acquisition of California Jockey Club/Bay Meadows Operating Company. Starwood Lodging, on the other hand, was one of the original grandfathered entities.

This paired-share status means that the shares of both the REIT and its management company trade as one. The net effect is that these hotel REITs do not have to lease their properties to third party management organizations, but rather can manage them directly. This means greater control over the operations of such facilities, as well as lower operating expenses.

The other hotel REITs that do not enjoy this paired-share status must lease their properties to third party organizations, which are then responsible for managing the assets. It is essential that these REITs carefully select competent and experienced management organizations, because the revenues they derive from their holdings depends on the ability of these third party managers to profitably operate the hotel properties.

Under the hotel lease agreements, the REITs receive either a specified base rental payment, percentage rent, or a combination of the two. A specified percentage of the gross revenues is normally set aside in a capital refurbishment or improvement fund and is utilized by the lessee to maintain and replace furniture, fixtures, and equipment. Setting aside an adequate amount of funds for such improvements is important because it will determine whether or not these hotels will be able to continue to meet the operating standards imposed by the chains with which they are affiliated.

A number of the hotel REITs have lease agreements with entities which are entirely or partially owned and controlled by one or more of the principals of the REIT. Such an arrangement creates a conflict of interest in the negotiation of the lease agreement between the REIT and the lessee, because the objective of both parties is to secure as much of the hotel's profits for themselves as possible. Wall Street has generally frowned on such arrangements. The management of REITs that have entered into such arrangements have generally attempted to allay Wall Street's concerns by acquiring significant ownership interests in the REIT, thereby balancing their interests more evenly between the REIT and the lessee. Others have simply sold their management companies to third parties.[8]

The hotel sector of the REIT industry has been one of the more active ones in recent years. The existing REITs have been fairly aggressive in expanding their portfolios and, unlike other sectors of the REIT industry, a number of new hotel REITs have entered the fray since the beginning of 1996. This activity is largely the result of the attractive buying opportunities that have existed in the lodging industry.[9] The overbuilding that took place in the industry in the 1980s, combined with the economic downturn in the early 1990s and the fact that many hotel properties were overleveraged, resulted in a host of properties being put on the market in the mid-1990s. Many were hotels that had been taken over by lenders through foreclosure action.

The net result was that hotel properties were available for prices well below their replacement cost. The hotel REITs, with their access to capital, were able to take advantage of these market conditions just at a time when the industry's prospects were improving. This is why this segment of the REIT industry recorded such positive return figures in 1995 and 1996.

More recently, as improved market conditions have resulted in higher asking prices for hotel properties, most of the hotel REITs have changed their focus to acquiring properties whose value can be enhanced through renovation and/or repositioning. Equity Inns, Felcor Suite Hotels, and Winston Hotels, Inc., have entered into alliances with Promus, the largest franchiser of hotels in the United States, to develop and convert certain acquired properties to Promus brand hotels. Equity Inns has focused on Hampton Inns and Homewood Suites, Felcor has concentrated its efforts in the Embassy Suites brand, and Winston Hotels has specialized in developing Homestead Suites.

Boykin Lodging was a spin-off of a hotel management company, The Boykin Group, which was founded in 1959 and which manages most of the REIT's hotel properties. Boykin Lodging concentrates its activities in the full-service sector where it believes there is minimal risk of overdevelopment in the near future due to funding constraints. Boykin seeks properties which will benefit from renovation and repositioning.

Hospitality Properties Trust, which was a 1995 spin-off of health care REIT Health and Retirement Properties Trust, has focused its acquisitions on Courtyard by Marriott hotels. Unlike some of the other hotel REITs that look to install new management in the properties they acquire, Hospitalities Properties Trust has sought to acquire hotels where the existing management organization wants to stay on. Their acquisitions, therefore, usually take the form of a purchase/leaseback.

Innkeepers USA Trust concentrates in the upscale extended-stay market. It is the largest owner of Marriott Residence Inn hotels in the country and has an agreement with a major hotel developer, The Impac Hotel Group, to acquire any Residence Inn property developed by that company.

Jameson Inns has taken a different approach in its planned growth. Instead of acquiring existing hotels, it develops all of its properties. They are small (generally 40-60 rooms in size), Colonial-style, limited service hotels designed to appeal to the price and quality conscious business person. By developing all of its properties with the same look and amenities, Jameson Inns seeks to offer customers in its targeted markets (in the Southeastern United States) with consistent and predictable accommodations.

The remaining hotel REITs—American General Hospitality, RFS Hotel Investors, Patriot American, and Starwood Lodging—invest in diversified portfolios of upscale, mid-priced and limited service hotels.

American General Hospitality Corporation was a spin-off of American General Hospitality, Inc., one of the largest hotel management companies in the United States. It has primarily focused on acquiring full-service hotels in need of significant renovation and upgrading. In most situations, the company has converted the hotels to different national brands so they could benefit from the new franchisers' national brand recognition, reservation systems, and group sales organization.

RFS Hotel Investors invests in a diversified mix of full service and limited service hotel properties. Like many of the other hotel REITs, RFS has received a significant equity investment from a major hotel operating company, the Doubletree Corporation, under an agreement which provides Doubletree with the right to manage all properties acquired or developed by RFS.

Patriot American Hospitality and Starwood Lodging have been

the most aggressive hotel REITs in terms of their expansion and the scope of their operations. That's largely due to the fact that they are able to both own and manage their hotel properties.

Patriot American went public in late 1995 with the largest ever public offering for a hotel REIT. In early 1997, it completed the acqusition of California Jockey Club/Bay Meadows Operating Company, which provided it with the ability to manage its own properties. It has largely focused its acqusitions on full-service hotels in major U.S. cities and resort areas. Those acquisitions have included a $1 billion deal to purchase the Wyndam Hotel Corporation and certain hotels controlled by real estate developer Trammel Crow and a $217 million acquisition of Carefree Resorts, an owner and operator of high-end resorts.

Starwood Lodging has also focused its efforts on full-service hotel properties. The higher level of management that is required in operating such properties makes them attractive to a company like Starwood which is able to manage them directly. The company owns such premier hotels as the Boston Park Plaza, the Ritz Carlton in Philadelphia, the Westin Hotel in Washington, D.C., and the Westwood Marquis in Los Angeles.

Its aggressive growth strategy has enabled it to become one of the largest REITs in the industry, with a market capitalization as of April 1997 of $2.6 billion. That included a $439 million investment in early 1997 by Prisa II, a real estate investment fund managed by Prudential Real Estate Investors.

Hotel REITs

American General Hospitality
5605 MacArthur Blvd., Suite 1200
Irving, TX 75038
(972) 550-6800

Exchange: New York (AGT)
Initial Public Offering: July 25, 1996
Initial Offering Price: $17.75
Geographical Focus: National
Competitive Strategies: Focus on full-service hotels located in major markets and tourist areas; renovation, repositioning, and re-

branding of hotels to enhance revenue growth; aggressive management and marketing programs to improve operational performance.

Special Notes: Formed to continue and expand the hotel acquisition and development activities of American General Hospitality, Inc., the nation's fourth largest hotel management company.

Investment Performance:

	Close	Gain/Loss	Dividend	% Yield	Annual Return
1996	$23.75	—	$0.68	—	—

Boykin Lodging Company
50 Public Square, Suite 1500
Cleveland, OH 44113-2258
(216) 241-6375

Exchange: New York (BOY)
Initial Public Offering: November 4, 1996
Initial Share Price: $20.00
Geographical Focus: National
Competitive Strategies: Focus on full-service hotels that serve both business and leisure travelers and are operated under franchise agreements with national hotel franchisers such as Marriott, Radisson, Hilton, Hyatt, Westin, Omni, Doubletree, Sheraton, Hilton Inn, and Quality Suites; Acquisition of properties whose value can be enhanced through conversion to a new hotel brand, new marketing strategies, and/or physical renovation or redevelopment.

Special Notes: Successor to the Boykin Group, an organization founded in 1959 to develop and manage hotels. It was one of the first franchisees of Marriott Hotels and an early franchisee of Howard Johnson's Hotels.

Investment Performance:

	Close	Gain/Loss	Dividend	% Yield	Annual Return
1996	$24.00	—	$0.28	—	—

Equity Inns Inc.
4735 Spottswood, Suite 102
Memphis, TN 38117
(901) 761-9651

Exchange: New York (ENN)
Initial Public Offering: March 1, 1994
Initial Offering Price: $10.00
Geographical Focus: National
Competitive Strategies: Focuses on the acquisition and ownership of limited-service and extended stay hotels affiliated with established, nationwide hotel chains; the company believes these two industry segments enjoy high consumer acceptance and are more resilient during economic downturns. Equity Inns is the nation's largest owner of Hampton Inn hotels.
Special Notes: In 1996, formed a strategic alliance with Promus Hotel Corporation(NYSE:PRH), the franchiser of Embassy Suites, Hampton Inns, and Homewood Suites, under which Promus agreed to purchase up to $15 million in newly issued shares of Equity Inns over the subsequent three years.
Investment Performance:

	Close	Gain/Loss	Dividend	% Yield	Annual Return
1994	$11.25	—	$0.70	—	—
1995	$11.50	2.2%	$1.00	8.9%	11.1%
1996	$13.00	13.0%	$1.12	9.7%	22.7%

Felcor Suite Hotels, Inc.
545 John Carpenter Freeway, Suite 1300
Irving, TX 75062
(972) 444-4900
(http://www.felcor.com)

Exchange: New York (FCH)
Initial Public Offering: July 28, 1994
Initial Offering Price: $21.25
Geographical Focus: National
Competitive Strategies: It is the largest owner of Embassy Suites in

the United States; since its IPO in 1994, the company has been primarily engaged in acquiring hotel properties and converting them to Embassy Suite Hotels.

Special Notes: Formed in 1994 by company Chairman Thomas Feldman and President Thomas Corcoran for the purpose of acquiring ownership interests in a diversified portfolio of hotel properties. Mr. Feldman was previously the president and chief executive officer of Embassy Suites hotels, from 1983 to 1990, and its chairman from 1990 to 1992. In 1996, Promus invested $75 million in FelCor and guaranteed a $25 million loan to assist the company in converting its Crown Suites hotels to Embassy Suites.

Investment Performance:

	Close	Gain/Loss	Dividend	% Yield	Annual Return
1994	$19.50	—	$0.66	—	—
1995	$27.75	42.3%	$1.84	9.4%	51.7%
1996	$35.38	27.5%	$1.92	6.9%	34.4%

Hospitality Properties Trust
400 Centre Street
Newton, MA 02158
(617) 964-8389

Exchange: New York (HPT)
Initial Public Offering: August 22, 1995
Initial Offering Price: $25.00
Geographical Focus: National
Competitive Strategies: Has elected to fill what it believes is a niche in this segment of the REIT industry—that of providing capital to hotel operators who want to sell their real estate while remaining in the hotel business as lessees. Therefore, unlike many of the other hotel REITs that have affiliates manage their holdings, the company seeks to enter into sale/leaseback arrangements where the previous hotel owner stays on to operate the facility.

Special Notes: Formerly a subsidiary of health care REIT Health and Retirement Properties Trust (NYSE:HRP), Hospitality Properties Trust was spun off as a separate operating REIT in August 1995.

Investment Performance:

	Close	Gain/Loss	Dividend	% Yield	Annual Return
1994	$26.75	—	$0.55	—	—
1995	$29.00	8.4%	$2.28	8.5%	16.9%

Innkeepers USA Trust
306 Royal Poinciana Plaza
Palm Beach, FL 39480
(561) 835-1800

Exchange: New York (KPA)
Initial Public Offering: September 20, 1994
Initial Offering Price: $10.00
Geographical Focus: National
Competitive Strategies: Focuses on acquiring limited service hotels such as Hampton Inn, Comfort Inn, Holiday Inn Express, and Fairfield Inn hotels, and limited service, extended-stay hotels such as Residence Inn, Hampton Inn & Suites, and Homewood Suites hotels. Entered into a strategic alliance with Impac Hotel Group, Marriott Corporation's Developer of the Year in 1995 under which the trust will have a right of first refusal to acquire any Residence Inn developed by Impac.
Special Notes: Commenced its operations in September 1994. It was founded by Jeffrey Fisher who, since 1986, had served as President and Chief Operating Officer of JF Hotel Management.
Investment Performance:

	Close	Gain/Loss	Dividend	% Yield	Annual Return
1994	$ 7.25	—	$0.19	—	—
1995	$ 9.13	25.9%	$0.84	11.6%	37.5%
1996	$13.88	52.1%	$0.90	9.9%	62.0%

Jameson Inns, Inc.
8 Perimeter Center East, Suite 8050
Atlanta, GA 30346-1603
(770) 901-9020

Exchange: NASDAQ (JAMS)
Initial Public Offering: January 27, 1994

Initial Offering Price: $9.00
Geographical Focus: Southeast
Competitive Strategies: Develops all of its hotel properties to look alike and to be managed in the same manner under the Jameson Inn name; The company creates brand awareness by restricting its focus geographically to secondary markets in the Southeastern United States which have a strong industrial or commercial base; New property development capabilities.
Special Notes: Successor to an organization founded in 1987. The company believes the markets in which it develops its properties are underserved by hotels.
Investment Performance:

	Close	Gain/Loss	Dividend	% Yield	Annual Return
1994	$ 7.25	—	$0.69	—	—
1995	$ 8.88	22.5%	$0.82	11.3%	33.8%
1996	$13.25	49.2%	$0.87	9.8%	59.0%

Patriot American Hospitality Inc.
3030 LBJ Freeway, Suite 1550
Dallas, TX 75234
(214) 888-8000

Exchange: New York (PAH)
Initial Public Offering: September 27, 1995
Initial Share Price: $24.00
Geographical Focus: National
Competitive Strategies: Goal is to acquire, re-develop, and reposition hotels in major U.S. business centers and tourist destinations; the company's strategy is to acquire a portfolio of hotel properties that are diversified by type and location with a focus on full-service hotels.
Special Notes: The company's 1995 IPO, which raised more than $350 million, was the largest ever public offering for a hotel REIT and the largest REIT IPO in 1995. In early 1997, it acquired the California Jockey Club/Bay Meadows Operating Company and their unique paired share status which enabled Patriot American to not only own hotel properties, but manage them as well. Created in

1991 as a vulture fund to buy undervalued hotel and resort properties from the Resolution Trust Corporation.
Investment Performance:

	Close	Gain/Loss	Dividend	% Yield	Annual Return
1995	$25.75	—	$0.48	—	—
1996	$43.13	67.5%	$2.10	8.2%	75.7%

RFS Hotel Investors, Inc.
889 Ridge Lane Blvd., Suite 220
Memphis, TN 38120
(901) 767-7005

Exchange: New York (RFSI)
Initial Public Offering: August 13, 1993
Initial Offering Price: $10.00
Geographical Focus: National
Competitive Strategies: To invest in a diversified mix of hotel properties with the goal of having a portfolio equally divided between full-service hotels, limited-service hotels, and limited-service/extended stay properties.
Special Notes: Was the first REIT-structured hotel company to go public in the 1990s. In February 1996, Doubletree Corporation made an $18.5 million investment in RFS Hotel Investors through its purchase of newly-issued convertible preferred stock in exchange for a 10-year right of first refusal to lease hotels acquired or developed in the future by RFSI. Hotel chains represented in RFSI's portfolio include: Comfort Inn, Hampton Inn, Holiday Inn, Holiday Inn Express, Ramada Inn, and Residence Inn.
Investment Performance:

	Close	Gain/Loss	Dividend	% Yield	Annual Return
1993	$14.75	—	$0.11	—	—
1994	$14.63	(0.8)%	$0.97	6.6%	5.8%
1995	$15.78	5.1%	$1.18	8.1%	13.2%
1996	$19.75	28.5%	$1.39	8.8%	37.3%

Starwood Lodging Trust
2231 East Camelback Road, Suite 410
Phoenix, AZ 85016
(602) 852-3900

Exchange: New York (HOT)
Initial Public Offering: 1980
Geographical Focus: National
Competitive Strategies: Focuses on the acquisition of mid-scale and upscale hotels in major metropolitan areas throughout the United States that can be purchased for less than replacement cost; acquisition criteria focuses on hotels where management believes it can increase profitability through more efficient management and/or capital improvements; the trust specifically targets markets with significant barriers to entry or markets with stable demand generators such as universities, government agencies, or large companies.
Special Notes: Initially founded as Hotel Investors Trust. Changed its name in early 1995 when it reorganized its operations with those of Starwood Capital Group, L.P. Under the reorganization, Starwood Capital contributed its portfolio of hotel properties, as well as $12.6 million in cash, to the reorganized entity. Starwood Lodging Trust has a unique structure. Its shares are "paired" on a one-for-one basis with the common stock of Starwood Lodging Corporation, the entity that leases and manages most of the trust's hotel properties. This structure was adopted in 1980. In 1984, the IRS issued new regulations prohibiting future pairing of a REIT and management company.
Investment Performance:

	Close	Gain/Loss	Dividend	% Yield	Annual Return
1991	$ 3.50	(22.2)%	$0.00	0.0%	(22.2)%
1992	$ 4.00	14.3%	$0.00	0.0%	14.3%
1993	$10.50	162.5%	$0.00	0.0%	162.5%
1994	$11.50	9.5%	$0.00	0.0%	9.7%
1995	$19.83	72.5%	$0.94	5.4%	77.9%
1996	$36.75	85.3%	$1.36	6.9%	92.2%

3 for 2 stock split in January, 1997

Winston Hotels, Inc.
2209 Century Drive, Suite 300
Raleigh, NC 27612
(919) 510-6010

Exchange: NASDAQ (WINN)
Initial Public Offering: June 2, 1994
Inital Offering Price: $10.00
Geographical Focus: Southeast
Competitive Strategies: Focus on limited service hotels in high growth markets; Has an agreement with Promus, Inc. under which Winston will acquire or develop up to $100 million of Homestead Suites through the year 2000 in exchange for an investment of up to $15 million by Promus; Winston also has an agreement with the Equitable to co-invest in hotels which require significant rehabilitation and possibly rebranding.
Investment Performnace:

	Close	Gain/Loss	Dividend	% Yield	Total Return
1994	$10.00	—	$0.48	—	—
1995	$11.88	18.8%	$0.93	9.3%	28.1%
1996	$13.63	14.7%	$1.02	8.6%	23.3%

CHAPTER THIRTEEN

Mortgage REITs

AT ONE TIME, MORTAGE REITs dominated the REIT industry, especially in the late 1960s and early 1970s when mortgage REITs replaced commercial banks as the primary lending source for developers. A recession in 1973, combined with higher interest rates, however, proved to be the death knell for a number of mortgage REITs and an end to the first boom in the REIT industry's history.

While mortgage REITs made a comeback in the 1980s, today, they represent less than 4 percent of the REIT industry on the basis of their stock market capitalization.[1] Current mortgage REITs have a far different investment focus than those of the 1960s and 1970s. They generally include one or more of the following:

- The origination of mortgage loans secured by first deeds of trust on existing, income-producing commercial real estate and single family homes,

- The acquisition of interests in individual mortgages or pools of mortgages on commercial properties and single family homes,

- The purchase of interests in government insured, private insured, and private non-insured mortgage-backed securities,

- The procurement of single family mortgage loans from mortgage bankers and the repackaging of such mortgage loans into securitized instruments.

In short, the focus of current mortgage REITs is much more conservative than that of the mortgage REITs that existed over two decades ago. This is because they loan money on existing real estate as opposed to properties that are under development.

Today's mortgage REITs, however, still have to be concerned with the quality of their borrowers. Real estate investment trusts that originate mortgage loans address this issue at the underwriting stage by establishing standards that borrowers have to meet in order to receive a loan. This involves a review of both the credit standing of the borrower as well as an evaluation of the collateral. The mortgage REIT can also address the credit risk of a loan at the funding stage or at the time the loan is sold in the marketplace by obtaining either government insurance or private insurance.

Government mortgage insurance protection originated in the 1930s as part of the federal government's effort to pull the nation out of the Depression. Although there was some initial private sector opposition to the government's involvement in the mortgage industry, the availability of FHA insurance over the years has had a favorable impact on the industry because it has created an active national market for a variety of mortgage instruments and made more capital available for real estate.

Private mortgage insurance is provided by one of a select number of major mortgage insurance companies. Private mortgage insurance is often preferred over government insurance by originators due to more flexible terms (such as a lower down payment by borrowers).[2]

Another method that REITs utilize to facilitate the sale of their mortgage loans in the secondary market is to secure an investment grade rating from one or both of the major rating agencies: Standard & Poor's and Moody's Investor Services. Just as investors are more comfortable investing in a pool of AAA corporate bonds, they have a similar comfort level investing in a pool of real estate mortgage loans with the same rating.

Generally, the mortgage REITs that originate loans retain a portion of their originated mortgage loans and sell the remainder in the secondary market. The potential buyers of such securitized loans are numerous and include government entities such as the Federal National Mortgage Association (FNMA), the Government National Mortgage Association (GNMA), and the Federal Home Loan Mortgage Association (Freddie Mac), as well as private entities such as insurance companies, pension funds, REITs, and brokerage firms.

Other mortgage REITs prefer to purchase mortgage loans in the secondary market from such institutions as :

- Savings and loans
- Mortgage bankers
- Commercial bankers
- Mutual savings banks
- Credit unions
- Government entities
- Mortgage REITs

Secondary markets have developed not only for mortgage loans on single family homes, but for multifamily residential properties (classified as buildings with five or more units) and commercial properties as well. FNMA and Freddie Mac, for instance, guarantee mortgage loans on multifamily properties as part of their mission of fulfilling the nation's housing needs. Private sector financial institutions have also played a key role in creating and maintaining an active market in both multifamily and commercial property mortgage loans. These include banks, brokerage firms, and mortgage bankers.[3]

The other half of the risk equation associated with mortgage loan investments is interest rate risk. Today, this is the more significant concern of investors who are considering an investment in mortgage REITs because it was not very long ago (1994, in fact) that mortgage REITs suffered from increasing interest rates. A number saw their stock values decline by about 50 percent. As a result, many shifted a large percentage of their assets from fixed rate loans to adjustable rate mortgage loans.

An adjustable rate mortgage (ARM) is a loan that has an interest rate that is usually adjusted every six months or yearly according to some predetermined index. The interest rate is based on an index that mirrors the lender's cost of funds. Lenders utilize various indices to determine the periodic rate adjustments. Generally, the only stipulations regarding the chosen index is that it must be beyond the control of the lender and it must be verifiable by the borrower. The index, of course, is used as a basis for determining the interest rate to be charged. This is basically the lenders cost of funds. To this base amount, lenders add a margin, which represents their profit.

While the periodic interest rate adjustments on variable rate loans provide the lender with some protection against rising interest rates, they do not provide full protection because there are caps on the rate adjustments. These caps are normally 200 basis points (2 percent) in any year and 600 basis points (6 percent) over the life of the mortgage loan. Thus, if the base rate of the loan is 10 percent, it cannot be increased beyond 12 percent in its first full year and beyond 16 percent at any time during the life of the mortgage loan.[4]

To obtain full protection from interest rate increases, the lender can obtain insurance that will cover a portion or all of the interest costs above the capped level. The insurance is needed only if the lender is borrowing capital to fund its loans, because this would be the only situation where an actual "loss" would be incurred.

Another way to mitigate the risks of increasing interest rates is for the lender to obtain a participation in the increasing revenues of the mortgaged property and/or in its increased value over the term of the mortgage loan. In an environment where interest rates are increasing, property cash flow and values normally increase as well. By securing an agreement enabling it to participate in such profits, the lender will realize additional interest on its mortgage loan.

Equity participation loans were common in the 1980s due to the high level of interest rates and inflation that existed at the time. For borrowers, such agreements generally resulted in a lower base interest rate on their mortgage loans. In a high interest rate environment, this reduced rate was often the only way an investor was able to profitably acquire a property with the desired leverage. It also provided the borrowers with protection that their interest rate would not rise to a level that would create an operating loss, as could be the case with an adjustable rate mortgage.

Equity participation mortgage loans are not as prevalent in the 1990s due to lower market interest rates, the employment of less leverage in property acquisitions, and lender concerns regarding the future appreciation potential of real estate investments. (An understandable concern after the decline in real estate prices in the late 1980s and early 1990s.)

While investors who acquire interests in mortgage investments have to be concerned with increasing interest rates, they must also be concerned with the other possibility: decreasing interest rates. This is because when there is a significant decline in interest rates, many property owners refinance their mortgages. The net result is that investors are unable to reap the benefits associated with their high yielding mortgage investments and, instead, are faced with the dilemma of having to reinvest such proceeds in lower yielding instruments.

To combat the prepayment problem, collateralized mortgage obligations (CMOs) were devised. These instruments divide a pool of mortgage loans into various classes. The highest class investors receive all of the principal realized from prepayments until they receive back their investment. Then, the second class of holders receive all principal payments until payback, and so on. This division of a pool of mortgages into various classes provides investors with a higher degree of certainty as to the duration of their investment.

The real estate mortgage conduit (REMIC) was introduced in 1986. It is comparable to the CMO in structure, but has certain tax and balance sheet advantages for its sponsors.[5]

Within the mortgage sector of the REIT industry, there are basically three types of REITs: (1) those that invest in small business loans secured by real estate, (2) those that invest in non-government insured mortgage loans, and (3) those that invest primarily in government guaranteed mortgage loans.

Allied Capital and PMC Capital are part of organizations that specialize in making business loans. These REITs also make business loans, except their loans are collateralized by real estate. Both companies have focused their investments in the lodging industry, which are more operating businesses than pure real estate.

Commercial Assets, CWM Mortgage Holdings, and Dynex Capital invest in uninsured mortgage loans. CWM Mortgage concentrates in the single family market, Commercial Assets in the multifamily market, and Dynex Capital in both segments.

The remaining three mortgage REITs: Capstead, CRIIMI MAE, and Thornburg, invest primarily in government guaranteed mortgage loans on single family homes. Much of their portfolios are acquired with borrowed funds with the objective of realizing a profit on the spread between their cost of funds and the earnings on the acquired mortgage loans.

Mortgage REITs

Allied Capital Commercial Corporation
1666 K Street, 9th Floor
Washington, D.C. 20006
(202) 331-1112
(http://www.alliedcapital.com)

Exchange: NASDAQ (ALCC)
Initial Public Offering: July, 1992
Initial Offering Price: $15.00
Focus: Invests in portfolios of small business commercial real estate mortgages. The company also purchases interests in mortgage pools from banks, government agencies, wholesalers, and insurance companies with the objective of realizing current income plus capital gains from the prepayment of discounted mortgages.
Competitive Strategies: As part of its mission of providing funds for small businesses, the company specializes in mortgage financing for entrepreneurs whose business is the primary source of revenue rather than the real estate itself; seeks niches in the marketplace that are not being adequately served by other financial entities, such as the hotel/motel industry.
Special Notes: Managed by Allied Capital Advisers, which also manages six other public and private investment entities all of which are engaged in lending to and investing in small businesses. Under its advisory agreement with the company, Allied Capital Advisors evaluates, structures and closes investments, arranges debt financing, and is responsible for monitoring the company's investments.
Investment Performance:

	Close	Gain/Loss	Dividend	% Yield	Annual Return
1992	$17.88	—	$0.40	—	—
1993	$16.63	(7.0)%	$1.00	5.6%	(1.4)%
1994	$16.63	0.0%	$1.47	8.8%	8.8%
1995	$19.75	18.8%	$1.78	10.7%	29.5%
1996	$23.25	17.7%	$1.98	10.1%	27.8%

CWM Mortgage Holdings, Inc.
35 North Lake Avenue
Pasadena, CA 91101-1857
(800) 669-2300
(http://www.inmc.com)

Exchange: New York (CWM)
Initial Public Offering: September 6, 1985
Focus: Invests in fixed and adjustable rate mortgage loans secured by single family homes and in mortgage backed securities. The company also operates a mortgage loan conduit that purchases jumbo mortgages and repackages such mortgages into collateralized mortgage obligations or REMICs that are then sold in the secondary market.
Competitive Strategies: Obtains its investments primarily through its subsidiary, Independent National Mortgage Corporation (Indy Mac). Indy Mac purchases jumbo and nonconforming mortgage loans on a nationwide basis from S&Ls, credit unions, and mortgage bankers and then securitizes such mortgage loans; has two other affiliates which provide it with loans for its investment portfolio: One makes construction loans and the other provides financing to individuals buying or refinancing a new or existing manufactured home.
Special Notes: Prior to 1993, CWM was a passive investor in the mortgage business. It became an active investor in 1993 through the creation of its subsidiary, Independent Natioinal Mortgage Corporation.
Investment Performance:

	Close	Gain/Loss	Dividend	% Yield	Annual Return
1991	$ 6.13	36.1%	$0.79	17.6%	53.7%
1992	$ 5.38	(12.2)%	$0.48	7.8%	(4.4)%
1993	$10.00	86.1%	$0.48	8.9%	95.0%
1994	$ 8.63	(15.9)%	$1.04	10.4%	(5.5)%
1995	$17.00	97.0%	$1.17	13.6%	110.6%
1996	$21.50	26.5%	$1.56	9.2%	35.7%

Capstead Mortgage Corporation
2711 North Haskell Avenue, Suite 900
Dallas, TX 75204

(800) 358-2323
(214) 874-2323
(http://www.capstead.com)

Exchange: New York (CMO)
Initial Public Offering: 1985
Initial Offering Price: $8.89
Focus: Operates as a mortgage conduit that purchases, securitizes and invests in various types of single family residential mortgage loans most of which are guaranteed by Fannie Mae, Fredie Mac, or Ginnie Mae. The company has also formed a mortgage servicing unit to function as the primary mortgage servicer for loans and mortgage servicing rights it acquires.
Competitive Strategies: Expanded into mortgage servicing and CMO administration in 1994 to offset the volatility caused by swings in interest rates. Whereas the company's investment portfolio does well when interest rates remain stable or decline, the mortgage servicing and CMO administration businesses perform better if interest rates remain stable or rise.
Special Notes: Founded in 1985, the company was managed by Lomas Mortgage USA, through October 1, 1993, after which it became fully self-administered. For the five year period ending December 31, 1996, shareholders realized an average annual return of 25.1 percent.
Investment Performance:

	Close	Gain/Loss	Dividend	% Yield	Annual Return
1991	$13.05	109.9%	$1.14	18.3%	128.2%
1992	$17.44	33.6%	$1.45	11.1%	44.7%
1993	$18.22	4.5%	$1.63	9.3%	13.8%
1994	$ 7.44	(58.8)%	$1.43	7.8%	(51.0)%
1995	$15.25	104.8%	$1.09	14.7%	119.5%
1996	$24.00	57.4%	$2.12	13.8%	71.2%

3 for 2 stock split in October 1995 and July 1996

Commercial Assets, Inc.
3600 South Yosemite Street
Denver, CO 80237
(303) 773-1221

Exchange: American (CAX)
Initial Public Offering: 1993
Initial Offering Price: $7.48
Focus: Engaged in the acquisition and management of debt instruments backed by mortgage loans on multifamily properties. The company generally acquires a class of bonds that are the most subordinate in position in the event of a borrower's default.
Competitive Strategies: Focuses on mortgage loans on multifamily properties and manufactured home communities, market segments that it believes have traditionally had more stable property values than other types of real estate.
Special Notes: Was incorporated as a subsidiary of Asset Investors (NYSE:AIC) in August 1993. In October of the same year, Asset Investors distributed approximately 70 percent of the outstanding stock to its shareholders.
Investment Performance:

	Close	Gain/Loss	Dividend	% Yield	Annual Return
1993	$ 6.25	—	$ 0.07	—	—
1994	$ 5.75	(8.0)%	$ 0.53	8.5%	(0.5)%
1995	$ 5.63	2.2%	$ 0.68	12.4%	10.2 %
1996	$ 6.75	20.0%	$ 0.68	12.1%	32.1%

CRIIMI MAE, Inc.
The CRI Building
11200 Rockville Pike
Rockville, MD 20852
(800) CMM-0535
(301) 816-2300

Exchange: New York (CMM)
Initial Public Offering: 1989
Focus: Invests in government insured and guaranteed mortgages secured by multifamily properties and in uninsured mortgages and mortgage-related investments backed by multifamily and other commercial mortgages.
Competitive Strategies: Utilization of its in-house real estate, mort-

gage and financial expertise to evaluate and acquire pools of subordinated securities and to issue uninsured mortgages.

Special Notes: Formed in 1989 as part of the merger of three federally insured mortgage funds sponsored by CRI. In mid-1995, the company become a self-managed REIT through a merger with its advisor. It enabled CRIIMI MAE to acquire mortgage servicing, loan origination, and advisory services and to expand its holdings into uninsured mortgages and mortgage related investments.

Investment Performance:

	Close	Gain/Loss	Dividend	% Yield	Annual Return
1991	$ 8.75	29.6%	$1.08	16.0%	45.6%
1992	$10.00	14.3%	$1.08	12.3%	26.6 %
1993	$11.13	11.3%	$1.12	11.2%	22.5%
1994	$ 6.75	(39.4)%	$1.16	10.4%	(29.0)%
1995	$ 8.38	24.1%	$0.92	13.9%	38.0%
1996	$12.63	50.7%	$1.22	14.6%	65.3%

Dynex Capital, Inc.
10900 Nuckols Road, 3rd Floor
Glen Allen, VA 23060
(804) 217-5800

Exchange: New York (RMR)
Initial Public Offering: 1988
Initial Offering Price: $10.00
Focus: Originates, services, and securitizes residential mortgage loans and invests in a portfolio of mortgage loans and securities on single family homes, multifamily properties, and manufactured homes.

Competitive Strategies: The company targets "non-conforming" loans, where the borrowers cannot easily qualify for a loan from federal mortgage agencies; Is attracted to this market segment because of the greater profit opportunities it presents and the expertise the company has developed in this market.

Special Notes: Formed in 1988 as a spin-off of The Ryland Group (NYSE:RYL), one of the nation's largest homebuilders, the company was initially called RAC Investment Mortgage and was advised by Ryland Acceptance Corporation, a subsidiary of the Ryland

Group. In 1992, RAC Investment Mortgage terminated its agreement with Ryland Acceptance, became a self-managed REIT, and changed its name to Resources Mortgage Capital. In April 1997, the company changed its name again, to Dynex Capital.

Investment Performance:

	Close	Gain/Loss	Dividend	% Yield	Annual Return
1991	$ 5.25	104.9%	$0.77	30.0%	134.9%
1992	$10.13	92.9%	$1.30	24.8%	117.7%
1993	$14.32	41.4%	$1.53	15.1%	56.5%
1994	$ 5.32	(62.9)%	$1.38	9.6%	(53.3)%
1995	$10.00	88.0%	$0.84	15.8%	103.8%
1996	$14.69	46.9%	$1.14	11.4%	58.3%

2 for 1 stock split in May 1997

Imperial Credit Mortgage
20371 Irvine Avenue
Santa Ana Heights, CA 92707
(714) 474-8500

Exchange: American (IMH)
Initial Public Offering: November 1995
Initial Offering Price: $13.00
Focus: Is primarily engaged in investing in non-conforming residential mortgage loans, securitizing and selling interests in non-conforming loans, and providing short-term loans to buyers of real estate.
Competitive Strategies: Invests in non-conforming residential mortgage loans, many of which are acquired by its subsidiary, ICI Funding Corporation, and in mortgage-backed securities.
Investment Performance:

	Close	Gain/Loss	Dividend	% Yield	Annual Return
1995	$13.25	—	—	—	—
1996	$23.75	79.3%	$1.99	15.0%	94.3%

PMC Commercial Trust
PMC Capital Building
17290 Preston Road

Dallas, TX 75252
(972) 380-0044

Exchange: American (PCC)
Initial Public Offering: December 28, 1993
Initial Offering Price: $15.00
Focus: Is primarily engaged in originating loans to small businesses which are secured by first liens on real estate.
Competitive Strategies: Focuses on the origination of loans to owner occupied hotels whose net worth, asset, income, or other limitations exceed applicable Small Business Administration programs or exceed the SBA limit of $1.1 million.
Special Notes: Founded in 1993 as an affiliate of PMC Capital, a publicly owned company (ASE:PMC) founded in 1979. Lending criteria includes the following: (1) first lien real estate mortgages which do not exceed 70 percent of the lesser of the appraised value of a property or its cost, (2) the borrower has proven management capabilities and a satisfactory credit history, and (3) the loan meets specified debt coverage ratios based on historical operating results.
Investment Performance:

	Close	Gain/Loss	Dividend	% Yield	Annual Return
1993	$15.00	—	—	—	—
1994	$11.75	(21.7)%	$1.02	6.8%	14.9%
1995	$16.25	38.3%	$1.38	11.7%	50.0%
1996	$17.75	9.2%	$1.56	9.6%	18.8%

Thornburg Mortgage Asset Corporation
119 E. Marcy Street, Suite 201
Santa Fe, NM 87501
(505) 989-1900
(http://www.thornburg.com/tmac.htm)

Exchange: New York (TMA)
Initial Public Offering: July 25, 1993
Initial Offering Price: $15.00
Focus: Combines equity capital with borrowed funds to invest in adjustable rate mortgage securities and generates income based on

the difference between the interest rates it charges borrowers and its cost of capital.

Competitive Strategies: The company's general strategy is to reduce interest rate risk by investing only in adjustable rate mortgage securities that re-price at least once a year and in hedging agreements that result in the company being reimbursed when the market interest rates on its borrowings exceed a contractually specified interest rate on its investment mortgages.

Special Notes: To limit credit risk, the company seeks to invest at least 70 percent of its assets in mortgage securities that are either issued or guaranteed by an agency of the U.S. Government or are rated within one of the two highest ratings categories by either Standard & Poor's or Moody's Investor Services.

Investment Performance:

	Close	Gain/Loss	Dividend	% Yield	Annual Return
1993	$16.50	—	$ .29	—	—
1994	$ 7.38	(55.3)%	$1.00	6.1%	(49.2)%
1995	$15.75	113.6%	$ .93	12.6%	126.2%
1996	$21.38	35.7%	$1.65	10.5%	46.2%

CHAPTER FOURTEEN

Miscellaneous REITs

IN THE MISCELLANEOUS CATEGORY, there are only two REITs to discuss, both of which invest in golf courses.

National Golf Properties was formed in August 1993 to continue and expand the golf course ownership business of David Price, a well-known investor in golf courses throughout the United States. Golf Trust of America went public in February 1997 with a portfolio of properties developed by Larry Young, a prominent developer of golf courses in the southeastern United States.

As is the case for hotel REITs and health care REITs, these golf REITs cannot manage their own properties. Instead, they lease their facilities to golf course operators who manage the courses under agreements that require the payment of both base rent and percentage rent.

The two REITs in this sector have different stragegies with regard to the leasing of their properties. Most of National Golf Properties leases are with American Golf Corporation, an entity primarily owned by David Price. While this arrangement presents a potential conflict of interest, it is mitigated by the fact that Price also owns a substantial interest in the Operating Partnership through which National Golf Properties owns its investments. Thus, he has significant holdings in both the lessee and the lessor.

Golf Trust of America generally leases the golf courses it acquires back to affiliates of the previous owners under long-term operating agreements.

National Golf Properties has interests in a variety of courses, including daily fee, private club, and resort courses. Daily fee courses are open to the public and generate revenue principally based on green fees, golf cart rentals, and driving range charges. Private club courses are generally closed to the public and generate revenue principally through initiation fees, membership dues, golf cart rentals, and guest green fees. Resort courses are generally located in destination vacation areas where play comes primarily from tourist traffic. Such courses are open to the public and generate revenue principally based on green fees, golf cart rentals, and driving range charges. These courses can typically command higher green fees, but their business is more seasonal in nature and more susceptible to economic downturns.[1]

Golf Trust of America's plan is to invest primarily in upscale club and resort golf courses. The company's founder, Larry Young, has developed some premier golf courses, including six Grand Strand golf courses (three of which are located at the Legends complex). The company either acquires golf courses directly through a purchase/leaseback transaction or provides financing for the acquisition of courses.

In May 1997, Golf Trust of America took the latter route in making a $69.9 million loan to Starwood Capital Group for the acquisition of the Innisbrook Resort, a 63-hole destination golf and conference facility near Tampa, Florida, and the Tamarron Resort, an 18-hole destination golf and conference facility near Durango, Colorado. The loan provides for a base rate of interest with minimum interest rate increases annually through the first five years as well as a participating interest feature throughout the loan term based on the growth in revenues over the base year.

The golf course industry has several characteristics that make it an appealing market segment:[2]

Positive growth trends—Between 1982 and 1992, the number of golfers increased from 16 million to 24.8 million, a 55 percent increase. The number of rounds of golf played in the United States also increased by approximately 33 percent. Despite this tremendous growth, the number of golf courses grew in total by only 8.5 percent.

In the mid-1990s, the situation has changed. New golf courses have continued to be developed, while the number of golfers has remained flat. The demand/supply equation could change again in the near future, though, as baby boomers mature and start playing more golf.

Highly fragmented industry—At the end of 1996, it was estimated that there were more than 15,700 golf courses in the United States.[3] Only a small fraction of those facilities fit the acquisition criteria of the two REITs that focus in this sector. It is estimated that the top 15 operators own or lease fewer than 5 percent of all U.S. courses, with most courses owned by real estate developers, families, and financial institutions as a result of foreclosures. This situation presents attractive buying opportunities for companies like Golf Trust of America and National Golf Properties.

Lack of management expertise in the industry—Most golf course operators do not manage a large number of properties. National Golf Properties estimates that there are less than 10 operators who manage more than 20 courses and only 2 that manage more than 75 courses. As a result of this large fragmentation of management, few companies have developed sophisticated management systems that will enable them to maximize the profit potential of the courses they manage.

Golf Trust of America
14 North Adger's Wharf
Charleston, SC 29401
(803) 723-4653

Exchange: American (GTA)
Initial Public Offering: February 7, 1997
Initial Offering Price: $21.00
Focus: It is engaged in both the acquisition and ownership of a portfolio of upscale golf courses and in the issuance of participating mortgage loans on such golf courses.
Competitive Strategies: Seeks to acquire upscale golf courses that can be leased back to the former owners under a long term operating agreements that provide for the payment of both a base rent as well as percentage rent; will also make participating loans to parties acquiring golf courses.
Special Notes: Formed by Larry Young, who developed six Grand Strand golf courses, including three at the Legends complex.

National Golf Properties, Inc.
2951 28th Street, Suite 3001
Santa Monica, CA 90405
(310) 664-4100

Exchange: New York (TEE)
Initial Public Offering: August 18, 1993
Initial Offering Price: $20.375
Focus: Is engaged in the acquisition and ownership of a diversified portfolio of golf courses. To comply with the regulations regarding the operation of a REIT, the company leases such facilities to an operator who is responsible for managing the courses on a day-to-day basis.
Competitive Strategies: The company's business strategy is to: (1) acquire golf courses in urban areas or resort locations that demonstrate the potential for significant revenue and cash flow increases, (2) select capable golf course operators to manage these assets under triple net leases that provide for payment of a base rent plus percentage rent, (3) work with the golf course operators to increase property values through maintenance efforts and capital improvements, and (4) monitor the operating performance of the golf courses and their compliance with the terms of the leases.
Special Notes: Formed to continue and expand the golf course business of David Price. The company is the second largest overall owner of courses in the nation.
Investment Performance:

	Close	Gain/Loss	Dividend	% Yield	Annual Return
1993	$22.25	—	$0.16	—	—
1994	$22.13	(0.6)%	$1.49	6.7%	6.1%
1995	$22.88	3.4%	$1.61	7.0%	10.4%
1996	$31.63	38.3%	$1.66	7.3%	45.6%

CHAPTER FIFTEEN

Diversified REITs

DIVERSIFIED REITs CAN GENERALLY be divided into two camps: (1) those that commenced operations before 1990, when diversification was considered important in the construction of REIT portfolios, and; (2) those that have gone public in the 1990s and which are geographically focused, but diversified by asset type.

One of the diversified REITs, Property Capital Trust, determined that its traditional method of operating, as a passive entity investing in a diversified portfolio of assets, was so out of line with the current practice of actively managed, highly focused REITs, that it elected to go out of business. Other REITs that have faced the same dilemma have been attempting with varying degrees of success to modify their operations to more closely conform with the accepted REIT structure of the 1990s.

The pre-1990 REITs include a mixture of companies that have experienced significant financial problems as a result of the industry downturn at the outset of this decade and companies that have changed their investment strategies in recent years to enhance their growth prospects.

BRT Realty is one of the financially strained REITs. It was originally created as a mortgage REIT in 1972. As a result of the real estate recession in the late 1980s and early 1990s, it repossessed a significant percentage of its mortgaged assets. Its focus since then has been to reduce its outstanding debt. This is why it did not pay any dividends from 1990 through 1996.

First Union Real Estate, which has been around since 1961, also experienced financial challenges in the early 1990s. This forced it to reduce its dividends by more than half from 1991 to 1994. Since then, the REIT has come under new management that has sought to more narrowly define the trust's scope to retail and multifamily properties in the Pacific Northwest, Upper Midwest, and Southeast, and to a new investment property type, parking facilities. First Union is one of four REITs with a paired share structure under which their management companies trade as one with the REIT. First Union is taking advantage of this structure to acquire and actively manage parking facilities.

PennREIT has also changed its strategy in the 1990s. From its beginnings in 1960, it was a passive investor acquiring interests in properties through joint ventures. In the mid-1990s it elected to focus its efforts on acquiring direct property interests in apartment communities and retail facilities and to directly manage these holdings.

EastGroup Properties has traditionally been a small REIT with a narrow geographical focus. This has started to change in recent years after the company acquired two other REITs: LNH REIT in 1995 and Copley Properties in 1996.

Sizeler Property Investors has also expanded its operations in the 1990s both in size and geographical coverage. From 1990 through the end of 1996, the company's asset base increased from $86 million to more than $300 million.

In 1992, the board of trustees for Boddie-Noell Properties decided it also needed to expand its operations. The company's initial investments were in a portfolio of Hardees restaurants. While providing a solid and stable return for shareholders, these triple net lease properties failed to provide any dividend growth. Company management, therefore, elected to expand into the multifamily sector to provide Boddie-Noell shareholders with some capital appreciation potential.

Washington REIT has also sought to diversify its portfolio since it went public in 1960, but it has done so in a targeted geographical area: the Washington D.C./Baltimore corridor. The company has acquired a portfolio of office properties, shopping centers, high-rise apartment buildings, and industrial properties that have produced consistent earnings over the years.

MGI Properties road has not been as direct as that taken by Washington REIT. It started out as a mortgage REIT in 1971, and later in the decade converted to an equity REIT. Since then, it has shifted its attention from one market to another depending upon regional economic conditions. This strategy has produced mixed results. The trust, however, may have hit gold with its recent emphasis on its home state, Massachusetts. It took advantage of depressed real estate conditions that existed in the Northeast in the early 1990s to acquire primarily R&D and office buildings at prices well below replacement value.

Cousins Properties has been a public company since 1962 and a REIT since 1987. Although Cousins has investments in retail and apartment properties, its primary focus over the years has been office buildings located in the Southeastern United States. Most of its properties were developed by the company, many on a joint venture basis with major corporations such as Coca-Cola, IBM, and NationsBank.

The remaining major diversified REITs are relatively new to the marketplace. Most have sizable portfolios that are geographically focused. Colonial Properties Trust, which went public in 1993, is focused in the Southeast. It has three separate divisions, multifamily, office, and retail, each of which is responsible for developing, acquiring, and managing its own properties. Duke Realty Investments' portfolio includes office, industrial, and retail facilities located in the Midwest. It is also actively engaged in developing new properties, primarily on a build-to-suit basis. Pacific Gulf Properties is a spin-off of another REIT, Santa Anita Realty Enterprises. It started out in 1994 with a geographically diversified portfolio of multifamily and industrial properties. Since that time, it has sought to narrow its geographical focus to the West Coast, acquiring apartment properties geared toward families and senior citizens, as well as industrial properties.

Glenborough Realty Trust is a REIT which is pursuing a strategy completely different from most other real estate investment trusts. It is diversified not only by asset type, but geographically.

Formed at the end of 1995 through the consolidation of eight limited partnerships, Glenborough has elected to fill what it believes is a potentially profitable niche in the industry—that of acquiring entire real estate portfolios from existing limited partnerships managed by others. Most of these partnerships were formed in the 1980s and their investors are generally anxious to have the opportunity to "cash out". The problem for these partnerships is that there are few entities interested in acquiring their entire portfolios of real estate and the cost of selling such assets on a piecemeal basis is significant.

227

Therefore, the opportunity exists for a company like Glenborough to advantageously acquire real estate portfolios owned by existing limited partnerships. Since many of these portfolios will generally be diversified both by asset type as well as geographically, Glenborough intends to continue to go against the specialization trend in the REIT industry.

The diversified REITs will likely have a mixed future. The larger ones will gain attention primarily because of their size and, to a lesser extent, because of their geographical focus. The smaller diversified REITs are generally too small to gain any significant following on Wall Street. They are likely to be acquisition or merger candidates. However, because they maintain diversified portfolios of real estate, many of the REITs that focus in specific property sectors may not be interested.

Diversified REITS

BRT Realty Trust
60 Cutter Mill Road, Suite 303
Great Neck, NY 11021
(516) 466-3100

Exchange: New York (BRT)
Initial Public Offering: 1972
Geographical Focus: New York and Texas
Competitive Strategies: Monitor its portfolio of mortgage loans, maintain and enhance the cash flow of real estate and prepare it for eventual sale, and utilize such sale proceeds, as well as interest and principal payments from its loan portfolio, to reduce bank debt.
Special Notes: Formed in 1972 to make primarily short-term mortgage loans on existing, income-producing real estate. As a result of the industry downturn in the late 1980s and early 1990s, the company foreclosed on many of its mortgaged properties. In September 1992, BRT entered into an agreement with its banks to pay down the outstanding balances on its loans with proceeds from the sale of properties and any operating profits.
Investment Performance:

	Close	Gain/Loss	Dividend	% Yield	Annual Return
1991	$2.13	(10.5)%	$0.00	0%	(10.5)%
1992	$3.38	58.2%	$0.00	0%	58.2%
1993	$3.75	11.1%	$0.00	0%	11.1%
1994	$3.75	(0.0)%	$0.00	0%	(0.0)%
1995	$4.25	13.3%	$0.00	0%	13.3%
1996	$6.63	55.9%	$0.00	0%	55.9%

Boddie-Noell Properties, Inc.
3710 One First Union Center
Charlotte, NC 28202-6032
(704) 333-1367

Exchange: American (BNP)
Initial Public Offering: April 1987
Geographical Focus: Southeast
Competitive Strategies: Third party management operations; geographically focused; achieve steady income from restaurant leases and growth potential from investments in multifamily properties.
Special Notes: Founded in 1987 as Boddie-Noell Restaurant Properties, it originally invested in net leases on 47 Hardees restaurant properties located in Virginia and North Carolina. In 1992, after a review of ways to increase shareholder value, Boddie-Noell's Board elected to diversify the company's assets through the acquisition of multifamily properties. The company's name was changed to Boddie-Noell Properties at that time.
Investment Performance:

	Close	Gain/Loss	Dividend	% Yield	Annual Return
1991	$12.88	35.6%	$1.30	13.7%	49.3%
1992	$13.38	3.9%	$1.24	9.6%	13.5%
1993	$15.00	12.1%	$1.24	9.3%	21.4%
1994	$12.50	(16.7)%	$1.24	8.3%	(8.4)%
1995	$12.50	0.0%	$1.24	9.9%	9.9%
1996	$12.50	0.0%	$1.24	9.9%	9.9%

Colonial Properties Trust
2101 6th Avenue North, Suite 750
Birmingham, AL 35203
(205) 250-8700
(http://www.colonialprop.com)

Exchange: New York (CLP)
Initial Public Offering: September 29, 1993
Initial Offering Price: $23.00
Geographical Focus: Southeast
Competitive Strategies: Geographically focused, but diversified by
property type with investments in multifamily, retail, and office buildings; growth strategy is to seek investment opportunities through
both acquisitions and development; special acquisition opportunities
such as the purchase of properties repossessed by lenders.
Special Notes: Formed to succeed the interests of Colonial Properties, Inc., a developer, owner, and manager of real estate in the
Southeastern United States since 1970. The company has three dis-
tinct operating divisions, multifamily, retail, and office, that are responsible for their own development, acquisition, management,
and leasing activities.
Investment Performance:

	Close	Gain/Loss	Dividend	% Yield	Annual Return
1993	$21.50	—	—	—	—
1994	$22.50	4.7%	$1.73	8.0%	12.7%
1995	$25.50	13.3%	$1.90	8.4%	21.7%
1996	$30.38	19.1%	$2.00	7.8%	26.9%

Cousins Properties Inc.
2500 Windy Ridge Parkway, Suite 1600
Atlanta, GA 30339-5683
(770) 955-2200

Exchange: New York (CUZ)
Initial Public Offering: 1962
Geographical Focus: Southeast
Competitive Strategies: Strong new property development capabili-
ties; acquisition and development of raw land into either retail

properties or office buildings; highly focused geographically in major markets in the Southeast.

Special Notes: A public company since 1962, Cousins elected REIT status in 1987. From 1962 through 1996, produced a total stock return averaging better than 20 percent per year; a $10,000 investment in Cousins in 1977 would have been worth over $1.2 million in March 1996. Many of the company's investments are made through joint ventures with other real estate investors or with the major tenant of developed properties. Joint venture partners have included Coca-Cola, IBM, and NationsBank.

Investment Performance:

	Close	Gain/Loss	Dividend	% Yield	Annual Return
1991	$11.88	18.8%	$0.60	6.0%	24.8%
1992	$14.50	22.0%	$0.62	5.2%	27.2%
1993	$16.50	13.8%	$0.73	5.0%	18.8%
1994	$17.38	5.3%	$0.90	5.5%	10.8%
1995	$20.25	16.5%	$0.99	5.7%	22.2%
1996	$28.13	38.9%	$1.12	5.5%	44.4%

Duke Realty Investments, Inc.
8888 Keystone Crossing, Suite 1200
Indianapolis, IN 46240
(317) 846-4700

Exchange: New York (DRE)
Initial Public Offering: October, 1993
Initial Offering Price: $23.75
Geographical Focus: Midwest
Competitive Strategies: Focused geographically, but diversified by asset type with investments in office buildings, industrial facilities, and retail properties; new property development capability.
Special Notes: Successor to an organization formed in 1985. In late 1995, formed a 50/50 joint venture with an institutional investor under which the company contributed 19 existing properties, two properties under development, and 13 acres of undeveloped land and the institution contributed cash equal to the value of the company's investment. The venture then acquired an additional 25

properties, bringing the overall joint venture portfolio to 46 industrial properties.
Investment Performance:

	Close	Gain/Loss	Dividend	% Yield	Annual Return
1993	$22.25	—	$1.68	—	—
1994	$28.25	27.0%	$1.84	8.3%	35.3%
1995	$31.38	11.1%	$1.92	6.8%	17.9%
1996	$38.50	22.7%	$2.00	6.4%	29.7%

EastGroup Properties
300 One Jackson Place
188 East Capitol Street
Jackson, MS 39201-2195
(601) 354-3555
(http://www.eastgroup.net)

Exchange: New York (EGP)
Initial Public Offering: December 1969
Geographical Focus: South
Competitive Strategies: Diversified property holdings in industrial, retail, and multifamily.
Special Notes: The trust is the largest of six real estate companies comprising the Eastover Group. In 1995, it merged with LNH REIT, Inc. (NYSE-LHC) and in 1996, acquired Copley Properties, a Boston-based REIT, that owned a portfolio of industrial and office properties in Florida, Arizona, California, and Maryland.
Investment Performance:

	Close	Gain/Loss	Dividend	% Yield	Annual Return
1991	$ 8.67	6.1%	$1.01	12.4%	18.5%
1992	$11.33	30.8%	$1.01	11.7%	42.5%
1993	$13.83	22.1%	$1.03	9.1%	31.2%
1994	$12.09	(12.6)%	$1.06	8.4%	(4.2)%
1995	$14.25	17.9%	$1.23	10.1%	28.0%
1996	$18.25	28.1%	$1.28	9.2%	37.3%

2 for 1 stock split in March 1997

First Union Real Estate Investments
55 Public Square, Suite 1900
Cleveland, OH 44113
(216) 781-4030

Exchange: New York (FUR)
Initial Public Offering: 1961
Geographical Focus: Northwest, Midwest, and Southeast
Competitive Strategies: Use its paired share REIT status to acquire and actively manage parking facilities; focuses its other investments in retail and apartment properties in the Pacific Northwest, the upper Midwest, and the Southeast; upgrade the appearance and size of its retail facilities to make them more competitive within their respective markets; uses internally generated profits to fund capital improvements and acquisitions (payout ratio is less than 50 percent, one of the lowest in the industry).
Special Notes: One of the original REITs formed in the industry. Through 1993, the trust invested in a diversified portfolio of real estate, including equity and mortgage investments. Since that time, it has adopted a strategy to focus on equity investments in the retail and multifamily property sectors.
Investment Performance:

	Close	Gain/Loss	Dividend	% Yield	Annual Return
1991	$ 7.00	5.1%	$0.93	14.0%	8.9%
1992	$ 9.13	30.4%	$0.72	10.3%	40.7%
1993	$ 9.63	5.5%	$0.72	7.9%	13.4%
1994	$ 6.63	(31.2)%	$0.40	4.2%	(27.0)%
1994	$ 7.00	5.7%	$0.41	6.2%	11.9%
1996	$12.50	78.6%	$0.44	6.3%	84.9%

Glenborough Realty Trust
400 South El Camino Real, Suite 1100
San Mateo, CA 94402-1708
(415) 343-9300

Exchange: New York (GLB)
Conversion Date: December 31, 1995
Opening Trading Price: $12.00

Geographical Focus: National

Competitive Strategies: Primary goal is to advantageously acquire entire portfolios of real estate owned by existing limited partnerships managed by others and by purchasing the General Partner interests in limited partnerships.

Special Notes: Formed at the end of 1995 through the merger of eight limited partnerships and the Glenborough Corporation. In its first year of existence as a REIT, Glenborough's total market capitalization increased from $110 million to more than $250 million.

	Close	Gain/Loss	Dividend	% Yield	Return
1996	$17.63	46.9%	$0.90	7.5%	54.4%

MGI Properties
One Winthrop Square
Boston, MA 02110
(617) 422-6000

Exchange: New York (MGI)

Initial Public Offering: 1971

Geographical Focus: National

Competitive Strategies: Shifts its investment focus by region and property type based upon buying opportunities; targets properties in the $2 million to $10 million range—a marketplace not usually visited by institutional buyers. The acquired properties are usually substantially occupied at rent levels that are below current market rates, enabling the company to realize a significant increase in cash flow as leases are renewed.

Special Notes: In existence as a REIT since 1971, making it one of approximately 20 REITs that have been around for more than two decades. Initially the trust was called Mortgage Growth Investors and engaged in mortgage lending activities. It now focuses on equity investments. As is the case for many of the older REITs, MGI has maintained a portfolio that is diversified by both property type as well as location.

Investment Performance:

	Close	Gain/Loss	Dividend	% Yield	Annual Return
1991	$11.50	56.0%	$0.80	10.9%	66.9%
1992	$11.38	(1.0)%	$0.80	7.0%	6.0%
1993	$13.63	19.8%	$0.81	7.1%	26.9%
1994	$14.00	2.7%	$0.86	6.3%	9.0%
1995	$16.75	19.6%	$0.90	6.4%	26.0%
1996	$22.00	31.3%	$0.98	5.9%	37.2%

Pacific Gulf Properties
363 San Miguel Drive, Suite 100
Newport Beach, CA 92660
(714) 721-2700

Exchange: New York (PAG)
Initial Public Offering: February 18, 1994
Initial Offering Price: $18.25
Geographical Focus: Southern California and the Pacific Northwest
Competitive Strategies: Its apartment communities cater to families, making it one of the few REITs focusing on this segment; their complexes generally contain such amenities as pools, recreation areas and "tot lots" for children; plans to focus much of its future residential property acquisitions in the senior's market due to the attractive demographics of this segment in the company's target markets.
Special Notes: Established as a spin off of Santa Anita Realty Enterprises (NYSE:SAR). Concurrent with its IPO, Pacific Gulf acquired from Santa Anita interests in 10 multifamily residential properties containing 2,654 units and three industrial properties containing 185,000 square feet.
Investment Performance:

	Close	Gain/Loss	Dividend	% Yield	Annual Return
1994	$15.00	—	$1.35	—	—
1995	$16.25	8.3%	$1.57	10.5%	18.8%
1996	$19.50	20.0%	$1.61	10.1%	30.1%

Pennsylvania Real Estate Investment Trust
455 Pennsylvania Avenue, Suite 135
Fort Washington, PA 19034
(215) 542-9250

Exchange: American (PEI)
Initial Public Offering: 1960
Geographical Focus: Mid-Atlantic and Florida
Competitive Strategies: Geographically focused
Special Notes: Founded in 1960, the Trust traditionally acquired joint venture interests in properties that were managed by either the joint venture partner or a third party. In recent years, Penn REIT has started to acquire direct interests in apartment and retail properties and has established management operations to run these properties.
Investment Performance:

	Close	Gain/Loss	Dividend	% Yield	Annual Return
1991	$20.50	35.5%	$1.72	11.4%	46.9%
1992	$24.75	20.7%	$1.29	6.3%	27.0%
1993	$24.13	(10.2)%	$1.78	7.2%	(3.0)%
1994	$18.63	(22.8)%	$1.86	7.7%	(15.1)%
1995	$20.75	11.4%	$1.88	10.1%	21.5%
1996	$24.38	17.5%	$1.88	9.1%	26.6%

Sizeler Property Investors, Inc.
2542 Williams Blvd.
Kenner, LA 70062
(504) 471-6200

Exchange: New York (SIZ)
Initial Public Offering: October 28, 1986
Geographical Focus: South and Southeast
Competitive Strategies: To attain a balanced portfolio of retail and apartment properties.
Investment Performance:

	Close	Gain/Loss	Dividend	% Yield	Annual Return
1991	$11.13	25.4%	$1.00	11.3%	36.7%
1992	$10.75	(3.4)%	$1.01	9.1%	5.7%
1993	$11.25	4.6%	$1.05	9.8%	14.4%
1994	$10.50	(6.7)%	$1.10	9.8%	3.1%
1995	$ 8.88	(15.5)%	$1.12	10.7%	(4.8)%
1996	$ 9.63	8.5%	$0.88	9.9%	18.4%

Washington Real Estate Investment Trust
10400 Connecticut Avenue
Kensington, MD 20895
(301) 929-5900

Exchange: American (WRE)
Initial Public Offering: 1960
Geographical Focus: Washington D.C./Baltimore corridor
Competitive Strategies: Investments in a diversified portfolio of office buildings, shopping centers, apartment properties, and industrial facilities in a focused market area; maintenance of a conservative balance sheet with little to no debt.
Special Notes: One of the older REITs in the marketplace, having started its operations in 1960. The Trust increased its funds from operations every year from 1967 through 1996. Additionally, through the end of 1996, the company had paid consecutive quarterly dividends for the prior 34 years and had increased its annual dividend every year since 1970.
Investment Performance:

	Close	Gain/Loss	Dividend	% Yield	Annual Return
1991	$17.67	58.2%	$0.79	7.1%	65.3%
1992	$20.13	13.9%	$0.84	4.8%	18.7%
1993	$20.50	1.9%	$0.89	4.4%	6.3%
1994	$16.13	(24.4)%	$0.92	5.7%	(18.7)%
1995	$15.88	(1.6)%	$1.00	6.2%	4.6%
1996	$17.50	10.2%	$1.04	6.6%	16.8%

CHAPTER SIXTEEN

The Price
Is Right

HOW DO YOU KNOW whether a REIT is a bargain, or whether it is overpriced? The main criteria analysts use in evaluating REITs are their current dividend yield, their dividend coverage, the quality of their balance sheet, their anticipated earnings growth, and the quality of their management.

In the financial marketplace, REITs compete with other income alternatives, such as money market funds, Treasury securities, corporate bonds, and utility stocks. The price an investor is willing to pay for a given REIT share will be largely influenced by the yields of those income alternatives.

Since the mid-1960s, REIT dividend yields have closely tracked yields for ten-year Treasury securities as shown in Exhibit 16-1.

The close parallel between interest rates and REIT dividend yields is not surprising. REITs benefit when interest rates decline because such an event makes their high dividends more appealing to investors. This results in increased demand for REIT stocks, and higher prices.

Declining interest rates in the early 1990s, in fact, were an important reason why so many real estate companies went public in 1993 and 1994. At the time, low interest rates made the yields of most income alternatives look anemic. As a result, the new REITs, with their 7 to 9 percent dividend yields, were welcomed by income-oriented investors.

Just as declining rates have a positive impact on REIT share

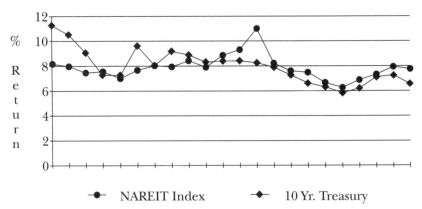

Exhibit 16-1 Ten-Year T-Note versus NAREIT Division Yield (1985–1975) SOURCE: National Association of Real Estate Investment Trusts

prices, increasing rates can have the opposite effect. Although REIT stock prices usually decline in a marketplace where interest rates are on the rise, they tend to suffer less than the overall stock market. This is because of three factors: their high dividend yields, the fact that they are able to increase their dividends by raising rents at the properties they own, and because real estate values tend to increase more during an inflationary period due to the higher costs of building new properties.

Another related factor that analysts look at when evaluating REITs is their dividend coverage, or as it is more commonly referred to in the industry, their payout ratio. Before we discuss payout ratios, however, it is important to review how REITs measure their profitability because it is different from the measure used by most companies due to one factor, depreciation.

It is standard practice in business that when a company acquires property that will be available for use for a number of years, called a capital asset, it depreciates or expenses that asset over its anticipated life. For example, if a telephone company acquires trucks for its installers to drive on the job, it depreciates the cost of these trucks over their expected lives; perhaps five years. (The depreciation schedule a corporation uses for reporting its profits and losses to shareholders is often different than the depreciation schedule it uses for reporting its taxable income or loss to the government. This is the difference between financial and tax accounting.)

When a REIT acquires an apartment property for its portfolio, it also depreciates the cost of the apartment community's buildings (the value of the land cannot be depreciated because land is not deemed to have a limited useful life like a building). Many REITs use a 40 year depreciable life. Therefore, if the value of its buildings total $4 million, a REIT would deduct $100,000 a year from its income to arrive at its net income.

For most companies, net income is the measure of their profitability. This is not true for REITs because the main asset of a REIT, real estate, does not necessarily diminish in value like a telephone company repair truck, but rather rises or falls with market conditions. To account for this fact, the REIT industry has developed a new term to explain the profitability of its companies: funds from operations (FFO). Funds from operations is basically a REIT's net income, excluding gains or losses from the sale of property or debt restructuring, plus depreciation deductions taken on its real estate holdings. Exhibit 16-2 gives an example of this.

When a REIT reports its FFO, it is simply reporting its earnings.

There are other terms that are also used within the industry to explain a REIT's profits. One of these terms is funds available for distribution, or FAD.

Funds available for distribution (FAD) is FFO less certain other expenses, primarily capital improvements. There has been an ongoing debate in the REIT industry about what improvements should be ex-

Revenues	$60,000,000
Expenses	
Property	$12,000,000
G&A Exp.	$ 4,000,000
Interest	$18,000,000
Depreciation	$10,000,000
Amortization	$ 600,000
Total Expenses	$44,600,000
Net Income	$15,400,000
Net Income	$15,400,000
Plus: Depreciation	$10,000,000
Funds from Operations	$25,400,000

Exhibit 16-2   Funds from Operations

241

pensed (i.e., deducted from the REIT's income in the year in which they are incurred) and which ones should be depreciated. Some companies expense items such as new carpeting, appliances, and interior painting, while other REITs depreciate these improvements. Since depreciation deductions are added back to net income to arrive at FFO, by depreciating such expenditures a REIT can improve its FFO results. However, these expenditures are actual cash outlays and therefore reduce the amount of funds that are available for distribution. Therefore, a number of REITs report their funds available for distribution as well as their funds from operations.[1]

The percentage of profits, or funds from operations, a REIT pays out to its shareholders is its payout ratio. As you may recall, one of the requirements a REIT must meet in order to qualify for favored tax treatment is it must distribute 95 percent of its taxable income.

A REIT's taxable income is different from its FFO. (It will also differ from its net income due to timing differences in the recognition of certain income and expense items). While REITs must distribute at least 95 percent of their taxable income, they generally distribute a much lower percentage of their FFO.

In Exhibit 16-3, the 95 percent taxable payout requirement would yield an FFO payout ratio of 60 percent. However, because REITs are generally viewed as income-oriented investments, most REITs have payout ratios that far exceed the 95 percent taxable income payout requirement. In fact, in the industry, the average FFO payout ratio is around 80 percent. However, it can be much less. Some REITs actually pay out less than 50 percent of their earnings.

As an investor, you should be leery of those REITs that have payout ratios in excess of 100 percent. This means they are paying out more than what they are earning. Some REITs were guilty of this

Net Income	$15,400,000
Plus: Amortization	$ 600,000
Taxable Income	$16,000,000
	× .95
Minimum Dividends	$15,200,000

$$\frac{\text{Minimum Dividends}}{\text{Funds From Operations}} \frac{\$15,200,000}{\$25,400,000} = \text{Payout Ratio of 60\%}$$

Exhibit 16-3   REIT Minimum Dividends versus FFO

when they first went public because they failed to correctly estimate their expenses as a public company.

Besides its profitability and payout ratio, the quality of a REIT's balance sheet will also impact its stock price. A heavily leveraged REIT with a significant amount of variable rate debt will be considered a higher risk investment than a REIT with a modest amount of fixed, low-rate debt. The amount of debt a REIT maintains on its balance sheet will impact its dividend-paying ability, especially when the interest rate on that debt is subject to change. An increase in market interest rates will, of course, result in a larger percentage of the REIT's cash flow being utilized to pay interest expenses. If the increase in interest expense is significant, it could force the REIT to reduce its dividends.

The earnings growth potential of a REIT is another important consideration in determining whether a given REIT is appropriately priced. Factors that impact a REIT's earnings growth include the type of properties the REIT owns, the location of these properties, its success in increasing the profitability of its existing holdings, the trust's ability to advantageously acquire additional real estate for its portfolio, and the level of new property development in which the REIT is engaged.[2]

Real estate investment trusts usually target properties of a specific quality level, what are known as Class A, Class B, or Class C properties. Class A properties are the premier properties, the type of real estate institutional investors generally want to own. Class B properties are one step below, while Class C properties are generally older properties that are the least competitive in the marketplace. If a market becomes overbuilt or an economic slowdown reduces demand, Class A and Class B properties will fare the best, while Class C properties will suffer the most.

At various times, certain property sectors will be more "in favor" than other sectors. For instance, in 1995 and 1996, the capital markets believed that the office sector was starting to recover from the overbuilding that took place in the 1980s. Excess space was being leased, and vacancy levels were steadily declining. As a result, REITs which invested in office properties recorded a 38.8 percent return in 1995 and a 51.8 percent return in 1996 versus a 15.3 percent and 35.3 percent gain registered by all equity-based REITs those two years.

Because economic conditions can vary substantially from one region to another, the geographical area in which a REIT focuses its operations will also impact the price of a REIT's stock. In the mid-1980s, the downturn in the oil markets negatively impacted major cities in the state of Texas. This was followed by a recession in the Northeast in the late 1980s and by an economic downturn in California in the early 1990s. When these market areas experienced recessions, property values declined. As they recovered from their economic doldrums, so did their real estate values.

The type of properties a REIT owns and the supply/demand outlook in their respective markets will impact the REIT's ability to increase rents. While market conditions are beyond the control of REIT management, there are steps that can still be taken to enhance earnings, including renovating properties, expanding them, or repositioning them in the marketplace to fit a special niche. All of these steps can provide certain properties with a new competitive advantage, which could lead to increased revenues and profits.

The popularity of particular types of real estate within the investment community as well as the location of such properties will impact the ability of REITs to advantageously acquire such assets. In the early 1990s, just about all real estate was out of favor. This is why so many REITs went public, so they could access the capital markets to take advantage of the special buying opportunities that existed at the time.

Advantageously acquiring real estate in the marketplace can enhance a REIT's operating results. For example, if a given REIT is realizing a 9% return from its existing portfolio of properties and it can acquire a property that will yield a 10% return, such an acquisition will be accretive to its funds from operations or, in other words, will enhance its overall profitability. A REIT should only acquire a property if the asset will enhance its profitability, either in the short term or over the long term.

Another measure that impacts a REIT's growth potential is whether it engages in new property development. Real estate investment trusts that undertake a significant amount of new property development will normally have higher growth rates than those REITs that restrict their investment activities to existing properties, at least in a stable real estate marketplace. This is because they are able to reap the profits associated with developing a property.[3]

As with all companies, the reputation of management plays a key role in how the firm is viewed in the capital markets. A management team that has the reputation of being accurate in its earnings forecasts, has issued a clearly defined strategy for the company and is effectively implementing that strategy, will be viewed more favorably than a management team that has been inexact in its forecasts, which is more reactive than pro-active, and that does not appear to have any clearly defined strategy for its company.[4]

Another factor that impacts the pricing of REITs is size. Shares of the largest REITs usually trade at a premium to those of smaller REITs. There are several reasons for this. First, a REIT with a large market capitalization usually accesses the capital markets more frequently for equity and debt capital. Such events require that Wall Street analysts provide their respective opinions on the REIT and the fairness of its stock price. This analyst coverage allows investors to make more informed decisions and ensures that the market value of a REIT more closely reflects the underlying value of its assets and management team.

Larger REITs also attract more attention from institutional investors because the movement of funds by such investors in and out of larger capitalized companies has a small to negligible impact on the stock price. If these same institutions were to invest significant funds in smaller REITs, the purchase or sale of shares could have a material impact on stock price because of demand/supply factors.

Another benefit of being large is that it is generally easier, and less expensive, to borrow money. Lending institutions like companies with lots of assets because there's more protection there for their loans. These lower borrowing costs enable the larger REITs to realize a higher profit margin on their property holdings.

All of these factors are important in properly evaluating a real estate investment trust. But, how do you determine the "right" price to pay?

Initially, you start with the REIT's current earnings (or funds from operations). Then, you evaluate the factors I have outlined above to estimate a projected earnings growth rate for the REIT. You can utilize some of the sources I will outline in Chapter 18 to help you in this regard.

Once you derive an estimated earnings growth rate, you are then in a position to calculate a REIT's "target" price. That target price can be arrived at a number of different ways.

The most popular methods are by capitalizing either a company's dividends or its earnings. The dividend discount model is used to capitalize a company's dividends. Under this method, you estimate a firm's dividends for a number of years and the price its stock can be sold at some point in the future. You then discount these figures to a present value to at arrive an appropriate price.

$$\text{Price} = \frac{D_1}{(1 + k_e)^1} + \frac{D_2}{(1 + k_e)^2} + \frac{D_3}{(1 + k_e)^3} + \frac{P_3}{(1 + k_e)^3}$$

Where: D_1 = Dividend for Year 1
D_2 = Dividend for Year 2
D_3 = Dividend for Year 3
P_3 = Price at the end of Year 3
k_e = The rate of return required by an investor

Let's use the following assumptions to determine the price an investor should be willing to pay for a given REIT's stock.

- The REIT is currently paying a dividend of $2.00 per share.
- It's dividend is projected to increase by 5% per year over the next several years.
- When the investor sells the stock after three years, the market will value it based upon an 8% yield.
- The investor requires a 12% annual rate of return from the investment.

What is the price this investor should be willing to pay for this stock?

$$\text{Price} = \frac{\$2.00}{(1 + .12)^1} + \frac{\$2.10}{(1 + .12)^2} + \frac{\$2.20}{(1 + .12)^3} + \frac{\$27.50}{(1 + .12)^3}$$

$$= \$1.79 + \$1.67 + \$1.57 + \$19.57$$

$$= \$24.60$$

If we were to change the assumed dividend growth rate from 5% per year to 10% per year, the price would change accordingly:

$$\text{Price} = \frac{\$2.00}{(1 + .12)^1} + \frac{\$2.20}{(1 + .12)^2} + \frac{\$2.42}{(1 + .12)^3} + \frac{\$30.25}{(1 + .12)^3}$$

$$= \$1.79 + \$1.75 + \$1.72 + \$21.53$$

$$= \$26.79$$

The second method which can be utilized to determine the right price to pay for a particular REIT's stock is to capitalize earnings. To accomplish this, you multiply a REIT's funds from operations (FFO) by an appropriate earnings multiple. The earnings multiple will be related to the company's estimated earnings growth rate. A high projected earnings growth rate will translate into a high earnings multiple and stock price.

Unfortunately, there is no specific formula which is available to arrive at this multiple. Most REIT industry analysts derive a number by comparing a given REIT's FFO multiple (which is based upon its current trading price and its expected earnings per share over the following 12 months) with the FFO multiple of comparable REITs. Other comparable REITs would be trusts that invest in similar types of properties as the subject REIT.

For instance, if a particular REIT was projected to record earnings of $2.50 per share over the next 12 months and it's stock is currently priced at $25.00 per share in the marketplace, its FFO multiple would be 10.

The REIT analyst will then compare this FFO multiple with comparable real estate investment trusts based upon the factors I've previously discussed—their current dividend yields, payout ratios, anticipated earnings growth, the quality of their respective balance sheet, and the reputation of their management. After reviewing these factors, the analyst may conclude that the REIT's current FFO multiple is too low and will therefore recommend the purchase of such shares. On other occasions, the analyst will conclude that the FFO multiple is appropriate, or that it is too high. These conclusions will lead to different investment recommendations.

Some analysts evaluate REIT shares by estimating the net asset value (NAV) of a REIT's properties and comparing these results to the REIT's price. Under this method, the analysts use market data to determine the fair market value for each of the REIT's properties. They then subtract from this total the REIT's debt to arrive at its NAV. The total NAV is then divided by the number of shares outstanding to arrive at an NAV/share.

Most REITs trade at a premium to their NAV. This is because, as discussed previously, today's REITs are more than just a collection of properties, but rather fully integrated real estate firms. Because of this fact, I regard the NAV approach to be of somewhat limited value in evaluating the appropriate price for a REIT. However, it can be a useful tool in gauging whether a given REIT's shares are overpriced. This would be the case if a REIT's shares were trading at a significant premium to its NAV while its competitors, with similar growth potential and revenue streams, were trading at lower premiums to their net asset values.[5]

CHAPTER SEVENTEEN

The Track Record of the REIT Industry

THE FIRST ISSUE TO address in discussing the track record of REITs is what is relevant? Is it relevant to evaluate the performance of REITs going back to their beginnings in 1960? Or, should one start with 1993 when the new wave of fully integrated REITs started to dominate the industry?

My vote would be for the latter because prior to 1993, the vast majority of REITs were simply portfolios of real estate, whereas today most are operating real estate companies that are actively engaged in managing and increasing the value of their assets. In fairness to those of you who may disagree with this conclusion, I present both the long term measures of performance as well as the more recent numbers.

Unfortunately, in its first 12 years of existence, no organization tracked the performance of the REIT industry. The industry association, the National Association of Real Estate Investment Trusts (NAREIT), started tracking performance in 1972. Based upon NAREIT's calculations, from 1972 through the end of 1996, equity REITs outperformed the Standard & Poor's 500 Index with a compound average annual gain of 13.76 percent versus a 12.54 percent return by the S&P 500.[1] Exhibit 17-1 shows how equity REITs and the S&P 500 Index returns compare over different time periods ending in 1996.

Time Period	Equity REITs	S&P 500
1 Year	35.3%	23.0%
3 Years	17.2%	19.6%
5 Years	16.6%	15.2%
10 Years	9.0%	15.3%
15 Years	12.2%	16.8%
20 Years	13.2%	14.6%

Exhibit 17-1   Average Annual Returns

In comparing NAREIT's Equity REIT Index and the S&P 500, it is interesting to note the similarity in the performance of the two indexes. As Exhibit 17-2 illustrates, the overall direction of returns recorded by REITs during the period 1980 through 1996 did not differ all that much from the Standard & Poor's 500 Index.

Various studies have concluded that there is a low correlation between REIT stock returns and those of the overall stock market.[2] That generally means that when the stock market goes up in value, REIT stocks will not increase in value as much as the overall market and, when the overall market declines in value, REIT stocks will not decline as much.

Nevertheless, Exhibit 17.2 clearly indicates that there is a correla-

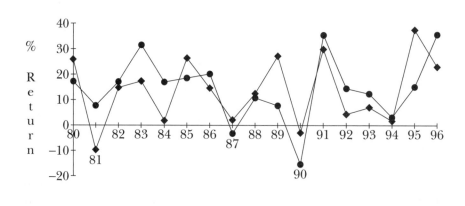

Exhibit 17-2   NAREIT versus S&P 500 Index (1980–1996) SOURCE: National Association of Real Estate Investment Trusts

tion between the direction of REIT stock prices and those of the S&P 500 Index. This observation conflicts with the contention that many have espoused over the years that real estate investments provide significant diversification to a stock portfolio. However, it should be noted that REIT returns have also varied with those of privately-owned real estate portfolios, as measured by the NCREIF Index, an index produced by the National Council of Real Estate Investment Fiduciaries (NCREIF). This index, which is based on property appraisals, has been a standard for the real estate industry for years.

As noted in Exhibit 17-3, real estate returns recorded by the NCREIF Index have varied from and have generally been more stable than those recorded by REITs over the 1980 through 1996 time period. This can be attributed to a number of factors:

- The stock market anticipates events such as a real estate market recovery or recession. Stock prices will generally rise before a recovery takes hold and decline before a recession occurs. The NCREIF Index, meanwhile, is based on appraisals, which are retrospective in nature. They examine prices received for real estate previously sold in the marketplace to determine the value of a property being appraised. Because

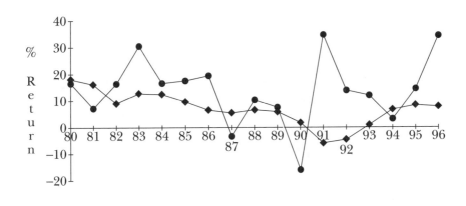

Exhibit 17-3 NAREIT versus NCREIF Index (1980–1996) SOURCES: National Association of Real Estate Investment Trusts and the National Council of Real Estate Investment Fiduciaries

the number of properties that are usually sold declines during a real estate recession, such appraisals may be based upon outdated information.

• The capital markets can run hot and cold on different investment sectors. One year high technology stocks are Wall Street's favorite, the next year Blue Chip stocks, and the third year, real estate stocks. It would be expected that investments that trade on the stock exchanges would be subject to greater volatility. Private real estate companies, which have traditionally relied on the NCREIF Index to gauge market conditions, are long-term players in the business and do not abandon the industry when market conditions decline for a period of time.

Despite the difficult time the real estate industry experienced in the early 1990s, REIT returns in this decade have compared favorably to those recorded by the S&P 500 as shown in Exhibit 17-4.

From the beginning of 1993, when fully integrated equity REITs started to dominate the REIT industry, through year-end 1996, equity REITs realized a compound annual return of 17.8 percent versus a 17.1 percent return for the S&P 500. These returns are the average for all equity REITs trading in the marketplace. The returns for individual REIT sectors have varied significantly from these averages. For instance, in 1995, factory outlet center REITs recorded an overall loss of 2.8 percent, while office REITs gained almost 39

Year	Equity REITs	S&P 500 Index
1990	(15.4)%	(3.3)%
1991	35.7%	30.4%
1992	14.6%	7.7%
1993	19.7%	10.0%
1994	3.2%	1.3%
1995	15.3%	37.5%
1996	35.3%	23.0%
Avg. Compound Annual Return	14.2%	14.4%

Exhibit 17-4 Equity REIT and S&P 500 Annual Returns (1990–1996)

percent. In 1996, factory outlets came in last again with a 3.5 percent return compared to a 51.8 percent gain realized by office REITs. This is shown in Exhibit 17-5.

The difference in returns registered by the various REIT sectors is the result of the market's perception of the respective sectors, the current profitability of REITs within these sectors, and their future earnings prospects.

In 1995, lackluster retail sales hurt most of the retail-oriented REITs. REITs that were especially hard hit in this sector were those that had a large number of properties leased to Kmart, which was teetering on the verge of bankruptcy at the time. A healthier retail environment in 1996, combined with Kmart's improved operating results, helped the retail sector of the REIT industry post some impressive gains in 1996.

Equity REIT Sector	1995 Results	1996 Results
Residential		
Apartments	12.3%	28.4%
Manufactured Housing	10.7%	34.9%
Retail		
Regional Malls	3.0%	44.6%
Strip Centers	7.4%	33.9%
Outlet Centers	(2.8)%	3.5%
Industrial/Office		
Industrial	16.2%	37.0%
Office	38.8%	51.8%
Mixed	—	40.8%
Self-Storage	34.4%	42.0%
Health Care	24.9%	19.9%
Specialty		
Triple Net Lease	31.6%	30.8%
Hotel	30.8%	49.2%
Diversified	21.2%	32.8%
Avg. Equity REIT Return	15.3%	35.3%
Avg. Mortgage REIT Return	110.8%	52.0%

Exhibit 17-5 Equity REIT Sector Returns:1995 and 1996 SOURCE: NAREIT

Real estate investment trusts focusing on office buildings and hotel properties did well both years because REITs in these sectors were aggressively buying assets for less than replacement value in a marketplace where property rents were increasing at an impressive rate.

Mortgage REITs, of course, had the most impressive gains in 1995 and 1996. This was after a disastrous 1994, when a number of them lost more than 50 percent of their respective values due to rising interest rates. In 1995 and 1996, these trusts were the beneficiaries of declining and moderating interest rates.

CHAPTER EIGHTEEN

Finding the
Right REIT
for You

BEFORE YOU INVEST IN any REITs, it is important that you remember the importance of sticking to the basics. This means that you should not be overly concerned with the recent track of the individual REIT sectors or, for that matter, with the results recorded by individual REITs. True, the stock performance is important in evaluating any public company, but just because a company's stock may have posted a 40 percent annual return each of the last two years does not mean it will do so again next year.

As discussed in an earlier chapter, real estate goes through cycles. Some years REITs will do very well, some years they will record "average" results, and other years they will perform poorly. Most analysts project that REITs should provide investors with a 10 to 15 percent annualized return through the end of the decade.[1] This was also what many of them projected for 1996 when equity REITs posted a 35.3 percent overall gain.

Just because these analysts missed the mark with their 1996 forecast does not mean you should ignore their projections for the future. In fact, what it really means is that 1996 was an unusually good year for the REIT industry. Level interest rates, concern about an over-inflated stock market, and an investor shift away from an increasingly uncertain utility sector,[2] were some of the primary causes of the REIT industry's stellar performance in 1996.

In your decision making process, you need to follow a disciplined approach of determining your investment objectives and risk tolerance and matching those results with the appropriate REIT or REITs.

The initial step is to determine your goals. Are you seeking a high level of current income, significant appreciation potential, or a combination of income and growth? How much risk are you willing to assume? Do you want a stock that will be a fairly predictable performer, or one that is "out of favor" and primed for a comeback? All of these factors will play a role in the REIT sectors you choose to invest in and the specific REITs you select in those sectors.

A look at the dividend yields of the various equity REIT sectors and mortgage REITs (Exhibit 18-1) will help you, as an investor, distinguish between sectors that are more income-oriented and those which are more growth-oriented.

Equity REIT Sector	1996 Year-end Dividend Yield
Residential	
Apartment	6.4%
Manufactured Housing	5.5%
Retail	
Regional Malls	6.6%
Strip Centers	6.5%
Outlet Centers	9.3%
Industrial/Office	
Industrial	5.2%
Office	5.1%
Mixed	5.4%
Self Storage	4.6%
Health Care	7.2%
Specialty	
Triple Net Lease	7.3%
Hotel	5.9%
Diversified	6.1%
Avg. Equity REIT Dividend Yield	6.1%
Avg. Mortgage REIT Dividend Yield	8.3%

Exhibit 18-1 Equity REIT Sector 1996 Year-end Dividend Yields
SOURCE: National Association of Real Estate Investment Trusts

The triple net lease and health care sectors had two of the highest dividend yields at the end of 1996. As I outlined in the chapter on net lease investments, these REITs can be expected to provide stable dividends along with modest earnings growth primarily through CPI-mandated rent increases. Most of the direct health care investments are also net leases, with the remainder being mortgage investments.

Mortgage REITs, of course, had an even higher dividend yield. This should be expected based on my discussion of such REITs as income-oriented vehicles. Investors seeking a high level of income should recall the risks of mortgage investments before investing in these REITs. An increase in interest rates can have a significant impact on the price of mortgage REIT stocks.

The average yields of regional mall, strip center, and apartment REITs all fell within a narrow range of 6.4 percent to 6.6 percent at the end of 1996. They are good targets for growth and income-oriented investors because of their above average REIT yields and their prospects for steady growth; however, within these sectors, there are companies that are more development-oriented (which makes them more suitable investments for growth-oriented investors) and companies that restrict themselves to buying only existing properties (which are better for the growth and income investor).

Although their dividend yields were lower at the end of 1996, three other REIT sectors that I would also include in the "growth and income" category are: manufactured housing, industrial, and self storage.

Manufactured housing is comparable to apartments. This sector had a lower dividend yield at the end of 1996 primarily because the few REITs in this segment of the industry all have successful operating histories, resulting in higher stock multiples and lower dividend yields; and there is less concern about overdevelopment.

Industrial REITs have been very popular investments over the last few years because of the perceived safety of these investments. This has driven up their stock values. Another factor that has reduced the dividend yield of industrial REITs is that most of them are fairly active in the development of new properties. This ties up some of their capital in properties that are not producing any current income.

The 1996 year-end self-storage sector dividend yield was somewhat misleading in that the low payout ratios of the Public Storage REITs distorted the dividend yield of the sector. Other REITs in the self storage segment had dividend yields in excess of 6 percent.

Two of the remaining sectors, office and hotels, are investments which have been very appealing to growth-oriented investors in recent years. This is because REITs focused in these sectors have generally been able to acquire properties for prices well below their replacement values.

The lower than average dividend yield of office REITs has generally been due to the below market lease rates that were still in effect at many of their properties. As the office markets stabilize further, look for office REITs to become more growth and income oriented investments.

Hotel REIT yields were below average largely because many of the companies in this industry segment were spending their cash to renovate and reposition their newly acquired assets. As acquisition opportunities become less attractive, look for hotel REITs to engage in more new property development. This will likely mean that their dividend yields will remain on the low end of the REIT spectrum and that they will continue to be more appealing to growth-oriented investors who understand and appreciate the cyclical nature of this segment.

Factory outlet center REITs had the highest 1996 year-end dividend yields due to the fact that they were generally out of favor. One factory outlet REIT in particular, FAC Realty, was especially out of favor as evidenced by its year-end 15.1 percent dividend yield. This was largely because of the fact that its stock declined in value by almost 50 percent in 1996 due to operational problems and a cut in its dividend. The factory outlet sector, therefore, is one that contrarian investors might want to look at.

When evaluating individual REITs, you should give preference to equity REITs that have some or all of the following characteristics:

Self-administered—The REIT administers all of the operations associated with running a company, including: asset management, financial affairs, investors relations, etc.

Self-managed—The REIT manages its own properties as opposed to contracting out such services to other property management companies.

Fully integrated—The Trust handles all real estate services: acquisition of properties, management, construction and re-construction, and property sales.

High quality assets—Assets that will fare well in both a solid real estate market as well as "soft" markets.

Geographic and asset focus—These are some of the key differences between the REITs of the 1990s and those of years past. Today's REITs are usually specialists; focusing on the ownership of one particular type of property in a given region of the country.

I should note that some of the larger—and more successful—REITs in the industry are not geographically focused, while other REITs have no focus either geographically or by asset type. The non-geographically focused companies generally maintain regional office operations, however, which enable them to gain a better insight into market conditions in specific areas of the country. REITs that are not focused by asset type are usually focused geographically. Therefore, they become experts in the dynamics of the markets in which they invest.

Those REITs which are not focused either geographically or by asset type—such a New Plan Realty—are substantial in size and have enough holdings in specific asset types to qualify them as major industry players in those segments. Therefore, within their ranks, these firms have the necessary experience and skill to acquire and manage assets in each category in which they have investments.

Successful track record with experienced management—The real estate industry has traditionally been very cyclical; therefore, investors like to place their money with people who have been through several cycles and who have not only lived to tell about their experiences but who have also won stars and stripes as a result of the job they did during the down cycles.

High insider ownership—Many of today's REITs were formerly privately held real estate companies owned primarily by the firm's senior management. In the majority of cases, the managers retained their ownership interests when these companies went public.

Payout ratio of around 80 percent—A payout ratio of approximately 80 percent generally provides a REIT with sufficient funds to cover its capital expenditure needs and to invest some of its profits in new property investments. It normally also results in a dividend payment which is sufficiently competitive to appeal to most income conscious investors. If a REIT's payout ratio is much higher, there is obviously a greater risk that its dividend will be reduced if the trust experiences setbacks (i.e., declining revenue from lower occupancy levels, higher capital expenditures, higher interest expenses, etc.)

The exception to the 80% rule would include net lease and health care REITs, since they do not pay for the operational costs of their properties; and mortgage REITs, since they do not have any depreciation deductions (therefore, their taxable income is approximately equal to their funds from operations.)

Within the industry, there has been an overall trend toward reducing payout ratios. REITs have generally accomplished this by increasing their dividend payments at a lower rate than their growth in earnings. Therefore, a REIT whose earnings increased by 10% in a given year, might increase its dividend payment by only 7%. By reserving more of its profits, a REIT not only provides itself with a cheaper source of capital (since it does not have to go to the capital markets to raise these funds), it provides itself with a greater cushion in the event it experiences operational setbacks.

Modest level of low interest rate, fixed debt—The REITs of the 1990s generally carry less debt than REITs that existed in the 1970s and 1980s. This is primarily due to the fact that the capital markets are more cautious about the use of leverage after the real estate downturn of the late 1980s and early 1990s. In a low interest rate environment, however, the use of some debt is prudent, especially when a REIT can purchase properties that have cash-on-cash yield that exceeds the REIT's cost of debt.

Steady earnings and dividend growth—Ideally, a REIT should have a history of generating increasing profits as well as dividends. Those results, of course, will be impacted by market conditions. When real estate went through its downturn at the end of the 1980s and the early part of the 1990s, few markets were spared. Therefore, most real estate companies experienced declining revenues during this period.

Successful stock performance—Evaluating the historical stock performance of today's REITs can be difficult because of the fact that most have such short operating histories as public companies. As time goes on, however, a comparison of the stock performance of individual REITs with other trusts in their industry segments will become more and more meaningful, especially after we have gone through a full real estate cycle.

Another way of narrowing your choices is to identify REITs that are located in your marketplace or that invest in the area where you live. This approach has a number of advantages.

First, because you live in the market area, you will be better equipped to assess the investments made by the REIT in your city. You may be able to visit these properties to evaluate their locational advantages and disadvantages, physical appearance, and competitive position.

Secondly, you will have an understanding of the marketplace in terms of the business climate. Is the local economy expanding or contracting? If the REIT is located in your city, it will also be easier for you to attend the company's annual meeting. At this gathering, you will have an opportunity to hear first-hand a report of the REIT's operating results for the previous year and its plans for the following year. Additionally, you will have the opportunity to ask questions of the REIT's senior management team and visit with company's staff members.

CHAPTER NINETEEN

Making the Investment

IF YOU ARE CONSIDERING an investment in one or more real estate investment trusts, there are several avenues you can pursue. One option is to invest through a securities broker or investment advisor. If you select this option, you would be well advised to go through a brokerage firm that conducts research on the REIT industry. Many of the major companies do so, including: Merrill Lynch, Paine Webber, Prudential Securities, and Dean Witter. Regional firms which follow the industry include: Alex Brown & Sons, J.C. Bradford, A.G. Edwards, and The Robinson-Humphrey Company.

Brokers employed by these firms have access to research reports on various REITs. These reports are prepared by company analysts who specialize in the industry. These individuals not only dissect financial information released by the various trusts, but they have regular discussions with the senior management of the firms they track. These relationships provide the analysts with a first-hand opportunity to evaluate the competence and credibility of the management.

Other financial advisors who are not affiliated with these brokerage firms may also have the requisite expertise and knowledge to recommend REIT investments. They may subscribe to reports issued by independent research firms and they may also do their own industry analysis.

A second option you can pursue as an investor is to conduct your own analysis and invest through a discount broker. There are a number of sources of information you can access to evaluate individual REITs.

My first suggestion is that you stay abreast of real estate market conditions and the outlook for the various sectors. You can do this by reading the business news on a consistent basis. *The Wall Street Journal, Business Week, Fortune, Forbes, Financial World,* and *Investor's Business Daily* are some of the publications that have articles on real estate and REITs in particular. Some of these publications have an annual issue covering the investment marketplace. In this issue, there is usually an article on real estate investments.

Barron's has a fairly regular article on REITs. It provides some valuable and insightful information on topics of current interest in the REIT industry, including which sectors are "in favor" or "out of favor" and which REITs are garnering attention within the investment community.

The Wall Street Journal has a weekly article on the REIT industry covering a range of topics including initial and secondary stock offerings, performance results, and merger and acquisition activity.

Real Estate Review, a quarterly publication published by Warren Gorham Lamont, contains some excellent articles on the real estate industry as well as on REITs. These articles are written by real estate practitioners and academicians specializing in real estate.

An annual report that I have found to be informative in analyzing real estate conditions throughout the country and in the various segments of the industry is *Emerging Trends in Real Estate* published jointly by the Real Estate Research Corporation (RERC) and Equitable Real Estate Investment Management. The *Emerging Trends* report reviews current investment trends in the real estate industry, the sources of investment capital, the market conditions in various major metropolitan areas, and prospects for the various asset classes.

RESEARCH INFORMATION

In evaluating individual REITs, you should seek to obtain current financial and performance information on any REITs you are considering for investment. There are several organizations that publish information that will be of value to you at this stage: *Value Line and Standard & Poor's.*

Value Line has the most analytical reports. It provides a solid overview of the REIT marketplace. Its reports are also valuable reading in gaining a better understanding of some of the key issues that analysts evaluate in reviewing REITs. The drawback is that *Value Line* only reports on approximately 15 REITs.

Standard & Poor's has the most comprehensive coverage of REIT stocks. It divides its reports into three sets of volumes, one covering the New York Exchange, a second reviewing American Stock Exchange stocks, and a third set covering a large number of over-the-counter stocks.

The *Standard & Poor's* reports are factual in nature. They provide a summary of the REITs, their investment portfolios as of the last fiscal year-end, and information on major announcements made by the REITs during the course of the year. They also provide pertinent financial information on the REITs' capitalization, balance sheet data, income statement results, and ratio analyses.

Value Line and *Standard & Poor's* also provide valuable information on the performance of individual REITs. They do this through graphs that chart the price per share over a specified time frame. Both *Value line* and *Standard & Poor's* can be found in most major libraries.

Another source of quality information is the National Association of Real Estate Investment Trusts (NAREIT). NAREIT has a web site (http://www.nareit.com) that has information on the overall industry. It has a listing of performance data that is available from its fax service, and it also has connections to the web sites of most of the REITs that have their own individual web sites. (Unfortunately, at the end of 1996, there were a relatively small percentage of REITs that had web sites).

REAL ESTATE INVESTMENT TRUST REPORTS

After you have had a chance to review some of the publicly available information on REITs and have narrowed down your choices, you should then obtain information directly from the individual REITs. Most trusts have an investor package they will forward to you containing the latest annual report, quarterly reports, and recent press releases. Some will also provide you with copies of analysts' reports on the REIT.

You should also request the company's most recent proxy statement in which the REIT provides shareholders with a comparison of its performance with certain other performance measures, such as the S&P 500 Index and/or the NAREIT Equity Index. This comparison is in the form of a graph, although many REITs also provide a numerical comparison as well. (A few REITs do include this type of graph in their annual reports.)

The annual report should be valuable in helping you to make a decision. In reviewing a host of annual reports for this book, I found a high correlation between the quality of the reports and the quality of the REITs issuing the reports.

An annual report should be more than just a review of a company's operating results for the prior year. It should tell you about the company: what its business is, what the competitive forces are in its industry segment and/or market areas, what its strategy is in competing in the marketplace, and the measures of performance against which it grades its efforts.

The annual report is an opportunity for the management of a publicly owned company to sell itself to existing and prospective shareholders. It should make current shareholders proud to be part-owners of the company and entice interested parties to become stockholders. Unfortunately, there are a number of REITs that either do not understand that concept, understand it but choose not to take advantage of the opportunity, or simply feel as if they have little to sell.

In compiling my research for this book, I came across some insightful comments which were made in the early 1960s by two investment professionals, comments that I believe are still quite applicable today. Richard Swesnik, who was president of the securities firm of Swesnik and Blum noted that:

> Like any other business, the real estate investment trust business must be organized and operated by men who are technically competent and ethically tuned to their responsibilities as organizers and managers. An investor seeking advice may very well weigh his decision 25 percent as to the quality and location of the property and 75 percent as to the men who must select and operate the property. If this formula appears lopsided and needs correction, let us do it now. Make it 10 to 90 percent. In other words, invest in persons, not things . . . things never make money.[1]

The second statement was by Louis Glickman, a long-time real estate investor who became involved in the REIT industry in 1961. He observed that:

> Managing properties for syndications, real estate corporations, and trusts, means servicing a new type of master. That master is the millions of thrifty Americans who have set aside part of their incomes to invest in the skylines of our cities. And I am one who believes that this is a trust. I realized . . . that I was no longer managing properties for my own account, but that I was the guardian of the cherished investment of others.[2]

An annual report can tell you a lot about the management team of a REIT. Do they view themselves as "guardians" of your investment dollars, or do they come across as real estate investors who believe that, by going public, they simply allowed other investors to join in on their success? This is why I believe that annual reports should be more than simply a review of the financial results of the prior year. These reports should provide you with a sense of who you are investing with, the principles that are important to the company's management, their strategic objectives, and how they are attempting to achieve those objectives.

In reviewing hundreds of annual reports for this book, I was amazed at the number of REIT's whose stock had performed poorly during the previous year and who not only failed to address that issue in their reports, but whose reports gave the impression that the REIT had actually experienced nothing but success the prior year. Even the best REITs will have bad years. Some will suffer from overbuilding in their particular markets; some will own properties that will be out-of-favor at a given point in time; and some will experience declining share prices due to no fault of their own (i.e., as a result of higher market interest rates). Real estate investment trusts, and all companies, should be obligated to review their stock performance in their annual reports. This review should include not only the previous year, but a number of years (perhaps five) so that shareholders can gain a perspective on the company's longer term performance results.

In summary, my recommendation is that if you read an annual report on a company and, after reading it, do not have a clear understanding of what the company is all about, don't invest. Chances are that the management team does not have a clear idea of where it is leading the company. What's that old saying—if you don't know where you're headed, any road will do?

MUTUAL FUNDS

If you are not interested in selecting your own portfolio of real estate investment trusts, you can hire a mutual fund manager to do it for you. If you should elect this path, you will not be alone. From the beginning of 1995 through January 1997, assets in real estate-oriented mutual funds rose from $1.55 billion to $7.18 billion.

There are a number of mutual funds that specialize in the REIT industry:

Alliance Real Estate Investment Fund
Alliance Fund Services
P.O. Box 1520
Secaucus, NJ 07096-1520
(800) 221-5672

CGM Realty Fund
CGM Capital Development, Inc.
One International Place
Boston, MA 02110
(800) 345-4048

Cohen and Steers Realty Income Fund
Cohen and Steers Realty Shares
Cohen and Steers Total Return Realty
757 Third Avenue
New York, NY 10017
(212) 437-9912

Columbia Real Estate Equity
1301 S.W. Fifth
P.O. Box 1350
Portland, OR 97207
(800) 547-1707

Crabbe Huson Real Estate Investment Fund
121 Southwest Morrison
Suite 1400
Portland, OR 97204
(800) 541-9732

Davis Real Estate
P.O. Box 1688
Santa Fe, NM 87504-1688
(800) 279-0279

Delaware REIT Portfolio Fund
One Commerce Square
Philadelphia, PA 19103
(800) 231-8002

DFA/AEW Real Estate Securities
1299 Ocean Avenue
11th Floor
Santa Monica, CA 90401
(310) 395-8005

Evergreen Global Real Estate Equity
& Evergreen U.S. Real Estate Equity
2500 Westchester Avenue
Purchase, NY 10577
(800) 807-2940

Fidelity Real Estate Securities Fund
P.O. Box 193
Boston, MA 02101
(800) 544-8888

First American Real Estate Investment Funds
601 Second Avenue South
Minneapolis, MN 55402
(800) 637-2548

Franklin Real Estate
777 Mariners Island Blvd.
San Mateo, CA 94404
(800) 342-5236

Grandview Funds
P.O. Box 164
East Glastonbury, CT 06025-1064
(800)525-3863

Heitman Real Estate Funds
900 N. Michigan Avenue
Chicago, IL 60611
(800)435-1405

INVESCO Realty Fund
P.O. Box 173706
Denver, CO 80217-3706
(800) 610-9337

INVESCO Advisor Real Estate Fund
1315 Peachtree Street NE
Atlanta, GA 30309
(800) 972-9030

Longleaf Realty Fund
6075 Poplar Ave., Ste. 900
Memphis, TN 38119
(800) 445-9469

Morgan Stanley Real Estate Fund
1221 Avenue of the Americas
21st Floor
New York, NY 10020
(800)548-7786

Munder Real Estate Equity Investment Funds
480 Pierce Street
Burmingham, MI 48009
(800)438-5789

Pheonix Real Estate Securities Funds
100 Bright Meadow Blvd.
Enfield, CT 06082
(800) 243-4361

Pioneer Real Estate Group
P.O. Box 9017
Boston, MA 02205
(800) 225-6292

The RREEF Funds
875 North Michigan Avenue
41st Floor
Chicago, IL 60611
(312)266-9300

Templeton Real Estate Securities
700 Central Avenue
St. Petersburg, FL 33701
(800)292-9293

United Services Real Estate
P.O. Box 781234
San Antonio, TX 78278
(800) 873-8637

Van Kampen American Capital Real Estate
P.O. Box 418256
Kansas City, MO 64141-9526
(800) 421-5666

The Vanguard REIT Index Portfolio
P.O. Box 2600
Valley Forge, PA 19482
(800) 662-7447

INFORMATION RESOURCES

Barron's
200 Burnett Road
Chicopee, MA 01020
(800) 277-4136 x426

Business Week
The McGraw Hill Companies
P.O. Box 506
Hightstown, NJ 08520-9470
(800) 635-1200

Emerging Trends in Real Estate
Real Estate Research Corporation
2 North La Salle, Ste. 730
Chicago, IL 60602
(312) 346-5885

Forbes
Forbes Inc.
60 Fifth Avenue
New York, NY 10011

Fortune
P.O. Box 61490
Tampa, FL 33661-1490
(800) 722-2853

National Association of Real Estate Investment Trusts
1129 Twentieth Street, N.W.
Washington, D.C. 20036-3482
(202) 785-8717
(800) 3NAREIT

Real Estate Review
Warren Gorham Lamont
One Penn Plaza
New York, NY 10119
(212) 971-5120

Realty Stock Review
179 Avenue at the Common
Shrewsbury, NJ 07702
(908) 389-8701

Standard & Poor's Stock Reports
25 Broadway
New York, NY 10004

The Value Line Investment Survey
Value Line Publishing, Inc.
220 East 42nd Street
New York, NY 10017-5891
(800) 833-0040

CHAPTER TWENTY

The Future

IT IS ALWAYS DANGEROUS to attempt to predict the future, especially when it involves the real estate industry. This is because the investment appeal of commercial real estate is impacted by a host of variables. Changing tax laws, inflation and interest rate levels, the stock market's performance, and the availability of capital, have influenced the performance of real estate investments in the past and will continue to do so in the future. In the 1990s, these variables have generally had a positive impact on the real estate industry. Tax laws have not encouraged speculative new construction like they did in the early and mid-1980s. Instead, new construction is the result of market demand.

Capital is available to the industry again, but in a more disciplined fashion now. This capital has also been obtainable on relatively favorable terms. Low interest rates have enabled real estate investors to once again buy properties in the marketplace with positive leverage. Low rates have also made it easier for REITs to raise capital because their dividend yields have generally been higher than those of other income alternatives.

The fact that the stock market has done well has not hurt either. Real estate investment trusts that raise their equity capital, and an increasing amount of their debt capital through Wall Street, have been the beneficiaries of the record amounts of money pouring into the stock market from individual investors. The REIT industry's transformation in the 1990s has enabled it to take advantage of these favorable market conditions. It has also enhanced its prospects for future growth and prosperity because it is more diverse and dynamic than at anytime in its history.

275

The REITs of today are not simply just portfolios of real estate like they were in decades past. Instead, the majority are actively managed companies just like General Motors, IBM, and Citibank. Most of the large REITs these days finance part of their operations with unsecured debt, just like other major public companies. In 1996, the REIT industry raised a record $5 billion in unsecured financing.[1]

It was not that many years ago that unsecured financing was unheard of in the industry. After all, REITs invested in assets that were financed with mortgages secured by real estate. Today, however, the capital markets recognize that most REITs make money not only from their real estate portfolios, but from new property development, third party management operations, and real estate advisory services. Additionally, their ability to increase the value of their real estate holdings is enhanced by the fact that the REITs can now manage their own assets as opposed to contracting out these responsibilities to a third party.

While the number of initial REIT offerings has declined significantly since the 1993 and 1994 rush, the industry is still a hotbed of offerings. The only difference is that these offerings are for existing REITs. In 1996, the industry raised a record $17.4 billion in secondary offerings. This means that the existing REITs have convinced the public markets they know what they are doing.[2]

The industry is also gaining increased recognition from institutional investors. The number of mutual funds specializing in real estate investments has jumped from a handful to more than two dozen this decade.

More and more pension funds are investing in REITs as well. In 1995, Aldrich, Eastman & Waltch, a major real estate advisory firm to pension plans, invested $50 million in Bedford Property Investments. In 1996, Stichting Pensioenfonds ABP, a Dutch pension fund, invested $75 million in Equity Residential and $35 million in Gables Residential; the Ohio State Teachers Retirement System entered into a $50 million joint venture with Developers Diversified Realty; and Meridian Industrial Trust was the beneficiary of investments from USAA Real Estate, J.P. Morgan Investment Management, as well as the Ohio State Teachers Retirement System. These are just a few of the institutional investments which have been made in the REIT industry. A lot more are likely to follow.

The largest public pension plan in the country, the California Public Employees Retirement System, has a $5.8 billion real estate portfolio. Recently, it has been exploring ways of reducing its direct investments in real estate and, instead, investing in real estate through REITs.[3] The California State Teachers' Retirement System has been doing the same thing.[4]

These pension plans are not alone in the institutional marketplace.[5] Major insurance companies and other pension funds that invested heavily in real estate in the 1980s, are looking for ways to benefit from improving market conditions here in the 1990s. This time around they would prefer not to invest in the large in-house staffs which are needed to directly acquire and manage such assets. They also would like to have greater liquidity in their real estate portfolios. This makes REITs an ideal alternative.

A number of REITs have been posturing themselves to benefit from this potential inflow of institutional dollars by building up their asset bases and market capitalizations. This is because large institutional investors prefer to invest in major real estate companies. It makes it easier to get their money out, if and when they decide to exit.

There will likely be more mergers and acquisitions in the REIT industry in the future. Most of the mergers and acquisitions to date have been in the multifamily sector. I expect there will be more in the retail sector in future years. There are a lot of smaller REITs in this segment, REITs that have had difficulty raising new capital and growing their operations. These REITs are generally ideal takeover targets.[6]

Don't expect a flurry of mergers and acquisitions, however. Most REITs were previously privately held companies built by the people who are still managing them. They have a lot of pride in the companies they built and are generally reluctant to sell out. They may have less of a reason to sell out if REITs continue to record the kind of results they have this decade. Two of the industry's best annual returns have been posted in the 1990s. In 1991, REITs realized an overall return of 35.7 percent, while in 1996 they recorded a 35.8 percent return. These returns are not the norm, however. In 1991, the markets perceived that the real estate industry would rebound from the overbuilding of the 1980s and bid up REIT stocks accordingly. In 1996, concern about an overvalued stock market led investors to the REIT industry where many individual REITs were undervalued.

I will not venture a guess on the industry's future performance numbers because those variables I mentioned earlier, tax laws, inflation and interest rate levels, the stock market's performance, and the availability of capital, are subject to change. A change in any of these variables can have a significant impact on the performance of REITs in the marketplace. The one thing I can say with confidence is that REITs will continue to be the dominate force within the real estate industry for the foreseeable future. The variety of REITs, their potential investment benefits, and their liquidity, make them very appealing.

One of the biggest risks of investing in REITs in future years is the possibility that they will become overpriced. One of the reasons for this concern is the increasing amount of attention which has been focused on the yields of REITs versus those of other stocks. In 1996, equity REITs had an average yield of just more than 6 percent versus 2 percent for the overall stock market. In comparing these yields, some industry observers forget to note that REITs pay out a significant percentage of their profits in dividends while most other public companies reinvest most of their profits back into their operations. This is why REIT dividend yields are so much higher.

From time to time, some REITs will become overpriced; however, there will still be other REITs that will be good values. In this book, I have provided you with tools to identify these REITs. I hope you will use them to your benefit. The REIT industry's future looks bright, so don't hesitate to join in.

ENDNOTES

Chapter One

1. *Emerging Trends in Real Estate:* 1997, New York: Equitable Real Estate Investment Management, Inc. and Real Estate Research Corporation (RERC) (October 1996).
2. Source: National Association of Real Estate Investment Trusts.
3. *Emerging Trends in Real Estate:* 1992, New York: Equitable Real Estate Investment Management, Inc. and Real Estate Research Corporation (RERC) (October 1991).
4. *Emerging Trends in Real Estate:* 1997, New York: Equitable Real Estate Investment Management, Inc. and Real Estate Research Corporation (RERC) (October 1996).
5. See Mitchell Pacelle, *"Real Estate Empires of Private Developers Face a Harsh New Era,"* Wall Street Journal (August 24, 1993).
6. Jeanne B. Pinder, *"Real Estate Funds Lure Investors,"* New York Times (April 29, 1993).
7. Source: National Association of Real Estate Investment Trusts.
8. Randall Smith and Mitchell Pacelle, *"Investors Rush To REITs in Sizzling New Issues Market,"* Wall Street Journal (August 24, 1993).
9. Mitchell Pacelle, *"Property Tycoon Seeks Wall Street Success,"* Wall Street Journal (January 9, 1997).
10. Randall Smith and Mitchell Pacelle, *"Investors Rush To REITs in Sizzling New Issues Market,"* Wall Street Journal (August 24, 1993).
11. Donald Seligman, *"Personal Investing: The Rise of the REITs. A New Road Into Real Estate,"* Fortune (January 1964).

Chapter Two

1. J. Richard Elliott, Jr., *"More Room at the Top: Real Estate Investment Trusts Have Come to Wall Street and Main Street,"* Barron's National and Business Financial Weekly (February 12, 1962). See also Dana L. Thomas, *"Misplaced Trust? Tight Money, Footloose Expansion Plague the Mortgage Funds,"* Barron's National and Business Financial Weekly (July 7, 1969).
2. J. Richard Elliott, Jr., *"More Room at the Top: Real Estate Investment Trusts Have Come to Wall Street and Main Street,"* Barron's National and Business Financial Weekly (February 12, 1962).

279

Endnotes

3. Morrissey v. Commissioner, 296 U.S. 344 (1935).
4. J. Richard Elliott, Jr., *"Fresh Appraisal: The Rewards and Risks in Real Estate Investment Trusts,"* Barron's National and Business Financial Weekly, vol. 145 (March 15, 1965).
5. Peter A. Schulkin, *"Real Estate Investment Trusts: A New Financial Intermediary,"* New England Economic Review (November/December 1970).
6. Kenneth D. Campbell, *America's Newest Billionaires,* New World Manufacturing Company, Inc., 1971.
7. *REIT Factbook 1978,* Washington, D.C.: National Association of Real Estate Investment Trusts, 1979.
8. *Real Estate Investment Trusts: The Low Risk, High Yield Asset-Growth Opportunity,* New York: New York Institute of Finance, 1988.
9. Ibid.
10. Ibid.
11. *REIT Factbook 1978,* Washington, D.C.: National Association of Real Estate Investment Trusts, 1979.
12. Source: The Stanger Report as reported by Peter Fass *et al.* in *Real Estate Investment Trusts Handbook,* Clark, Boardman, Callaghan, Derrfield, MI, 1996 edition.
13. *Emerging Trends in Real Estate:* 1987, New York: Equitable Real Estate Investment Management, Inc. and Real Estate Research Corporation (RERC) (October 1996).
14. Source: National Association of Real Estate Investment Trusts.
15. Ibid.
16. Philip S. Scherrer, *"The UPREIT: Solving The Tax Problem of Owners of Depreciated Property,"* Real Estate Review (Winter, 1996): Boston, Warren, Gorham & Lamont.
17. Source: National Association of Real Estate Investment Trusts.
18. Barry Vinocur, *"Sam Zell's Offer for Chateau Properties Exposes a Flaw in a Common REIT Structure,"* Barron's (August 26, 1996).
19. *"Why Invest in REITs?" A.G. Edwards Securities Research Report* (August 7, 1996), St. Louis, A.G. Edwards & Sons, Inc.

Chapter Three

1. See Neil Carn *et al., Real Estate Market Analysis: Techniques and Applications.* Prentice Hall, Englewood Cliffs, N.J., 1988.

Chapter Four

1. See Alvin L. Arnold and Daniel E. Feld, *Real Estate Investor's Handbook,* Warren Gorham & Lamont, Boston, 1987.
2. Source: The National Real Estate Index as published in *Real Estate Issues* (August 1996).

Chapter Five

1. Source: National Association of Real Estate Investment Trusts.
2. Neil Templin, *"Apartment Complexes Fall into New Hands, Up Go the Rents,"* Wall Street Journal (March 25, 1997).
3. See Alvin L. Arnold and Daniel E. Feld, *Real Estate Investor's Handbook,* Warren Gorham & Lamont, Boston, 1987.

4. Steve Bergsman, *"Multifamily Offers Unique Opportunities to Investors Looking for Solid Returns,"* National Real Estate Investors (July 1993).
5. Joseph Gyourko and Peter Linneman, *"Comparing Apartment and Office Investments,"* Real Estate Review (Summer 1993): Boston, Warren, Gorham and Lamont.
6. Ibid.
7. *Emerging Trends in Real Estate:* 1996, New York: Equitable Real Estate Investment Management, Inc. and Real Estate Research Corporation (RERC) (October 1997).
8. See *AMLI Residential 1995 Annual Report,* p. 12.
9. Ibid.
10. See Philip S. Scherrer, *"The Consolidation of REITs Through Mergers and Acquisitions,"* Real Estate Review (Spring, 1995): Boston, Warren, Gorham & Lamont. See also Steven E. Goodman and Peter H. Madden, *"Seven REIT Acquisition Targets,"* Real Estate Review (Spring, 1996): Boston, Warren, Gorham and Lamont.
11. Mark O. Decker and Burland B. East, *"The REIT Market: Offering Excellent Investment Opportunities in the Multifamily Sector,"* UNITS, vol. 20, no. 9 (November/December 1996).
12. Jane Adler, *"Apartments Still Investment Darling as REIT Buying Frenzy Continues,"* National Real Estate Investor (June 1994).

Chapter Six

1. Source: U.S. Department of Commerce.
2. See *Eric I. Hemmel and Steve Sakwa, "Manufactured Housing REITs: Strong Long-Term Fundamentals Support an Overweight Position,"* Real Estate Industry Overview (May 26, 1995): Morgan Stanley, New York.
3. Ibid.
4. Ibid.
5. Ibid.

Chapter Seven

1. See Alvin L. Arnold and Daniel E. Feld, *Real Estate Investor's Handbook,* Warren Gorham & Lamont, Boston, 1987. See also *Industry Trends: Specialty Retailers, Superstores as Industry Leaders,* Standard & Poors (May 6, 1996).
2. See Alvin L. Arnold and Daniel E. Feld, *Real Estate Investor's Handbook,* Warren Gorham & Lamont, Boston, 1987.
3. Ibid.
4. *Emerging Trends in Real Estate:* 1997, New York: Equitable Real Estate Investment Management, Inc. and Real Estate Research Corporation (RERC) (October 1996).
5. See *Kimco Realty 1995 Annual Report.*
6. *Industry Surveys: Retailing Outlook,* Standard & Poor's (June 15, 1996).
7. *Industry Surveys: Retailing, Demographic Trends and Consumer Attitudes* (June 15, 1996).
8. See Zina Moukheiber, *"Tempting the Jaded Shopper,"* Forbes (May 20, 1996).
9. See *Mills Corporation 1995 Annual Report.*
10. See *Mills Corporation 1996 Annual Report.*
11. See Marcia Berss, *"Oversupply Opens Opportunities,"* Forbes (April 8, 1996).

12. See *Federal Realty Investment Trust's 1995 Annual Report.*
13. See *New Plan Realty Trust's 1995 Annual Report.*
14. John McMahan, *"The Changing Real Estate Environment," Real Estate Issues* (April 1997).
15. Stephanie Anderson Forest, *"I Can Get It For You Retail," Business Week* (September 18, 1995).
16. Laura Bird, "Discounting Discounter: *Outlet Center Stocks Dip As Customers Go Elsewhere," Wall Street Journal* (April 3, 1997).
17. Ibid.

Chapter Eight

1. Source: National Association of Real Estate Investment Trusts.
2. Michael C. Sobolik and Jeanette I. Rice, *"A Tale of Recovery," Mortgage Banking* (July 1995): Boston, Warren, Gorham & Lamont. See also Neil Barsky, *"Commercial Property Market's Troubles May Deepen," Wall Street Journal* (November 5, 1992).
3. *Emerging Trends in Real Estate:* 1993, New York: Equitable Real Estate Investment Management, Inc. and Real Estate Research Corporation (RERC) (October 1994).
4. *Emerging Trends in Real Estate:* 1987, New York: Equitable Real Estate Investment Management, Inc. and Real Estate Research Corporation (RERC) (October 1988).
5. Source: *Koll National Real Estate Index.* See also Neil Templin, *"Real Estate Brokers See Big Jumps in Office Building Rents," Wall Street Journal* (December 6, 1996).
6. Ann Carns, *"Building Is Down but Boston Rebounds," Wall Street Journal* (November 11, 1996).
7. Ibid.
8. Jonathan R. Lang, *"Downtown Blues, Technological and Social Changes Cast A Cloud Over Urban Office Buildings," Barron's* (March 25, 1996). See also John McMahan CRE, *"The Changing Real Estate Environment," Real Estate Issues* (April 1997).
9. See Neil Carn *et al., Real Estate Market Analysis: Techniques and Applications.* Prentice Hall, Englewood Cliffs, N.J., 1988.
10. Ibid.
11. Ibid.
12. Michael C. Sobolik and Jeanette I. Rice, *"A Tale of Recovery," Mortgage Banking* (July 1995): Boston, Warren, Gorham & Lamont.
13. Bill Saparito, *"Real Estate's Low Rise Future," Fortune* (January 28, 1991).
14. Ann Carns, *"Office Workers Rub Elbows As More Workplaces Shrink," Wall Street Journal* (May 7, 1997).
15. Maggie Mahar, *"Turning Point? At Long Last, Commercial Real Estate Shows Signs of Recovery," Barron's* (October 4, 1993).
16. *Emerging Trends in Real Estate:* 1991, New York: Equitable Real Estate Investment Management, Inc. and Real Estate Research Corporation (RERC) (October 1992).
17. See Alvin L. Arnold and Daniel E. Feld, *Real Estate Investor's Handbook,* Warren Gorham & Lamont, Boston, 1987.
18. Robin M. Grugal, *"Reaping The Rewards of West Coast Recovery," Investor's Business Daily* (August 1, 1996).

Chapter Ten

1. Toddi Gutner, *"Self-storage: A Niche With Room To Grow,"* *Business Week* (April 22, 1996).

Chapter Eleven

1. *Industry Surveys: Healthcare Facilities,* Standard & Poor's (March 3, 1997).
2. *Healthcare Realty Trust 1995 Annual Report.*
3. Source: National Association of Real Estate Investment Trusts.
4. *Industry Surveys: Healthcare Facilities,* Standard & Poor's (March 3, 1997).
5. Ibid.
6. Ibid.
7. Ibid.

Chapter Twelve

1. Source: Smith Ravel Research.
2. Ibid.
3. Ibid.
4. Source: National Association of Real Estate Investment Trusts.
5. Pablo Galarza, *"Natural-Born Deal Maker,"* *Financial World* (August 12, 1996).
6. See Alvin L. Arnold and Daniel E. Feld, *Real Estate Investor's Handbook,* Warren Gorham & Lamont, Boston, 1987.
7. Kallie Jurgens, *"Low Rates and Declining Sales Prices Create Better Investment Climate,"* *National Real Estate Investor* (May 1993).
8. Neil Templin, *"Inside Deals Cloud Hotel Trusts,"* *Wall Street Journal* (May 7, 1997).
9. Patrick J. Corcoran, *"The Outlook for Hospitality Investments,"* *Real Estate Review* (Summer 1996).

Chapter Thirteen

1. Source: National Association of Real Estate Investment Trusts.
2. Alvin L. Arnold and Daniel E. Feld, *Real Estate Investor's Handbook,* Warren Gorham & Lamont, Boston, 1987.
3. Ibid.
4. Ibid.
5. Ibid.

Chapter Fourteen

1. *National Golf Properties 1995 Annual Report.*
2. Ibid.
3. Source: National Golf Foundation.

Chapter Sixteen

1. Neil Templin, *"Heard on the Street: Analysts Scrutinize Tactic Boosting REITs,"* *Wall Street Journal* (January 23, 1997).

Endnotes

2. See Philip S. Scherrer and Timothy Mathison, *"Investment Strategies for REIT Investors,"* *Real Estate Review* (Spring, 1996): Boston, Warren, Gorham & Lamont.
3. Ibid.
4. Ibid.
5. See Barry Vinocur, *"Are REIT Prices Inflated? Only if You Believe in Old-Fashioned Valuation Measures,"* *Barron's* (January 13, 1997).

Chapter Seventeen

1. Source: National Association of Real Estate Investment Trusts.
2. Petros S. Sivanideas, *"Why Invest in Real Estate: An Asset Allocation Perspective,"* *Real Estate Issues* (April 1997). See also Michael Paldino and Herbert Mayo, *"Investments in REITs Do Not Help Diversify Stock Portfolios,"* *Real Estate Review* (Summer, 1995): Boston, Warren, Gorham & Lamont.

Chapter Eighteen

1. Source: AEW Capital Management, Boston as reported by Frank Byrt in *Study Projects REITs Growth Through 2000,* Dow Jones News, June 3, 1997.
2. Barry Vinocur, *"REIT Rally Fueled by Cash from Utility Funds,"* *Barron's* (November 18, 1996).

Chapter Nineteen

1. Richard Swesnik, *"Realty Investment Trusts and The Potential Investor,"* *Commercial and Financial Chronicle,* Vol. 193 (April 6, 1961).
2. Louis J. Glickman, *"Management's Duties in Publicly Owned Real Estate,"* *Commercial and Financial Chronicle,* vol. 196 (July 19, 1962).

Chapter Twenty

1. Source: National Association of Real Estate Investment Trusts.
2. Source: National Association of Real Estate Investment Trusts.
3. See *"Prudential Prunes,"* *Wall Street Journal* (November 11, 1996).
4. Vaness O'Connell, *"REITs Grow Popular as Way to Diversify, But it Can Be Hard to Pick the Right Ones,"* *Wall Street Journal* (October 11, 1996).
5. Frank Byrt, *"Study Projects REITs Growth Through 2000,"* *Dow Jones News* (June 3, 1997). See also Barry Vinocur, *"Pension Funds Are Poised to Swap Property for Stocks,"* *Barron's* (July 1, 1996).
6. Philip S. Scherrer, *"The Consolidation of REITs through Mergers and Acquisitions,"* *Real Estate Review* (Spring, 1995): Boston, Warren, Gorham & Lamont. See also Steven E. Goodman and Peter H. Madden, *"Seven REIT Acquisition Targets,"* *Real Estate Review* (Spring, 1996): Boston, Warren, Gorham and Lamont.

INDEX